Franz J. L. Thimm

Shakspeariana from 1564 to 1864

An Account of the Shakspearian Literature of England, Germany, France...

Second Edition

Franz J. L. Thimm

Shakspeariana from 1564 to 1864

An Account of the Shakspearian Literature of England, Germany, France... Second Edition

ISBN/EAN: 9783337205010

Printed in Europe, USA, Canada, Australia, Japan

Cover: Foto ©Thomas Meinert / pixelio.de

More available books at **www.hansebooks.com**

Shakspeariana

from

1564 to 1864.

An Account

of the Shakspearian Literature

of

England, Germany, France

and other European Countries

During Three Centuries,

with Bibliographical Introductions

by

Franz Thimm.

Second Edition
Containing the Literature from 1864 to 1871.

———

London,
Franz Thimm,
Foreign Bookseller and Publisher
24 Brook Street, Grosvenor Square.
1872.

TO

THE SHAKESPEARE MEMORIAL LIBRARY

FOUNDED AT

BIRMINGHAM

IN 1864

AS A MONUMENT TO THE POET.

THIS SECOND EDITION

IS DEDICATED

BY

THE AUTHOR.

PREFACE

TO THE SECOND EDITION.

The members of the Shakespeare Memorial Library which has been established at Birmingham, have in a singular manner fulfilled the wishes which I expressed in my first Edition. It is their intention to collect every book, tract on, and Edition of Shakspeare, in all languages and they have already progressed so far that their determination will soon become an established fact.

That such a Library will eventually be the greatest Monument to Shakespeare is undeniable, and it reflects the utmost credit on those who have planned and carried out this design.

I have continued in the present Supplement the literature of the last eight years, together with other emendations and corrections since brought under my notice. The Supplement has been printed with the view of incorporating it with the first edition, so that the English part should be bound up after page 48; the German part after page 81; and the French part should be cancelled altogether, and the new sheets inserted instead. It is my intention to continue the literature from time to time.

FRANZ THIMM.

TO SHAKSPEARIAN SCHOLARS.

Bibliographers are aware that it is almost impossible to collect every known book on Shakspeare, I therefore appeal to the kindness of those who may use my book and find any thing missing, to inform me of any full titles, omissions or errors, which information will be received with thanks, and duly incorporated with future editions.

F. T.

I.

SKETCH OF THE PROGRESS OF SHAKSPEARIAN CRITICISM,

AND OF THE GRADUAL APPRECIATION OF SHAKSPEARE
IN
ENGLAND.

The history of Shakspearian criticism is one which goes hand in hand with that of the general literary and critical art of England: nay, Shakspeare's works would seem to have been particularly designed to test the march of English intellect. It will therefore be necessary to glance at the successive publications of his works, in order to show the effect they produced on English writers.

The separate plays of the great dramatist were issued during his life-time; in what consecutive order it is now impossible to say; though certain it is that Shakspeare himself could never have seen them, even separately, through the press. They appeared in a corrupt state from the beginning; for, being printed and published as *acting* plays, they were altered, corrected and "improved" by both actors and managers.

The first collected edition ("Editio princeps") appeared in folio in 1623, the editors being Heminge and Condell, both of whom were actors at the *"Globe"*, and Shakspeare's executors and friends. This edition was printed seven years after Shakspeare's death.

Its editors, in their
"Address to the Reader", speak as follows: —

"It had been a thing, we confess, worthy to have been wished, that the author himself had lived to have set forth, and overseen his own writings; but since it hath been ordained otherwise, and he by death departed from that right, we pray you do not envy his friends, the office of their care and pain, to have collected and published them; and so to have published them, as where (before) you were abused with diverse stolen, and surreptitious copies, maimed, and deformed, by the frauds and stealths of injurious impostors, that exposed them: even those are now offered to your view cured, and perfect of their limbs; and all the rest, absolute in their numbers, as he conceived them, etc.

"John Heminge".
"Henry Condell".

"It is by courtesy alone", says a writer of a very interesting article in Bentley's Quarterly No. 3, "that this folio can be termed an edition. "Edited, in any proper sense of the word, it is not. The errors of "the printer, and the corruptions of the players are put down to "Shakspeare's account, nor is there probably any Latin or Greek manu- "script more vitiated by sleepy and ignorant copyists, than this *editio* "*princeps* has been by its publishers. In spite of their vaunt about "using exclusively Shakspeare's manuscripts, it is palpable that they "availed themselves, when they could, of the quartos published in the "poet's lifetime, the text for which was, to all appearance, obtained sur- "reptitiously, either from copyists before the curtain, or from the "prompter, or theatrical library behind it. And this negligence is the more "inexcusable and provoking, because, according to general tradition, "Shakspeare's autographs were models of calligraphy, and Heminge "and Condell must have seen, and might therefore have printed from "them.

"Bad as the editing was, the printing of this volume was no bet- "ter. Verse is printed as prose, prose as verse. Priscian's head is "perpetually broken; words are omitted or transposed; the punctuation "is such that, had Dogberry and Verges turned compositors for the "nonce, they could hardly have made it worse. Nor was advantage taken "of a second edition to amend these gross, open, and palpable errors. "Some glaring blunders are corrected in the second folio; but new "blunders compensate for those which are removed. Of most ancient "authors there are three or four copies at least, fortunately not agree- "ing in their several corruptions, and capable, therefore, of being em- "ployed as correctives to one another. But the original text of Shak- "speare has no similar privilege: his fairly-written manuscripts have "vanished: no specimen of his handwriting, except his signature, exists: "and for one Medicean codex, we possess only this precious budget of "blunders which his friends and fellow-actors consecrated to their de- "ceased copartner's memory.

"The earlier editions — we still use the word by courtesy — of "Shakspeare unfortunately appeared in an age of remarkably careless "printing. When an author, indeed, severely corrected his own proofs, a "book, then, as now, would come forth from the press in fair condi- "tion. 'Shakspeare's Poems', for example, are nearly immaculate; for "these, the favourites, if not the first fruits of his mind, he grudged no "parental care". (Shakspearian Literature, Bentley's Quarterly No. III.)

The *second folio edition* appeared nine years after the first; viz. in 1632; the *third edition* thirty-two years later, in 1664, (some of its copies bearing the date of 1663); the *fourth and last folio* edition, twenty-one years after, in 1685; and this completes the list of the folio editions of the 17th century. The number of copies of which each of these editions consisted, when printed, is unfortunately quite un- known.

Books were then costly, bookbuyers and collectors few. The great mass of the public were illiterate; and a copy of Shakspeare was probably a thing beyond their reach. Moreover, the puritanical spirit of the time, which condemned all theatrical performances, had, naturally, the effect of diminishing the interest which the public took and had taken, from the very first, in the representation of Shakspeare's plays. Plays were denounced as immoral; theatres anathematized as very dens of wickedness; — nay, even pillaged and burnt. The Stage was in short *execrated* by the religious fanaticism of the time, as nothing less than the creation of hell. The Plague, and the terrible fire which followed it, had decimated the inhabitants of London, and destroyed both their trade and their property; and in the fire vanished no doubt many of the precious little 4to editions of Shakspeare's plays. Then came the Great Rebellion, and the Restoration; and, under the influence of the licentious taste of Charles II.'s time, no wonder the old dramatists were well nigh forgotten.

From 1685 until 1709 no new edition of Shakspeare was published; but with Rowe's edition begins an incessant and increasing stream of new editions of Shakspeare, which has now swelled into a perfect flood. Rowe's edition in 7 Volumes 8vo appeared in 1709—10.

"After an interval of nearly 25 years", says a Reviewer*, "Rowe "reminded the world of its intellectual hero. His edition of the Plays "was a step in the right direction. There was hope of Rowe. He "was a man of fortune, living to write, instead of writing to live. He "was a good scholar, and had a poetical taste. He possessed one ad- "vantage as an editor of Shakspeare, independently of all literary "gifts. At the period when he turned his attention to the subject, "traditions of Stratford and the 'Globe' were quickly disappearing; "memories of Shakspeare were dying out. What light yet lingered "— and it was very small — Rowe did his best to fix and detain. "As we said, in one respect he was peculiarly favoured. Rowe's first "tragedy was produced in 1702, when Betterton played the hero, and "we may assign his acquaintance with that actor to 1700. Betterton "knew Davenant. Who does not remember the story which Aubrey "tells, that when Davenant was pleased over a glass of wine, with an "'intimate' like 'Hudibras Butler', he would say that it seemed to "him that he 'writ with the very spirit of Shakspeare', and was not "unwilling to have people think that there was good cause for the "resemblance? Shakspeare died when Davenant was a boy of 11 years; "but we owe to him much of the little information about the poet "which we possess. The biographer of Rowe informs us that he neither "received much praise, nor seems to have expected it, for his Shak- "spearian labours; but that he at least contributed to the popularity "of his author."

After the publication of the 4th folio edition, Shakspearian criticism began to shew itself in England; and the first form it took was that of reviews of tragedies in general, combined with reflections on Shakspeare in particular, such as were published by Rymer, in 1693. His criticisms however were more the attacks of a querulous cynic than the comments of a sound thinker. Charles Knight remarks,** "We "cannot agree with the author of an able article in the Retrospective "Review, that 'these attacks on Shakspeare are very curious, as evincing "how gradual has been the increase of his fame'; that their whole

---

* Times, December 1860.
** Studies of Shakspeare.

"tone shows that the author was not advancing what he thought the "world would regard as paradoxical or strange'; that 'he speaks as "one with authority to decide'. So far from receiving Rymer's frenzied "denunciations as an expression of public opinion, we regard them as "the idiosyncrasies of a very singular individual, who is furious in the "exact proportion in which the public opinion differs from his own. "He attacks 'Othello' and 'Julius Caesar', especially, because Betterton "had for years been drawing crowds to his performance in those tra- "gedies. He is one of those who glory in opposing the general opinion."

Critics like Rymer, Gildon, Dennis etc.* began to establish an artistic code, based on the classical models of ancient Greece; and every Shakspearian drama was measured by its rules. It was the same error which crept into the German mind a century later, — when Aristotle's dogmas became the infallible standard of criticism for the modern drama, — and which gave rise to such eccentric and confused views regarding the greatness of Shakspeare. The idea that each century produces new capacities; — that the national mind is stamped upon the literature of each century; — that each poet must be judged by the amount of his own original powers, — never entered the heads of these critics. Yet, however singular may have been the turn which criticism took, the nation as a mass appears never to have been wanting for a moment, in admiration of its great poet; and therefore to say that Shakspeare was ever forgotten, ever neglected, is an error, which is at once refuted by the continual demand for more and better editions of his works. The fault finding commentators on Shakspeare began to show how little they were qualified to judge the poet, by their attempts to improve him. These "improvements" are the best evidence of their disqualification as critics." "Poetic justice", continues Charles Knight, "was one of the rules for which they clamoured. "Duncan and Banquo ought not to perish in 'Macbeth', nor Desdemona "in 'Othello', nor Cordelia and her father in 'Lear', nor Brutus in "'Julius Caesar', nor young Hamlet in 'Hamlet'. So Dennis argues: "— 'The good and the bad perishing promiscuously in the best of "Shakspeare's tragedies, there can be either none or very weak instruc- "tion in them'. — — The alteration of 'The Tempest' by Davenant "and Dryden, was an attempt to meet the taste of the town by music "and spectacle. Shadwell went further, and turned it into a regular "opera; and an opera it remained even in Garrick's time, who tried his "hand upon the same experiment. Dennis was a reformer both in "comedy and tragedy. He metamorphosed 'The Merry Wives of "Windsor' into 'The Comical Gallant'; and prefixed an essay to it, "on the degeneracy of the taste for poetry. Davenant changed "'Measure for Measure' into 'The Law against lovers'." The Essayists began to show better taste; for both the *Tatler* and the *Spectator* speak of Shakspeare as belonging to the first class of great geniuses, together with Homer; and Addison had a sounder appreciation of the beauties of the poet than even his predecessors.

Since the appearance of Rowe's edition, Shakspearian criticism in

---

* Knight's Shakspeare Studies.

England has been directed chiefly to the text. That higher aesthetical criticism which was to bring the greatness of Shakspeare more prominently into relief, by comparing him with the other giants of poetic thought, has been left to the Germans; as we shall presently see. These text criticisms, although numerous and of a higher standard than before, were as yet neither very conspicuous nor productive of much fruit. Proposals for new editions of Shakspeare, explanatory and critical notes on particular passages, answers to such criticisms, and rejoinders thereto, examinations of and remarks upon the text, volumes of selections, under the title "Beauties of Shakspeare", — these were the literary productions contributed by England towards the illustration of the dramatist's works.

Pope's edition, in 6 Vols 4to, appeared in 1725, handsomely printed, and with an admirable preface. It was chiefly interesting for the poet's criticism on Shakspeare and exhibits the progress of opinion and judgement respecting the great dramatist. The text itself was altered by Pope, as his fancy dictated; and it is therefore valueless.

Theobald's edition appeared in 7 Vols in 8vo in 1733; it was collated after the first editions, and had so high a stamp of correct text, that, according to Steeven's assertion, thirteen thousand Copies were sold of the first edition. *Warton* gives him his due praise, when he calls him the first publisher of Shakspeare who hit upon the rational method of correcting his author by reading such books as he had read.

Hanmer's edition appeared in 1744, in six splendid quarto volumes, printed at the Oxford University press; — but it was as valueless as that of Pope.

Pope's and Warburton's edition appeared in 1747; *Hugh Blair's* in 1753; *Johnson's* in 1765; who "did but little, and that little was not done well"; and *Steeven's* in 1766.

Dr. Farmer's eccentric "Essay on the learning of Shakspeare" appeared in 1767, and went through four editions. Dr. Johnson complimented Farmer in these words: — "You have done that which never was done before; that is, you have completely finished a controversy beyond all further doubt". Thus Dr. Farmer passed for a very learned and conspicuous man, and William Shakspeare for a very illiterate and obscure one.*

At about this period Shakspearian acting had risen to great eminence, through the genius of David Garrick, whose personification of Shakspearian characters was both novel and powerful. He appeared for the first time, in the Goodmansfield Theatre, of which Gifford was Lessee, in July 1741, and acted "Richard the 3rd" with such success that the great National Theatres stood empty, whilst the little theatre was literally besieged. In 1747 he took Drury Lane, and was there assisted by his fellow actors, Barry, Pritchard, and Cibber. It was a result of Garrick's admiration for the great dramatist that the celebrated "Jubilee" was held, in commemoration of the Bard, at Stratford on Avon, on the 6th of September 1769.

---

* Bentley's Quarterly Review. Part III.

John Kemble continued to keep up the public interest in Shakspearian acting; as did also his sister, Mrs. Siddons, the greatest tragic actress whom England has produced.

Shakspeare has perhaps never been treated with more care, nor have greater pains been expended upon his representation, than at this period.

A Glossary of the Plays of Shakspeare is extant, in which are explained technical terms, words which have become obsolete or uncommon, and common words used in an uncommon sense, by Richard Warner. This work has never been published, but the original manuscript, consisting of 71 Volumes in quarto and octavo, is preserved in the British Museum.* The original must have been written some time between 1750 and 1770. It was a gigantic undertaking; and would most likely have ruined any publisher who might have been bold enough to meddle with it. Separate essays on the characters of Hamlet, Sir John Falstaff, Richard the 3rd, and Lear, with critiques upon the faults of Shakspeare, occupied the literary world next. The extent, indeed, to which the censure of Shakspeare was carried at this period is both remarkable and characteristic; and shews the absence of any high literary or critical principles; for, though every one admired Shakspeare's genius, he was nevertheless constantly criticized on the score of his supposed exaggeration in the developement of character, his bombast, and his vulgarity.

In 1765 Johnson's edition of the great dramatist appeared, in 8 Vols 8vo. This was** "the foundation of the "variorum editions", the "principle of which has been to select from all, or nearly all existing "commentaries, various and conflicting opinions upon the same passage. "The respective value of the critics who had preceded him was fully "discussed by Johnson in his preface. This branch of the subject was "only of temporary interest. But the larger portion of Johnson's "preface not only to a certain extent represented the tone of opinion "in Johnson's age, but was written with so much pomp of diction, with "such apparent candour, and with such abundant manifestation of good "sense, that perhaps more than any other production, it has influenced "the public opinion of Shakspeare up to this day."

But the public admiration of Shakspeare was increasing in England; and men began to devote half a life-time to the collection of Shakspearian tracts and MSS. Capell, it is said, indeed, spent a whole life in the study of Shakspeare; and transcribed his works ten times with his own hand.

Capell's "Shakspeariana", which is of great interest to scholars, gives us a good idea of these collections; and still more so does the following notice of his life. Capell*** "was deputy-inspector of plays; and, as early as 1745, shocked at the licentiousness of Hanmer's plan, he first projected an edition of Shakspeare, of the strictest accuracy to be collated and published in due time "ex fide codicum". He immediately proceeded to collect and compare the oldest and scarcest

---

* MSS. Addit. 10,472 to 10,542.
** Knight's "Studies of Shakspeare".
*** Hartshorne, the Book Rarities in Cambridge.

copies: noting the original excellencies and defects of the rarest quartos, and distinguishing the improvements or variations of the first, second, and third folios. Three years after he put forth his own edition, in 10 volumes, small octavo, with an introduction which was printed (1768) at the expense of the principal booksellers of London, who gave him 300 pounds for his labours. There is not, even among the various publications of the present literary era, a more singular composition than this introduction. Its style and manner is actually more obsolete and antique than that of the age of which it treats. Taken in combination with the title page, it gives us, however, a perfect index to the contents of the work; and it began to rouse the attention of scholars, and to interest them in Shakspearian studies. In the title page is embodied the following announcement: — "Whereunto will be added, in some other volumes, notes, critical and explanatory, and a body of various readings entire." The introduction declared that these "notes and various readings" would be accompanied by another work, disclosing the sources from whence Shakspeare "drew the greater part of his knowledge in mythological and classical matters, his fable, his history and even the seeming peculiarity of his language", — "to which," says Capell, "we have given for title, 'The School of Shakspeare'." Twenty-three years had elapsed, in collection, collation, compilation, and transcription, between the conception and production of his projected edition; and even then it came, like its author, "naked into the world"; for it had neither notes nor commentary, save the critical matter dispersed through the introduction, and a brief account of the origin of the fables of the several plays; with a table of the different editions."

"But while he was diving into the classics of Caxton and working his way under ground, like the river Mole, in order to emerge at last with all his glories; — while he was looking forward, like the patient miner who has struck upon a vein unworked by others, to his coming triumphs; — certain other active spirits went to work upon his plan, and, digging out the promised treasures, laid them prematurely before the public, destroying, by this anticipation of them, the whole effect of our critic's discoveries. Stevens, Malone, Farmer, Percy, Reed, and a host of other literary ferrets, burrowed into every hole and corner of the warren of modern antiquity, and overran all the country which had been mapped out by Edward Capell. Such a contingency staggered the steady and hitherto unshaken perseverance of our critic, at the very eve of the completion of his labours; and, as his editor informs us, — (for, alas! at the end of nearly forty years, the publication, was posthumous, and the critic himself no more!) — he had almost determined to lay the work wholly aside. He persevered however; and after his death, in 1783, three large quarto volumes were published, under the title of "Notes and various Readings of Shakspeare": together with the "School of Shakspeare". He died on the 24th of January, 1781.*

Charles Knight** divides Shakspearian editors into two schools.

---

* Bibliographical Dictionary.
** Studies of Shakspeare.

"The earlier (to which belong Rowe, Pope, Theobald, Hanmer and Johnson), did not seek any very exact acquaintance with our early literature, and would have despised the exhibition, if not the reality, of antiquarian and bibliographical knowledge. A new school, however, subsequently arose, whose acquaintance with what has been called black-letter literature was extensive enough to produce a decided revolution in Shakspearian criticism. Capell, Steevens, Malone, Reed and Douce, are its representatives. The first school contained the most brilliant men; the second, the most painstaking commentators. The dullest of the first school, — who was branded as a mere dunce by his rival editor, — "poor, piddling Tibbald", — was unquestionably its best specimen. *Rowe* was indolent, *Pope*, flashy; *Warburton*, paradoxical; *Johnson*, pedantic."

In 1773 appeared the edition of *Johnson* and *Steevens*, in 10 vols 8°. This text of Steevens', in which the peculiar versification of Shakspeare, — with its freedom, its vigour, its variety of pause, its sweetness, its majesty, — is sacrificed to what he called "polished versification" has been received for nearly half a century as the standard text.* The year 1790 produced *Malone's* edition; and during the entire century, as many as thirty thousand copies of Shakspeare were dispersed through England.

The love of Shakspearian antiquity was indeed so great at this time, that dishonest men began to forge documents relating to the poet, with the object of foisting their trash upon his biographers and admirers. The fabrications of *Ireland* (published in 1795) belonged to this class. They created, at the time, a good deal of attention and controversy; but were at last detected for what they really were, — i. e. mere forgeries. The portraits known as the *Stace* Picture, and the *Bellow's* Picture of the poet, were also condemned as spurious.

If aesthetical criticism has come from Germany, England has at any rate not been behind hand in doing that which no foreigner could do for her national poet.

All that antiquarian research, and textual criticism could do, has been done in this country. Shakspeare's admirers and students here, have been, in truth, indefatigable. One of the most remarkable books which have been published is *Drake's "Shakespeare and his time"*; a work full of minute and valuable information respecting the manners, customs, and superstitions of Shakspeare's age, and is in its peculiar line, unrivalled to this day.

In the 19th century the best editions of the dramatist have been those of *Chalmer* in 1805, *Wood* in 1806, *Ballantyne* in 1807, *Malone's* edition, re-edited by *Boswell* in 1821, *Singer's* in 1826 and *Valpy's* in 1832.

A long period of time had passed, without the appearance of any edition worthy to be called a progress in Shakspearian editorship. It was not until 1839 that Charles Knight's "Pictorial Shakspeare" appeared. The historical introductions, explanations and illustrations which accompany this edition make it one of the most interesting ever published. Its editor indeed has distinguished himself as a great Shakspearian scholar. His life of the dramatist, his "Studies of Shakspeare"

* Knight's Studies.

and his various editions of his plays and poems have secured for Charles Knight a high and lasting position in Shakspearian literature.

In 1840 the "*Shakspeare Society*" was established, under the presidency of the Earl of Ellesmere. Its object was to publish books illustrative of Shakspeare and of the literature of his time. The Society lasted until 1853; and has published 48 volumes, some of them of great interest in a historical point of view.

In 1841 *Mr. Payne Collier* published his edition of Shakspeare, in 8 vols 8vo. It gave the collated text of the early editions in the possession of the Duke of Devonshire; of the unique first "Hamlet" of 1603, the first "Romeo and Juliet" of 1597, and many others. The task was executed with that success which great knowledge of the subject, and an intimate acquaintance with early English literature could alone ensure. There has indeed been no man more indefatigable than Mr. Collier in minute researches into Shakspearian lore. He has made Shakspearian research the task of his whole life; and literature owes him a lasting debt of gratitude. His "History of English dramatic Poetry, and Annals of the Stage", have given us materials which must form the foundation of Shakspearian inquiry for all future time. We refer to our Catalogue for a more particular account of Mr. Collier's labours.

In his biography of Shakspeare, he examined the original sources of information from the register of the poet's baptism, to the proof of his will.*

In 1853 appeared the 1st volume of Mr. J. O. Halliwell's splendid edition of Shakspeare, in 15 volumes folio, of which ten have already been printed. The text is formed from a new collation of the early editions; and the work includes the original novels and tales on which the plays are founded, copious archaeological annotations on each play, an essay on the formation of the text, and a life of the poet. The subscription for a single copy of this gigantic work, wholly unsurpassed in splendour, but from its costliness, inaccessible to the general public, amounted to 63 Pounds.

In 1853 appeared Mr. Collier's new edition of Shakspeare. The text was regulated by a newly discovered folio edition of 1632, containing many hundred early marginal emendations, in manuscript. With these "Notes and Emendations" a revolution began in the Shakspearian world, and a long controversy (known as the "Collier Controversy") resulted from their publication. The dispute was as hot as that respecting the *Ireland* forgeries, 70 years previous, and there was even frequent mention of that odious word. The most serious charges were brought against Collier by N. Hamilton in his well-known work entitled "An Inquiry into the Genuinness of the Manuscript Corrections in Mr. J. P. Collier's annotated Shakspeare of 1632, and of certain Shakspearian Documents likewise published by Mr. Collier."

Mr. Collier in a letter which appeared in the Athenaeum of the 18th February 1860, replied to these grave charges; and his reply (which he afterwards published as a distinct pamphlet)**, not only gives

---
* Collier's "Reasons for a new edition of Shakspeare".
** "Reply to Mr. N. Hamilton's Inquiry into the imputed Shakspeare Forgeries,

a historical account of this curious volume, but is in all respects satisfactory, and completely annihilates the charges of his assailants. There can be no doubt that the explanation which he gives is the true one; and that the corrections, frequently striking, are by an unknown hand, and a clever head.

In 1857 appeared Alexander Dyce's edition in 6 volumes 8vo and in 1858 Howard Staunton's carefully edited edition, in 3 vols, with illustrations. The year 1863 brought with it a new edition, by W. G. Clark and John Glover, known as the "Cambridge Edition"; which is, beyond all question, one of the best editions of Shakspeare which has ever been issued from the press.

For we think the time has indeed past when we should allow any literary dilettante to come forward and give us the text of Shakspeare according to his "new ideas", with his own new readings and corrections. We want no more such editors as these; for they are at best bad linguists, insufficiently acquainted with comparative philology; and are generally self-opinionated enough to substitute a bad word for one that is unintelligible. A man who has not proved himself to have the proper qualifications, and who is not moreover intimately acquainted with ancient English literature, has no pretention whatever to appear as a text-monger of Shakspeare. We want the texts of the early editions, however incorrectly they may have come down to us, with textual emendations in the form of notes, but no further *alterations* of the text, except such as may be based on early and well authenticated editions. This is a sound rule, we think, for all future editors of the great dramatist; and we are happy to say the Cambridge editors have set the example of adopting it. The plan which they have followed is to take a good early edition of each play, and to quote in the annotation the different readings of the other early editions. We have thus, for the first time, obtained a complete text of Shakspeare's dramas.

Whilst this edition is appearing, reprints of the early Quarto's, a "fac-simile" Shakspeare, and a host of new editions are being also ushered in, to complete the literary Monument of
Shakspeare's Tercentenary.

---

by J. Payne Collier." 1860. See, also, "Mommsen. Der Perkins - Shakspeare." Berlin, 1854.

THE EARLY QUARTO EDITIONS OF SHAKSPEARE'S PLAYS.

1594.

Titus Andronicus, entered at Stationer's Hall Feb. 6. 1593. Langbaine says the first edition was printed in 1594, but no copy of it is in existance. 2nd *Edition* 1600. 3rd *Edition* 1611 (in Capell's Collection).
Henry the Sixth part II. 1st *Edition* 1594 printed by Thomas Creede for Thomas Millington. In the Bodleian Library. 2nd *Edition* 1600. (In Capell's Collection, Cambridge.) 3rd *Edition* 1619 no date (Capell).

1595.

Henry the Sixth, part III. 1st *Edition* 1595.
2nd *Edition* 1600. British Museum and Bodleian Library.
3rd *Edition* (no date) 1619. do. do.

1597.

Romeo and Juliet, printed by John Danter.
1st *Edition* 1597. British Mus. Bodleian. Capell.
2nd *Edition* 1599. do. do. do.
3rd *Edition* 1609. do. do. do.
4th *Edition* (no date) 1615. do. do. do.
5th *Edition* 1637. do. do. do.
Richard the Second. Printed by Valentine Simmes for Andrew Wise.
1st *Edition* 1597. Capell.
2nd *Edition* 1598. British Mus. Bodleian. Capell.
3rd *Edition* 1608. With new additions of the Parliament Scene. Bodleian.
4th *Edition* 1608. British Mus. Capell.
5th *Edition* 1615. British Mus. Bodleian. Capell.
6th *Edition* 1624, 7th *Edition* 1629, 8th *Edition* 1634.
Richard the Third. Old play. London by Creede 1594.
1st *Edition* 1597. Printed by Valentine Sims for Andrew Wise. Bodleian. Capell.
2nd *Edition* 1598. Brit. Mus. Bodleian. Capell.
3rd *Edition* 1602. Brit. Mus. and Capell.
4th *Edition* 1605, 5th *Edition* 1612, 6th *Edition* 1621, doubtful, 7th *Ed.* 1622, 8th *Edition* 1629, 9th *Edition* 1634.

1598.

Love's Labour Lost. Printed by W. W. for Cuthbert Burby.
1st *Edition* 1598. Bodleian. Capell.
2nd *Edition* 1631. Brit. Mus. Capell.
King Henry the Fourth, part I. Printed by P. S. for Andrew Wise.
1st *Edition* 1598. Brit. Mus. Capell.
2nd *Edition* 1599. do. Bodleian. Capell.
3rd *Edition* 1604. (imperfect) do. do.
4th *Edition* 1608. Brit. Mus. do. do.
5th *Edition* 1613. do. do. do.
6th *Edition* 1622, 7th *Edition* 1632, 8th *Edition* 1639.

1600.

Henry the Fifth. Printed by Thomas Creede, for Thos. Millington and John Busby.
  1st *Edition* 1600. Brit. Mus. Bodleian. Capell.
  2nd *Edition* 1602. Capell.
  3rd *Edition* 1608. Brit. Mus. Bodleian. Capell.

The Merchant of Venice. Printed by J. R. for Thomas Heyes.
  1st *Edition* 1600. Brit. Mus. Bodleian. Capell. Entered at Stationer's Hall on July 22, 1598.
  2nd *Edition* Printed by J. Roberts. 1600. Brit. Mus. Bodleian. Capell.
  3rd *Edition* 1637. Brit. Mus. Bodleian. Capell.
  4th *Edition* 1652.   do.   and Capell.

A Midsommer Night's Dreame. Printed by James Roberts.
  1st *Edition* 1600. Brit. Mus. Bodleian. Capell.
  2nd *Edition* for Thomas Fisher 1600. Brit. Mus. Bodleian. Capell.

Much Adoe about Nothing. Printed by V. S. for Andrew Wise and William Aspley.
  1st *Edition* 1600. Brit. Mus. Bodleian. Capell.

1602.

Merry Wives of Windsor. Printed by T. C. for Arthur Johnson.
  1st *Edition* 1602. Bodleian L. Capell.
  2nd *Edition* 1619. Brit. Mus. Bodleian. Capell.
  3rd *Edition* 1630.   do.   do.   do.
  These Editions are all incomplete.

1603.

Hamlet. Printed for N. L. and John Trundell.
  1st *Edition* 1603. Only 2 incomplete Copies known. Brit. Mus. and Duke of Devonshire.
  2nd *Edition* 1604. 3 Copies known. Brit. Mus. and Duke of Devonshire.
  3rd *Edition* 1605. Brit. Mus. Capell.
  4th *Edition* 1607. no date, printed by W. S. for John Smethwicke. Brit. Mus. Bodleian. Capell.
  5th *Edition* 1611, 6th *Edition* 1637, 7th *Edition* 1683, 8th *Edition* 1695.

1605.

King Lear. Printed by Simon Stafford for John Wright.
  1st *Edition* 1605. Brit. Mus.
  2nd *Edition* 1608. printed for Nath. Butter, 41 leaves. British Museum. Bodleian. Capell.
  3rd *Edition* 1608. printed for Nath. Butter, 44 leaves. British Museum. Bodleian. Capell.
  4th *Edition* 1655. Bodleian. Capell.

1609.

Pericles. Imprinted for Henry Gosson.
  1st *Edition* 1609. Brit. Mus. Bodleian. Capell.
  2nd *Edition* 1609. corrected. Brit. Mus.
  3rd *Edition* 1611. Brit. Mus. Capell.
  4th *Edition* 1619. Brit. Mus. Bodleian.
  5th *Edition* 1630.   do.   do.
  6th *Edition* 1635.   do.   do.   7th *Edition* 1639.

Troilus and Cressida. Imprinted by G. Eld, for R. Bonian' and H. Walley.
  1st *Edition* 1609. (Title: The *famous* history of T. etc.).
  2nd *Edition* 1609. (Title: The history of T. etc.).

1622.

Othello. Printed by N. O. for Thomas Walkley.
  1st *Edition* 1622. Brit. Mus. Bodleian. Capell
  2nd *Edition* 1630.   do.   do.   do.
  3rd *Edition* 1655.   do.   do.   do.

1631.

Taming of a Shrew. An old play printed by Peter Short and sold by Cuthbert Burby 1594. Devonshire.
  reprinted   1607.   do.

1st *Edition* with Shakspeare's name, is dated 1631 printed by W. S. for John Smethwicke. Brit. Mus. Capell.

THE REPRINTS OF THE QUARTO'S.

Hamlet, exact reprints of the 1st and 2nd Edition of 1603 and 1604. 8º. London 1859. 1864.
—— do. with bibliographical preface by S. Timmins. 8º. 1860.
Romeo and Juliet, from the Edition of 1597 and 1599 by Mommsen. roy. 8º. 1859.
Reprints of the early quarto Editions in photo-lithographic copies, are about to be published, under the editorship of Mr. Staunton.

THE FOLIO EDITIONS OF SHAKSPEARE.

First Edition 1623.
Mr. William Shakespeare's Comedies, Histories and Tragedies. Published according to the true Original Copies. London Printed by Isaac Jaggard and Edward Blount. 1623. Portrait by Martin Droeshout.
This Edition has 36 plays, containing 17 which were not printed in 4º., excepting Pericles, which was added to the third Edition.

Second Edition 1632.
Printed by Thos. Cotes, for Robert Allot (title page varies). Portrait by Martin Droeshout.
"The Sources from which the numerous new readings in this edition were derived, are unknown. Ben Jonson and John Milton, are suggested as emendators."

Third Edition (Some Copies dated 1663). 1664.*
Printed for P. C. And into this Impression is added seven Plays, never before printed in folio, viz.: Pericles Prince of Tyre. The London Prodigal. The History of Thomas Ld. Cromwell. Sir John Oldcastle Lord Cobham. The Puritan Widow. A Yorkshire Tragedy. The Tragedy of Locrine.
"The greater part of this Edition is said to have been destroyed by the fire of London."

Fourth Edition 1685.
Printed for H. Herringman. E. Brewster. R. Chiswell and R. Bentley.

REPRINTS.

First Reprint of the First folio Edition 1807.
Second Reprint of the First folio in course of publication, small 4º. 1862—1864 by Lionel Booth.

VALUE OF THE EARLY EDITIONS.

In a sale of the Library of the late Mr. George Daniel which occured in August 1864 the Editions of Shakspeare fetched the following prices:

SHAKSPEARE.

"Shakspeare's Comedies, Histories, and Tragedies." Published according to the true original copies. The excessively rare first edition; brilliant portrait by Droeshout, with the verses by Ben Jonson; folio in beautiful old russia binding, preserved in a russia case. Printed by Isaac Jaggard and Ed. Blount, 1623. A marvellous volume of unrivalled beauty, unquestionably

---

* "This edition was first issued in 1663" and Copies with this date, do not contain the seven spurious plays. For minute details see: Lowndes Bibliographers Manual "Shakespeare."

the finest that has ever occured for public sale. This copy will to all future time possess a world-wide reputation. It was bequeathed by Daniel Moore, F. R. S., to William Henry Booth, who left it by will to John Gage Rokewode, from whom it passed to Mr. Daniel. Its beauty was first remarked on by Dr. Dibdin in his "Library Companion," 1824. Interesting letters attesting these facts are in the volume, and another from Mr. Lilly, offering the sum of 300*l*. for it. — 682 guineas (bought for Miss Burdett Coutts).

"Shakspeare's Comedies, Histories, and Tragedies." The second impression. Portrait by Droeshout, and verses by Ben Jonson; folio. In the original calf binding. Printed by Tho. Cotes, for Robert Allot, and are to be sold at his shop, at the signe of the blacke Beare, in Paul'schurchyard 1632. "This genuine and beautiful copy of the second folio edition of Shakspeare's plays was bought by Mr. Thorpe at the sale of the library at Neville Holt, Leicestershire, and bought of him by me this the 16th day of September (my Birth-day), 1848. I never saw its equal for soundness and size." - George Daniel, Canonbury. Of the purest quality from beginning to end, and the largest example known — 148*l*. (Boone).

"Shakspeare's Comedies, Histories, and Tragedies." The third impression. Portrait by Droeshout, the verses by Ben Jonson underneath. Folio, green morocco extra, with gilt borders inside, and joints, by C. Lewis. London, printed for P. C., 1664. . . . The publishers of the fourth edition of 1685 appear to have considered the destruction of the third edition so extensive, as to entitle them to treat it as a nonentity, and accordingly say upon their title-page, "unto which is added seven playes never before printed in folio," though they had been previously added to this issue of the third edition, a certain proof of its great rarity, even in those days. "The present copy is a remarkably fine, sound, and tall one, in the most genuine state." — Note by Mr. Daniel. It is certainly a copy of unmatchable beauty — 46*l*. (Lilly).

"Shakspeare's Comedies, Histories, and Tragedies." The fourth edition. Folio. Portrait by Droeshout, the verses underneath. Printed for H. Herringman, E. Brewster, and R. Bentley, 1685. A magnificent copy; blue morocco, richly gilt — 21*l*. 10s. (Boone).

VALUE OF THE SEPARATE PLAYS. THE ORIGINAL EDITIONS.

King Richard the Second, First Edition, 4°. 1597 — 325 guineas.
—— Second Edition, 4°. 1598 — 103 guineas (Halliwell).
King Richard the Third, First Edition, 4°. 1597 — the only Copy which has ever occurred for sale — 325 guineas.
Love's Labour Lost, First Edition, 4°. 1598 (the Copy was formerly Bindley's, and afterwards in the Heber Collection) — 330 guineas.
Henry the Fourth, Second Edition, 4°. 1599 — 110 guineas.
Romeo and Juliet, First Edition, 4°. 1599 — 50 guineas.
Henry the Fifth, First Edition, 4°. 1600 — 220 guineas.
The Merchant of Venice, First Edition, 4°. 1600 — 95 guineas.
Much Adoe about Nothing, First Edition, 4°. 1600 — 255 guineas.
Midsommer Nights Dream, First Edition, 4°. 1600 — 230 guineas.
—— Second Edition, 4°. 1600 — 36 Pounds.
The Merry Wives of Windsor, First Edition, 4°. 1602 (from the Bindley Collection) — 330 guineas.
King Lear, 4to 1608 — 28 guineas.
Pericles, Prince of Tyre, 4°. 1609 — 84 Pounds.
Troilus and Cresseid, First Edition, 4°. 1609 — 109 guineas.
Hamlet, 4°. 1611 – 27 guineas.
Titus Andronichus, 4°. 1611 — 30 guineas.
Othello, First Edition, 4°. — 155 guineas.
Lucrece, First Edition, 4°. 1594. Only three or four perfect copies are known to exist. — 150 guineas.
Venus and Adonis, Second Edition, 4°. 1594. The finest Copy known. Not more than three Copies exist. — 240 Pounds.
—— Second Edition, sm. 8°. 1596.

"This most precious volume is from the libraries of the late Sir W. Bolland and Mr. Robert Bright. At Sir W. Bolland's sale it was bought by Mr. Bright for 91*l*. At Mr. Bright's sale, on the 7th of Aripp, 1845, I became the purchaser for the sum of 91*l*. 10s." — MS. note by Mr. Daniel. A beautiful copy. The only other copy known is in the Bodleian — 300 guineas.

Shakspeare (W.). – Sonnets, never before imprinted. 4to, olive morocco extra, gilt edges. At London, by G. Eld, for T. T., and are to be solde by John Wright, dwelling at Christ Churchgate; 1600. A large and perfect copy of this most rare volume, and the one of only two perfect copies known with the above imprint. This precious little volume formerly belonged to Narcissus Luttrell and cost him one shilling. It was afterwards in the possession of George Steevens — 215 guineas.

Locrine, small 4°. 1595 — 105 Pounds.

THE DOUBTFUL PLAYS.

1. ARDEN OF FEVERSHAM.

The lamentable and true Tragedie of M. Arden, of Feversham in Kent. London printed for Edward White 1592. 4°. 1599. reprinted 1770 by Jacob. In the preface Shakspeare is mentioned as the Author.

2. ARRAIGNMENT OF PARIS.

The Araygnement of Paris, a Pastorall. Imprinted at London by Henrie Marsh. 1584. 4°. (written by George Peele).

3. THE BIRTH OF MERLIN.

The Birth of Merlin: or the Childe hath found his Father. Written by William Shakspeare and William Rowley. London T. Johnson, for Frances Kirkman and Henry Marsh. 4°. 1662.

4. EDWARD III.

The Raigne of King Edward the Third. Cuthbert Burby. 4°. 1596. 1599. — edited by Delius, Elberfeld 1854. 12°.

5. FAIRE EM.

A pleasant Comedie of Faire Em, the Millers Daughter of Manchester. London printed for John Wright. 4°. 1631.

6. LOCRINE.

The lamentable Tragedie of Locrine, the eldest sonne of King Brutus, etc. London printed by Th. Creede. 4°. 1595.

7. LONDON PRODIGAL.

The London Prodigall by William Shakspeare. London printed by T. C. for Nathaniel Butter. 4°. 1605.

8. LORD CROMWELL.

The true Chronicle Historie of the whole life and death of Thomas Lord Cromwell. Written by W. S. London printed by Thomas Snodham. 4°. 1613.

9. MERRY DEVIL OF EDMONTON.

The Merry Devill of Edmonton. London. 4°. 1608. 1617. 1626. 1631. 1655.

10. MUCEDORUS.

A most pleasant Comedy of Mucedorus, the Kings Sonne of Valencia and Amadine the Kings Daughter of Arragon. London. Printed for Francis Cotes. 4°. (no date, 1598). 4°. for W. Jones. 1610. 1613. 1615. 1634. etc.

11. SIR JOHN OLDCASTLE.

The first part of the true history of the Life of Sir John Oldcastle. Written by William Shakspeare. London. Printed for T. P. 4°. 1600. For Thomas Pauier (without Shakspeare's name). 1600.

12. THE PURITAN.

The Puritaine or the Widdow of Watling Street. London pr. by G. Eld. 4°. 1607.

13. THE TWO NOBLE KINSMEN.

The two noble Kinsmen; written by Fletcher and W. Shakspeare. London. Printed by T. Cotes for J. Waterson. 4°. 1634.

14. YORKSHIRE TRAGEDY.

A Yorkshire Tragedy. Written by Shakspeare. London. Printed by R. B. for Thomas Pauier. 4°. 1608. 1619.

SHAKSPEARE'S POEMS.

VENUS AND ADONIS.

London imprinted by Richard Field. 4°. 1593. Bodleian Library. *Second Edition* 1594. Bodleian. *Third Edition* by R. F. for John Harrison. sm. 8°. 1596. Bodleian L. *Fourth Edition* 1600. reprinted 16°. 1602, 12°. 1617, 18°. 1620, 8°. 1627, 8°. 1630, 32°. 1636, 8°. 1675.

LUCRECE.

London printed by Richard Field for John Harrisson. 4°. 1594. Bodleian. Brit. Mus. 1596, 1598, 18°; 1600, 24°; 1607, 8°; 1616, 8°; 1624, 16°; 1632, 12"; 1655, 16°.

THE PASSIONATE PILGRIME.

Printed for W. Jaggard sold by W. Leake. 16o. 1599. Capell. *Second Ed.* (not known). *Third Edition* by Jaggard. 16o. 1612.

SONNETS.

London by G. Eld for T. T. sold by John Wright. 4o. 1609. reproduced in facsimile. 4o. 1862.

POEMS.

Written by William Shakspeare. Printed at London by Cotes. 1640. (a collection chiefly by other hands.)

THE CHIEF COMPLETE EDITIONS OF SHAKSPEARE'S WORKS.

1623   The First Folio Edition.
1632   The Second Folio Edition.
1663–64   The Third Folio Edition.
1685   The Fourth Folio Edition.
1709   **Rowe's** Edition. 7 Vols. 8o.
1714   do. Second Edition. 9 Vols. 12o.
1725   **Pope's** Edition. 6 Vols. 4o.
1728   do. Second Edition. 10 Vols. 12o.
1731   do. Third Edition. 9 Vols. 18o.

1733	**Theobald's** Edition. 7 Vols. 8o.	
1735	Pope's Fourth Edition. 8 Vols. 12o. 1766. 1768.	
1740	Theobald's Second Edition. 8 Vols. 12o. 1752, 1757, 1762, 67, 72, 73.	
1744	**Hanmer's** Edition. 6 Vols. 4o.	
1745	do. Second Edition. 6 Vols. 8o.	
1747	do. Third Edition. 9 Vols. 18o. 1748, 1751, 1760. 1770.	
—	**Warburton's** Edition. 8 Vols. 8o.	
1753	Hugh Blair's Edition. 8 Vols. 12o. 1761, 1769, 1771, 1795.	
1765	**Sam. Johnson's** Edition. 8 Vols. 8o. 1768.	
1766	**Steeven's** Edition. 4 Vols. 8o.	
1767	**Capell's** Edition. 10 Vols. 8o.	
1771	Ewin's Edition (Dublin). 12 Vols. 12o.	
1773	**Johnson and Steeven's** Edition. 10 Vols. 8o. 1778, 1803.	
1774	Bell's Edition. 8 Vols. 12o. 1786, 1804.	
1784	Ayscough's Edition one Vol. roy. 8o. 1790, 1807.	
1785	Johnson and Steeven's Edition by **Reed**. 10 Vols. 8o. 1793, 1800, 1803, 1809, 1811. often reprinted.	
1783	John Nichol's Edition. 7 Vols. 12o. 1798.	
—	Rann's Edition. 6 Vols. 8o.	
1790	**Malone's** Edition. 10 Vols. cr. 8o. 1794.	
1791	Bellamy's Edition. 8 Vols. 8o.	
1797	Robinson's Edition. 7 Vols. imp. 8o.	
1800	Sharpe's Miniature Edition. 9 Vols. 24o. 1803, 1810.	
1802	Boydell's illustr. Edition. 9 Vols.	
1803	Wallis and Scholey's Edition. 10 Vols. 8o. 1807.	
1805	Chalmer's Edition. 9 Vols. 8o. 1811, 1818, 1823, 1826, 1837. etc.	
1806	Manley Wood's Edition. 14 Vols.	
1807	Ballantyne's Edition. 12 Vols. 8o.	
—	Heath's Edition. 6 Vols. 4o.	
1811	Miller's Edition. 8 Vols. 12o.	
1814	Life by Britten, Chiswick. 7 Vols. 18o.	
1818	Bowdler's Family Shakspeare. 10 Vols. 18o. often reprinted.	
1821	Johnson's, Steevens, Reed and Malone's Edition by **Boswell**. 21 Vols. 8o.	
1822	Corall's Miniat. Edition. 9 Vols. 48o. 1826, 12o. 1831.	
1824	Wheeler's Edition. 1 Vols. 8o.	
1825	Harness's Edition. 8 Vols. 8o. 1830, 1833.	
1826	**Singer's** Edition. 10 Vols. 8o.	
1827	Whittingham's Edition. 8 Vols. 32o.	
1832	Valpy's Cabinet Edition. 15 Vols. 1840.	
1838	T. Campbell's Edition. 1 Vol. roy 8o. 1852. often reprinted.	
—	Tilt's Miniat. Edition. 8 Vols. 32o. 1839.	
—	**Charles Knight's** Pictorial Edition. 8 Vols. roy. 8o. 1845, 1864.	
1839	Barry Cornwall's Edition (Illustr. by Meadows). 3 Vols. imp. 8o. 1846. etc	
1841	**J. Payne Collier's** Edition. 8 Vols. 8o.	
1842	Knight's Library Edition. 12 Vols. 8o.	
1847	do. Standard Edition. 7 Vols. roy. 8".	
1851	**Halliwell's** Edition. 4 Vols. 8o.	
—	Hazlitt's Edition. 5 Vols. 12o, 1853, 1859.	
—	Phelp's Edition. 2 Vols. roy. 8o. 1858.	
1852	Lansdowne Edition. 1 Vols. 8o. 1859.	
—	Knight's Edition. 1 Vols. 8".	
—	do. National Edition. 6 Vols. 8o.	
1853	**Halliwell's** magn. Edition. 15 Vols. Folio.	
—	Collier's amended Edition from M. S. notes of the Folio. 1632. 8 Vols. 8o.	
—	do. 1 Vols. imp. 8o.	
1857	**Alex. Dyce's** Edition. 6 Vols. 8o.	
—	R. Grant White's Edition (Boston). 12 Vols cr. 8o.	
1858	Collier's. 6 Vols. 8o.	
—	**Staunton's** Edition. 3 Vols.	
1860	Cowden Clarke's Edition (New-York). 1 Vol. roy. 8o.	
1862	Chamber's Household Edition. 10 Vols. 12o.	
1863	Bowdler's School Edition. post 8o.	
1864	**W. C. Clark and W. A. Wright's** "Cambridge Edition." 8 Vols. 8o.	
—	Dyce's Second Edition. 8 Vols. 8o.	

2

1864 Rowe's New Edition. 8⁰.
— Staunton's Edition with Notes. 4 Vols. 8⁰.
— Reprint of first Folio Edition by Booth.
— Reference Shakspeare by Marsh.
— First Folio of 1623 reproduced by Howard Staunton, Photo-Lithography.
— Charles and Mary Cowden Clarke's Edition. 4 Vols. 8⁰.
— do. roy. 8⁰.
— Cassell's Illustrated Shakspeare.
— Keigtley's Elzevier Edition. 6 Vols. 12⁰.
— Nimmo's Edition. 2 Vols. 12⁰.
—- Knight's Stratford Shakspeare.
—. do. Re-issue of the Pictorial Shakspeare.
— The Globe Edition of the Works of William Shakspeare, *edited from* the best texts by William George Blacke and William Aldis Wright. Cambridge one Vol. roy. fsc. 8⁰. 3s 6d.

ENGLISH

COMMENTARIES, ESSAYS AND PLATES.

A catalogue of pictures in the Shakspeare-Gallery. 8º. London 1787.
Account of the second commemoration of Shakspeare in 1830.
—— descriptive, of the Gala-Festival at Stratford-upon-Avon in commemor. of the natal day of Shakspeare. 8º. Stratf. 1827.
—— **descriptive** of the second Royal Gala-Festival in commemoration of the natal day of Shakspeare. 8º. Stratford-upon-Avon 1827 and 1830.
A comparative review of the opinions of Mr. James Boaden (editor of the Oracle) in February, March and April 1795 and of James Boaden Esq. (author of Fontainville forest etc.) in February 1796, relative to the Shakspeare manuscript, by a friend to consistency. 8º. London 1796.
Addison. The Spectator No. 40. 141. 279. 419.
A dictionary of quotations from Shakspeare. 12º. London 1824.
A disquisition on the scene, origin, date, etc. etc., of Shakspeare's Tempest. In a letter to Benjamin Heywood Bright Esq., from the Rev. Joseph Hunter. 8. London 1836.
Adresses, accepted; to which are added, Macbeth Travestie, and Miscellanies by different hands. 12º. London 1813.
A few concise examples of errors corrected in Shakspeare's plays. 8º. Lond. 1818.
Agreeable Variety, the, being a miscellaneous collection in prose and verse, from the Works of Shakspeare, Milton, etc. by a Lady. 8º. Lond. 1724.
Albert, [the Rev. John Armstrong] Sonnets (40) from Shakespeare. 8º. Lond.1791.
Album: or, Warwickshire Garland, Songs illustrating. 4º. 1862.
A letter to George Hardinge, Esq., on the subject of a passage in Mr. Steevens preface to his impression of Shakspeare (by Collins). 4º. Lond. 1777.
A letter from M. de Voltaire to the French Academy on the merits of Shakspeare, with a dedication to the Marquis of Granby, and a preface by the Editor. 8º. London 1777.
Allen, J. A. The Lambda-Nu. Tercentenary poem on Shakspeare. 1864.
Allot, Rob. England's Parnassus, or the choicest flowers of Modern poets. 8º. London 1600.
  "Extracts from Shakspeare."
A lyric ode on the fairies, aerial beings, and witches of Shakspeare. 4º. London 1776.
Analysis of the Illustrated Shakspeare of Thomas Wilson. Fol. 1820.
An answer to certain passages of Shakspeare in Mr. Warburton's preface of his edition of Shakspeare; together with some remarks on the many errors of false criticisms in the work itself. 8º. London 1748.
An essay on the character of Hamlet, as performed by Mr. Henderson, at the Haymarket. 8º. s. a.
Annotations by Johnson and Steevens, and the various Commentators upon Hamlet and Titus Andronicus. 8º. 1787.
—— on Plays of Shakspeare, Privately Printed. 8º. York 1819.
—— on the plays of Shakspeare. Publ. with Scholey's Edition. 2 Vols. 8º. London 1819.
Antiquary, the. A farce in two Acts (satire on Shak. Antiquaries. 12º. London 1808.

A parallel of Shakspeare and Scott. 12o. London 1835.
A poetical epistle from Shakspeare in Elysium to Mr. Garrick at Drury-Lane-Theatre. 4o. London 1752.
Apollonius of Tyre. The Anglo Saxon Version of the story of (upon which is founded) the Play of Pericles, attributed to Shakspeare, with a literal translation by B. Thorpe. 8o. 1834.
Arrowsmith, R. W. Letter to the Editor of "Notes and Queries" on the Questionable Credit of that Periodical, and the Shakspeare adulterations. 8o. London 1858.
A second appendix to Mr. Malone's supplement to the last of the plays of Shakspeare. 8o. London 1783.
As you like it, the Music composed by Sir H. Bishop. Folio. 1825.
—— Seven Ages, composed by C. Horn. Folio.
—— do. by Arne. Folio. 1740.
Attempt to rescue Maister Shakspeare "see Holt".
—— an, to illustrate a few passages in Shakspeare's Works. 1802.
Avon, a Poem. London 1758.
Ayscough, S. An index to remarkable passages and words made use of by Shakspeare. 8o. London 1790. Dublin 1791. Lond. 1807, 1827 and 1842.
Bacon, D. The Philosophy of the Plays of Shakespeare unfolded. 8o. London 1857.
Badham, C. Criticism applied to Shakspeare. 8o. Lond. 1846.
Bailey, S. The Received Text of Shakespeare's Dramatic Works and its improvement. 8o. Lond. 1842.
Baker, D. E. Biographia dramatica. Second Edition. Lond. 1812.
Balmanno, Mrs. see "Lines".
Barckley. Sir Richard. Discourse on the Felicitie of Man; or his Summum Bonum. 4o. Printed for William Ponsonby 1598. 1603.
   "This work contains at pp. 24 and 25, the story of the Induction to the Taming of the Shrew."
Barclay. An examination of Mr. Kenrick's Review of Dr. Johnson's edition of Shakespeare. 8. Lond. 1766.
Barret, J. Shakespeare Fresh Chiseled on Stone. 8o. n. d.
Baretti, J. Discours sur Shakspeare et sur Mr. de Voltaire. 8o. Lond. 1777.
Barnstorff, D. Key to Shakespeare's Sonnets, translated from the German by T. J. Graham. 6o. Lond. 1862.
Beale, M. Lecture on the Times and Play of Richard III. 8o. Lond. 1841.
Beauties, the, of Shakspeare and Sterne, with some account of his life. 2 Vols. 12o. London 1819.
—— of Shakspeare by Dodd. 24o. 1840. see Dodd.
——   ——   do.   12o. 1853 and 1860.
——   ——   Illustrated 12o. 1853.
Becket, A. A concordance to Shakspeare, suited to all the editions; in which the distinguished and parallel passages in the plays of that justly admired writer are methodically arranged: to which are added three hundred notes and illustrations entirely new. 8o. London 1787.
—— Proposals for printing by subscription, in two large vols. 8o. "Shakspeare set free; or, the language of the poet asserted." 8o. Lond. 1812.
—— Shakspeare's Himself Again: or, the language of the poet asserted: being a full but dispassionate examen of the readings and interpretations of the several editors. 2 Vols. 8o. London 1815.
Beeton. Shakespeare Memorial, a Collection of pictures and paragraphs about Shakespeare. folio. 1864.
Beisly, Sidney. Shakespeare's Garden, or the plants and flowers named in Shakspeare's Works, defined and described. 1864.
Bell. Shakespeare's Puck and his Folkslore, illustrated from the superstitions of all Nations, but more especially from the earliest religions and rites of northern Europe and the Wends. 1852.
—— The missing Years in the life of Shakespeare
Bellew, J. C M. Shakespeare's Home at New Place, Stratford upon Avon. Being a history of the "Great House" built in the Reign of King Henry VII by Sir Hugh Clopton, Knight, and subsequently the property of Sir William Shakespeare, Gent, wherein he lived and died. 8o. 1863.
Bible Truths, with Shakespearian Parallels. 12o Lond. 1862.

Bicknell, J. Laurens. Original Miscellanies (including an Analysis of Hamlet). 1820.
Birch, W. Inquiry into the Philosophy and Religion of Shakspeare. 8º. 1848.
Blackwood's Edinburgh Magazine V. p. 217. 226.
Blount, Sir Thomas Pope. Remarks upon Poetry with Characters and censures of the most considerable poets whether ancient or modern (a life and several notices of Shakspeare). 1694.
Boaden, J. A letter to George Steevens, Esq., containing a critical examination of the papers of Shakespeare, published by Mr. Sam. Ireland, with extracts from Vortigern. 8º. Lond. 1796.
—— An inquiry into the authenticity of various pictures and prints, which, from the poet to our own times, have been offered to the public as portraits of Shakespeare. Illustrated by accurate and finished engravings by the ablest artists from such originals as were of indisputable authority. 8º. Lond. 1824.
—— Remarks on the sonnets of Shakespeare, identifying the persons to whom they are addressed, and elucidating several points in the poet's history. 8º. Lond. 1837.
—— Comparative Review of the Opinions of Jac. Boaden in 1795 and in 1796 relative to the Shakespeare MSS. 8º. 1796.
Bohn, Henry, G. The Biography and Bibliography of Shakespeare, embellished with 19 illustrations. Printed for the Members of the *Philobiblon Society* (40 Copies) square 4º. Whittingham 1863.
Book, the, of Shakespeare Gems in a Series of 45 Landscape Illustrations of the most interesting Localities of Shakespeare's Dramas. 8º. Lond. 1845.
Bowdler, Thomas. A letter to the editor of the British Critic, occasioned by the censure pronounced in that work on the editions of Shakespeare by Johnson, Pope, Bowdler, Warburton, Theobald, Steevens, Reed and Malone, et hoc genus omne, all the herd of these and Mei-Cominses of the British School. 8º. Lond. 1823.
Boydell. Notice to the Subscribers of Boydell's Edition of Shakspeare. fol. Lond. 1791.
—— Account of the Origin of the Shakspeare Undertaking. 8º. Lond. 1791.
Bracebridge, C. H. Shakespeare no Deerstealer. 8º. Lond. 1862.
Brae, A. E. Literary Cookery with reference to matter attributed to Coleridge and Shakspeare. 8º. Lond. 1855.
—— Collier, Coleridge and Shakspeare, a Review. 8º. 1860.
British Curiosities in Art and Nature giving an account of Rarities both ancient and modern. 12º. London 1721 "with notice of Shakspeare and Stratford."
Britton, John. Essays on the Merits and Characteristics of Shakspeare's Writings. 8º. Lond. 1819.
—— Remarks on the Monumental-Bust of Shakespeare, at Stratford-upon-Avon, with two woodcuts representing front and profile views of the Bust. 8º. Lond. 1816.
—— Remarks on the Life and Writings of W. Shakespeare. 8º. Lond. 1814. revised 1818. privately printed.
Brooker, Luke. Springs of Plynlimmon. A poem with notes (relates to Henry V). 8º. 1834.
Brome, R. Antipodes, a Comedie, acted in the yeare 1638, at Salisbury Court in Fleet Street (a curious play, an allusion to Shakespeare, at sig. C. 2.) 1640.
Brown, C. A. Shakespeare's autobiographical Poems, being his Sonnets clearly developed, with his Character, drawn chiefly from his works. 8º. Lond. 1838.
Brough. see "Falstaff."
Bucknill, Dr. J. C. The Psychology of Shakspeare. 8º. Lond. 1859.
—— Remarks on the Medical knowledge of Shakespeare. Lond. 1860.
Burton. Shaksperiana Burtonensis; being a Catalogue of the extensive Collection of Shakspeariana of the late W. E. Burton of New-York. 8º. 1860.
Caldecott, T. "Hamlet" and "As You like it"; a specimen of an edition of Shakespeare. 8º. Lond. 1819. 2d. Ed. 1832.
Campbell, T. Remarks of Life and Writings of Shakspeare (Moxon's Edition of S.). 1833.
Campbell, Lord, John. The legal acquirements of Shakspeare considered. 12º. London 1859.

Capell, E. Notes and various readings of Shakespeare, or Extracts from diverse english Books that were in print in that author's time; evidently shewing from whence his several Fables were taken and some Parallel of his Dialogue. Also farther Extracts, or which contribute to a due understanding of his Writings or give a Light, to the History of his Life, or to the dramatic history of his Time. 4. London 1759. 2nd. edition, with additions, 3 vols. 1779—80.
—— Prolusions; or select pieces of Ancient Poetry, containing Edward the Third, a play thought to be made by Shakespeare. 8°. 1760.
Capell. A few Words in defence of Edward Capell, occasioned by a criticism in the Times Newspaper. 4°. Lond. 1861 (privately pr.).
Carey, G. Saville. Shakespeare's Jubilee, a masque. 8°. London 1769.
Caryl, J. English Princess, or the death of Richard the Third. 4°. 1667.
Catalogue of the Household furniture and Effects at New-Place, Stratford upon Avon 1861.
—— of Mr. Capell's Shakesperiana presented by him to Trinity College Cambridge and printed from an exact copy of his own Manuscript. London 1779.
—— of the pictures in Boydell's Shakespeare-Gallery, 8°. London 1792.
—— of some Books in the possession of H. Jadis Esq. in Bryanstone Square. Royal-8°. London. Privately printed. 1826.
—— of the books, paintings, etc. of the late Samuel Ireland Esq. 8°. London 1801.
—— of the various articles contained in *Clara Fisher's Shaksperian* Cabinet, with plates. 1830.
Caulfield, T. Vocal Music in Shakspeare's Plays.
Chalmeriana; a collection of papers occasioned by reading Chalmer's supplemental apology. 8°. London 1800.
Chalmers, A. Biographical Dictionary. Article: Shakspeare.
Chalmers, G. An apology for the believers in the Shakespeare papers, which were exhibited in Norfolk-Street. 8°. London 1797.
—— A supplemental apology for the believers in the Shakespeare-papers, being a reply to Mr. Malone's answer which was early announced, but never published, with a dedication to G. Steevens and a postscript to T. J. Mathias. London 1799.
—— An appendix to the supplemental apology for the believers in the supposititious Shakespeare papers. 8°. London 1800.
—— An inquiry into the incidents from which the title and a part of the story of Shakespeare's Tempest were derived, and its true era ascertained. 8°. London 1815. Only 40 Copies printed.
Chalmers. Antenor's Letter to George Chalmers, author of an apology for the believers in the Shakspeare Papers; and of a Postscript to the Apology. 8°. London 1800.
Characters, Modern, from Shakspeare, alphabetically arranged. 12°. 1778.
Chedworth, Lord. Notes upon some of the obscure passages in Shakespeare's plays. 8°. London 1805. (Privately printed.)
Chester, Rob. Love's Martyr, or Rosalin's Complaint etc. with some new Compositions of modern Writers. 4°. Lond. 1601.
   "Some of these Compositions are by Shakspeare."
Cibber, T. Familiar Epistle to W. Warburton. 8°. Lond. s. d.
—— Lives of the poets. Vol. I
—— A letter from Cibber to Pope. Lond. 1742.
—— A letter to Colley Cibber Esq. on his transformation of King John. 8°. Lond. 1745.
Citation and examination of W. Shakspeare, etc., touching deer-stealing. 12°. London 1834. see *Landor.*
Clarke. M, Cowden. Shakspeare Proverbs, or the Wise Saws of our wisest poet. 1847, 48, 49.
—— Mrs. Concordance to Shakspeare. roy. 8°. 1844—2nd. E. 1848.
—— Girlhood of Shakspeare's Heroines. 3 Vols, 12°. 1850—2.
—— Shakspeare's Characters chiefly subordinate. Demy. 8°. London 1863.
Clifford's Notes on Dryden's Poems (cont. notices of Shakspeare's plays). 1687.
Coleridge, S. T. Notes and Lectures upon Shakspeare, 2 Vols, 12°. London 1849.

Collection of Prints from pictures painted for the purpose of illustrating the dramatic Works of Shakspeare by the artists of Great Britain. Roy.-Fol. 2 Vols. London 1803.
Collier, J. P. New facts regarding the works of Shakespeare. 8°. London 1835.
—— New particulars regarding the writings of Shakespeare. 8°. London 1836.
—— Further particulars regarding the writings of Shakespeare. 8°. London 1840.
—— Shakespeare Library: a collection of the stories, novels, and tales, used by Shakespeare as the foundation of his plays. 8. London 1840—41.
—— Memoirs of Edward Alleyn, founder of Dulwich-College: including some new particulars respecting Shakespeare, Ben. Johnson, Massinger, Marston, Dekker etc. 8°. London 1841.
—— The Ghost of Richard the Third. 8° London 1844.
—— Diary of Philip Henslowe, from 1591 to 1609. From the Original at Dulwich-College etc. 8°. London 1845.
—— Memoirs of the Principal Actors in Shakespeare's Plays. 8°. London 1846.
—— A Dissertation on the imputed Portraits of Shakespeare. 8°. London 1851.
—— Life of Shakspeare, with a history of the early English Stage. 8°. Lond. 1844.
—— History of English Dramatic Poetry to the time of Shakespeare, and Annals of the Stage of the restoration. 3 Vols. 8°. 1831.
—— Extracts from the Registers of the Stationers Company. 1557—70, with notes and illustrations. 2 Vols. 1848/9.
—— Reasons for a new Edition of Shakspeare's Works. 2. Ed. 1842.
—— Reply to Mr. N. E S. A. Hamilton's "Inquiry into the imputed Shakspeare Forgeries. 1860.
—— New facts regarding the Life of Shakspeare. 1835. Privately printed.
—— Notes and emendations to the text of Shakspeare's Plays, from early Manuscript corrections in a Copy of the folio 1632 in the Possession of J. Payne Collier, Esq. forming a supplementary volume of the works of Shakespeare. 8°. London 1853.
Colman. Prose on several occasions. Vol. II. Lond. 1787.
Comedy of Errors, Music in, by Sir H. Bishop. Folio. 1819.
Commentary. Specimen of a Commentary on Shakspeare. 1794. 8°.
Congal and Fenella, a tale in the Story of Macbeth. 8°. 1791.
Conolly, John. Study of Hamlet. fsc. 8°. 1863.
Cooke, T. An Epistle (in verse) to the Countess of Shaftesbury, with a Prologue and Epilogue on Shakspeare and his writings. Folio. Lond. 1742.
Cooper, J. G. The Tomb of Shakespeare, a poetical vision. 4°. London 1755, — 2nd. edition 1755.
Corney, B. The Sonnets of Wm. Shakespeare: a critical disquisition suggested by a recent discovery. 8°. Lond. 1862. (Privately printed.)
Cornwallis, Sir W. Essayes of certaine Paradoxes. In Prose and Verse. 2 parts. 18°. London 1600—1. (Reference to Shakespeare.)
Courtenay, H. Commentaries on the historical plays of Shakespeare. 2 Vols. 8°. London 1840.
Cox, Frederick. Lecture on the Genesis, Life and Character of William Shakspeare. 8°. Leicester 1853. (Privately printed).
Craik, G. The English of Shakspeare; illustrated in a philological Commentary on his tragedy of "Julius Caesar." 8°. 1856.
Criticism. Cursory Criticism on the Edition of the Works of Shakspeare published by Ed. Malone. 1792.
—— Of Verbal Criticism, an Epistle to Mr. Pope, occasioned by Theobald's Shakespeare, and Bentley's Milton. Folio. 1733.
Croft, J. A. Select collection of the beauties of Shakespeare, with some account of the life of Shakespeare. 8°. York 1792.
—— Annotations on plays of Shakespeare; Johnson and Steevens edition. 8°. York 1810. (Privately printed.)
Croft, Z. (C. Kelsall.) The first sitting of the committee on the proposed monument to Shakespeare; taken in short-hand. 8°. Cheltenham 1825.
Croker, T. Crofton. Walk from London to Fulham (cont. a Shakespeare paper). 1860.
—— Remarks on an Article inserted in the papers of the Shakespeare Society on Massinger's play. Believe as you list. 8°. Lond. 1849. Privately printed.
—— New Readings of Shakespeare's Tempest. 12°. n. d.
Cumberland, R. The Observer. No. 55—58, 86.

Cunningham, P. A Selection from Oldys's Mss. Notes to Langbaine's Dramatic Poets. 8°. London 1851.
Cupid's Cabinet Unlock't, or the New Academy of Complements, Odes, Epigrams, Songs and Sonnets, Poesies, Presentations etc., with other various fancies, created partly for the delight, but chiefly for the use of all Ladies, Gentlemen and Strangers, who affect to speak Elegantly, or write Queintly. 12°. n. d.
"Falsely attributed to Shakespeare."
Curiosities of Shakspearian Criticism. 1853.
Curling, H. Shakespeare the poet, the lover, the actor, the man. A Romance. 3 Vols. 8°. 1849.
Davenant (Sir W.). Madagascar, with other Poems. Second Ed. 1648.
"At page 34 is an Ode "In Remembrance of Master William Shakespeare."
Davies (John). Microcosmos, the Discovery of the Little World, with the government thereof; 4°. Oxford 1603.
"At page 215 mention is made of Shakespeare and Burbage, as actors."
—— A Scourge for Paper-Persecutors. 4o. London 1824. 1825.
"Allusions to Shakspeare's Venus and Adonis."
Davies, Th. Memoirs of Garrick. 2d. Ed. Lond. 1780. (Vol. I p. 113—18, 277, Vol. II 275.)
—— Dramatick Micellanies, consisting of critical observations on the plays of Shakespeare: with a Review of his principal Characters, and those of various eminent writers, as represented by Mr. Garrick and other celebrated Comedians. With Anecdotes of dramatick Poets, Actors etc. 3 Vols. 8°. London 1784.
Denman, T. see Edinburgh Review. May 1828.
Dennis, J. The impartial Critic; or, some observations on Mr. Rymer's late book, entitled: "A Short view of tragedy" 4°. London 1692, 1693, 1697.
"One of the earliest and rarest of Shakespeariana; it is a reply to Rymer's attack on Shakespeare."
—— An essay on the Genius and writings of Shakespeare, with some letters of criticism to the Spectator. 8. London 1712.
—— Life of Dennis the Renowned Critick, in which are some observations on most of the poets (incl. Shakespeare) not written by Mr. Curll. (8°. London 1734.)
Deverell, Rob. Hieroglyphic and other Antiquities, in treating of which many favourite Pieces of Butler, Shakespeare etc. are explained. 6 Vols. 8°. London 1816.
Dictionary of Quotations from Shakespeare. 12°. London 1843.
Dirill, Ch. (Richard Sill). Remarks on Shakespeare's Tempest containing an investigation of Mr. Malone's attempt to ascertain the date of that play; and various notes and illustrations of obscure readings and passages. 8o. London 1797.
Dodd, Wm. B. A. The Beauties of Shakespeare, regularly selected from each play. 2 Vols. 12°. London 1752.
Dolby, Th. The Shakesperian Dictionary, forming a general index to popular expressions and striking passages in Shakespeare. 8". Lond. 1832.
Dolby, T. F. The Apotheosis of Shakespeare (in verse). 8°. Lond. 1848.
Done, John. Polydoron; or a Miscellanea of Morall, Philosophicall and Theological Sentences 12°. Printed at London by Tho. Cotes for George Gibbes. 1631.
"Notice of Shakespeare at page 32."
Donne, J. Poems (Epitaph on Shakespeare at page 165) 1633.
Douce, Francis. Illustrations of Shakespeare and of ancient manners: with dissertations on the clowns and fools of Shakespeare; on the collection of popular tales entitled Gesta Romanorum and on the English Morris dance. gr. 8°. Lond. 1839.
Douglas, Hypolitus, Earl of, containing some Memoirs of the Court of Scotland, with the Secret History of Mackbeth, King of Scotland. 8°. 1708.
Downes. Roscius Anglicanus. Review of the english Stage. Lond. 1789.
Drake, J. Ancient and Modern Stages survey'd (cont. curious early specimens of Shakspearian criticism). 1699.
Drake, Nathan. Shakespeare and his time, including the biography of the poet, criticism on his genius and writings, a new chronology of his plays, a disquisition on the object of his sonnets, and a history of the manners,

customs and amusements, superstitions, poetry and elegant literature of his age. With a portrait and autograph. 2 Vols. 4°. Lond. 1817.
Drake, Nathan. Noontide Leisure, including a Tale of the days of Shakspeare. 2 Vols. 8°. 1824.
—— Memorials of Shakespeare with Essay and Notes or Sketch of his character and genius by various writers. 8°. Lond. 1828.
Dramatic Magazine. Lond. 1830. pag. 12, 357—60; 1831. pag. 12, 44—50.
—— Souvenir: being Literary and graphic Illustrations of Shakspeare and the British Drama. 8°. Lond. 1841.
Dryden, J. Essay on dramatic poesy. Lond. 1668.
Dubois, E. The Wreath; selections from Sappho, Theocritus, Bion and Moschus, Greek and English; to which are added Remarks on Shakespeare. 8°. Lond. 1799.
Duff, W. Critical observ. on the writings of original genius. 2 Vols. Lond. 1767—70. (pag. 127—153.)
Dyce, A. The Old Play of Timon. Now first printed etc. 8°. Lond. 1842.
—— Remarks on Collier's and Knight's Shakespeare. 8°. Lond. 1830.
—— A few Notes on Shakespeare; with occasional Remarks on the Emendations of a Copy 1632 in the Possession of Mr. Collier. 8°. Lond. 1853.
—— Strictures on Mr. Collier's New Edition of Shakespeare. 1859.
—— Memoir of Shakespeare. Preface to the Poems of Shaks. Lond. 1832.
Dyce's Edition of Shakespeare. Article Quarterly Review No. 209. Jany. 1859.
Eaton, T. R. Shakespeare and the Bible. 1858. 1860.
Eccles, Am. Illustrations and Variorum Commentaries on three plays of Shak. viz: King Lear, Cymbeline, and the Merchant of Venice. 12°. Lond. 1792—1805.
Edinburgh Review. 1817. 472—88. 1829. No. 93 and 94. 1840 Febr.
Edwards, Th. The Canons of Criticism and Glossary; being a supplement to Mr. Warburton's Edition of Shakespeare, collected from the Notes in that celebrated work, and proper to be bound with it. 8°. Lond. 1747. 1748. 50. 58. 85.
Egestorf, G. On Hamlet. Literary Gazette Octbr. 1827.
Elwin, H. Shakespeare Restored. Macbeth, with a Comment. 4.° Norwich 1853. (100 Copies priv. printed.)
Encyclopedia Metropolitana, Lond. Article Shakespeare.
Encyclopedia of Wit — Prolegomena to the dramatic works of Shakespeare. Portrait. 1788.
Epistle, an, from Shakespeare to his Countrymen. 4°. Lond. 1777.
—— an, from Little Captain Brazen to the worthy Captain Plume, to which is added an answer to the said Epistle. In which the character of Iago is set forth, so as to be understood by the meanest capacity. folio. Lond. n. d.
—— an, to Mr. Pope, on verbal criticism, occasioned by Theobald's Shakespeare and Bentley's Milton. folio. 1773.
Essay. Prize Essay on the historical Plays of Shakespeare. 8°. Lond. 1830.
—— on the Jubilee at Stratford upon Avon. 4°. 1769.
—— towards fixing the true Standards of Wit, Humour, Raillery etc. and an Analysis of the Sir John Falstaff etc. 8°. 1744. (see "Morris").
—— an, on the character of Hamlet, as performed by Mr. Henderson. Lond. 1770. 1797.
Essays, by a Society of Gentlemen at Exeter. Exeter. 1796.
—— on the character of Macbeth. 8o. Lond. 1846.
Etchings to the illustrated Shakespeare: designed by Kenny Meadows. Roy.-8. London n. d.
Etymologist, a Comedy in three acts; dedicated to all the Commentators that ever wrote, are writing or will write on Shakespeare. 1785.
Euphues Golden Legacie, found after his death in his Cell at Silexedra, bequeathed to Philautus Sonnes, nursed up with their father in England, fetcht from the Canaries by T. L. Gent.
4o. imprinted at London for John Smethwicke. 1634.
„The foundation novel of the Comedy of As You Like It".
Evans, I. A. M. The progress of human life: Shakespeare's seven ages of man, illustrated by a series of extracts in prose and poetry; introduced by a brief memoir of Shakespeare and his writings. 8. Chiswick 1818.— 2d. Edition London 1820.

Exegesis, new, of Shakespeare. Interpretations of his principal characters and Plays on the Principle of Races. 8o. Edinb. 1859.
Facsimile, of the letter mentioning Shakespeare in the Collection of the Earl of Ellesmere. Privately printed.
Facsimiles (six) of all the known Autographs of Shakespeare, drawn by Harris, on a 4to. Sheet.
Faed, Thomas. Shakespeare and his Contemporaries. Print.
Fairholt, Home of Shakespeare illustrated and described. Engravings. Lond.1847.
Falstaff. The diverting history of the life, memorable exploits, pranks and droll adventures etc. of Sir John Falstaff and miraculous escapes from the wanton contrivances of the Merry Wives of Windsor as written by Shakspeare. 8o. (1750) 2nd Ed. 1789.
—— The Life and Exploits of that Extraordinary Character of Sir John Falstaff, the Hero of Shakespeare, and companion of Henry, Prince of Wales; with an account of the numerous Robberies and Offences committed by them; particulars of his amorous Adventures and Gallanteries at Windsor, with Mrs. Ford and Mrs. Page; his conduct as a Captain at the Battle of Shrewsbury, between Percy and Hotspur, a humorous Description of his Soldiers, Trial and Conviction at Maidstone etc. With the Portrait of Falstaff. 8o. Lond. n. d.
—— Original Letters etc. of Sir John Falstaff and his friends, now first made public by a Gentleman, see "White".
—— Life and Humours of Sir John Falstaff. 8o. Lond. 1829.
—— The Life of Sir John Falstaff, illustrated by George Cruikshank, with a biography of the Knight from authentic sources by Rob. Brough. 8o. Lond. 1857.
Falstaff's Jests, or the Quintessence of Wit and Humour, with a collection of Buckish Songs. 12o. Lond. 1761. 1762.
—— Wedding. 1760.
Farmer, Rich., D. D. An essay on the learning of Shakespeare. 8. Lond. 1767. 2nd 1767, 1789, 1821.
Farrago; containing Essays on Shakespeare, Boxing and other things, 2Vols 8o. Tewkesbury. 1792.
Farren, G. An essay on Shakespeare's character of Shylock. 8. London 1833.
—— Observations on the laws of Mortality and disease, with an Appendix on the progress of Mania, Melancholia, Craziness and Demonomania, as displayed in the Characters of Lear, Hamlet, Ophelia and Edgar. Printed for the Author. 1829.
—— Facts and Reasons in answer to Farren. 1833.
Fate of Majesty exemplified in the Barbarous Treatment of the Kings and Queens of the Royal House of the Stuarts. 8o. J. Roberts in Warwick Lane, n. d.
„Story of Macbeth"
Fechter's Version of Othello critically analysed see Ottley, Wilmot.
Felton, Sam. Imperfect hints towards a new edition of Shakespeare. 4. Lond. 1787. – 2nd Part 1788.
Fennel, J. H. The Shakespeare Repository. 8. London 1853.
—— Shakespeare Cyclopaedia, or a classified and elucidated Summary of Shakespeare's knowledge of the Works and Phenomena of Nature. (in 20 parts.) 8o. 1862.
Fergusson, Dr. On the Madness of Hamlet (Article in the Quarterly Review on Sir Henry Holford's Essay).
Finegan, F. T. An attempt to illustrate a few passages in Shakespeare's works. 8o. Bath 1802.
Fisher, Clara. Catalogue of the various articles in Clara Fisher's Shakespearian Cabinet. 8o. Lond. 1860.
—— Remembrance of Shakespeare. Wood engravings of all the models. 8o. 20 engrav. n. d.
Fletcher, G. Studies on Shakespeare with observations and the Criticism and acting of certain plays. 8o. Lond. 1847.
Footsteps of Shakespeare, or ramble with the Early Dramatists. roy. 12o. London 1861.
Forster, R. H A few remarks on the Chandos Portrait of Shakespeare, bought for the Earl of Ellesmere. 8o. Lond. 1849. (50 Copies.)

Fragments, Curious, from a Manuscript Collection, ascribed to Shakspeare. London 1811.
Friswell, Hain. Life Portraits of William Shakspeare: a history of the various representations of the poet; with an examination into their authenticity. Illustrated by Photographs. roy. 8⁰. London 1864.
Froude, J. A. History of England, the Volume containing: The Reign of Elizabeth. London 1863.
Fullom, S. W. The history of W. Shakspeare, the Player and Poet, with new traits and traditions. 8⁰. London 1862.
Gardenstone. Shakspeare compared with Corneille. In Drake's Memorials p. 274—9.
Garland of Shakspeariana (only 25 Copies printed, privately 1854).
Garrick, Dav. Ode upon dedicating a building, and erecting a statue to Shakespeare at Stratford-upon-Avon. 4. London 1769.
—— Vagary, or England run mad; with Particulars of the Stratford Jubilee. 8. 1769.
—— Letter to Garrick concerning a Glossary to the Plays of Shakespeare, with a Specimen. 1768.
—— A poetical Epistle from Shakspeare in Elysium to Mr. Garrick at Drury Lane Theatre. 4⁰. London 1752.
—— An Ode to Garrick. 8⁰. London 1749.
Gems of Shakespeare. In Tilt's Miniature Classics. London n. d.
Genius, the, of Shakspeare, a Summerdream. London 1793.
Gerard. An Essay on Genius. London 1747. (page 71, 363.)
Gervinus, G. G. Shakspeare Commentaries, translated by F. E. Bunnett. 2 Vols. 8. London 1862.
Gilchrist, O. An examination of the charges maintained by Messrs. Malone, Chalmers, and others, of Ben. Johnson's enmity, &c., towards Shakespeare. 8. London 1808.
Gildon, Ch. Some reflections on Mr. Rymer's „Short view of tragedy" and an attempt at a vindication of Shakespeare. 1694. (In the miscellaneous letters and essays. 8. 1694.)
—— Remarks on the plays of Shakespeare. Reprinted at the end of 7*th* Vol. of Rowe's Ed. 1709.
—— Complete Art of Poetry, and Shakespeariana, or the most beautiful topics and characters in all Shakspeare's plays. 12⁰. London 1718.
—— Comparison between the two Stages, with an examen of the generous Conqueror (includes Shakspearian critiques) 1702.
Giraud. The Flowers of Shakspeare. 30 plates. 4⁰. 1845.
Godwin. The life of Chaucer. (Vol. I. p. 499, 509, 512, Vol. IV. pag. 189.)
Goldsmith, O. Vicar of Wakefield. Ch. II. pag. 18.
Goodall's. Shakspeare's Tercentenary Playing Cards. 1864.
Gough, H. T. Ode, inscribed with reverend Regard to the Memory of William Shakspeare, the Immortal Bard. 4*to* 1848.
Graves, H. M. Essay on the Genius of Shakspeare, with critical remarks on the characters of Romeo, Juliet and Ophelia. 8⁰. 1826.
Green, C. F. The Legend of Shakspeare's Crab-Tree. Plates. 1857.
Green (Robert). Groatsworth of Witte, bought with a Million of Repentance. 4*to* London 1592 (contains a notice of Shakspeare) reprinted with preface by Sir E. Brydges. 4⁰. 1813.
Gregory, Letters on Literature, taste and composition. Vol. II. pag. 252.
Grey, Zach. A word or two of advice to William Warburton, a dealer in many words by a friend. With an appendix containing a taste of William's Spirit of railing. 8. London 1746.
—— A free and familiar letter to that great refiner of Pope and Shakespeare the Rev. Mr. Wm. Warburton. 8. London 1750.
—— Critical, historical and explanatory notes on Shakespeare, with emendations of the text and metre. 2 Vols. 8. Lond. 1752. — 2. Edit. 1754. — 3. Edit. 1755.
—— Remarks upon a late (Warburton's) edition of Shakespeare, with a long string of emendations, borrowed by the celebrated editor from the Oxford edition without acknowledgement; to which is prefixed a defence of the late Sir Thomas Hanmer, Bart. 8. London 1751.
Griffith, Mrs. Elizabeth. The morality of Shakespeare's dramas illustrated. London 1775. 8. 2 Vols 1777.

Grimaldi. Notes and Emendations on the plays of Shakespeare, from a recently discovered annotated Copy of the late Joseph Grimaldi Esq. Comedian. 8º. (a humorous squib on the late Shakspeare Emendations. 1854.)
Grinfield, C. V. Pilgrimage to Stratford on Avon. 12º.
Grinfield, C. V. Remarks on the moral Influence of Shakspeare's Plays; with illustrations from Hamlet. 8º. 1850.
Guizot. Shakespeare and his Times, translated from the french. 8. London 1852 & 1857.
Guthrie, W., Essay on English Tragedy, with Remarks on the Abbé Le Blanc's Observations on the English Stage. 8. London 1747, 1749.
Hackett, J. H. Falstaff, a Shaksp. Tract. privately printed. 1840.
Hall, J. Illustrations of Shakspeare. 8º. London 1773.
Hall, John. Select observat. on English Bodies; or cures both empericall and historicall, performed upon very eminent persons in desperate diseases transl. from Latin into English by James Cooke. 12º. London 1657, 1679, 1683.
„Hall married Shak. daughter Susanna in 1607, notices several family connexions."
Hall, Spencer. Letter to Mr. Murray on a New Edition of Shakspeare. 1841.
Hallam, H. Introduction to the Literature of Europe. Vol. II. & III.
Halliwell, J. O. The life of Shakespeare. 8. London 1827.
—— An introduction to Shakespeare's Midsummer-Night's Dream. 8. London 1841.
—— Shakesperiana. A catalogue of the early editions of Shakespeare's plays and of the commentaries and other publications illustrative of his works. 8. 'London 1841.
—— Illustrations of the Fairy Mythology of Shakespeare. 8. London 1845.
—— The life of Will. Shakespeare; including many Particulars respecting the Poet and his Family never before published. 8. London 1848.
—— The Remarks of M. Karl Simrock on the Plots of Shakespeare's Plays. With Notes etc. 8. London 1850.
—— A lyttle Boke givinge A True and Brief Accounte of some Reliques and Curiosities added of late to Mr. Halliwell's Shakspeare Collection facsimile 1617. Only 25 Copies printed. 4o. 1856.
—— Essay on the Character of John Falstaff. 12º.
—— Observations on the Character of Falstaff. 12º. 1841.
—— Some Account of the Antiquities, Coins, Manuscript Documents etc. illustrative of Shakspeare in the possession of J. O. Halliwell Esqr. Facsimile and woodcuts; only 80 Copies printed. 1852.
—— Traditionary Anecdotes of Shakspeare collected in Warwickshire in 1693. London 1838.
—— Account of the only known Manuscript of Shakspeare's plays, compr. some important variations and corrections in the Merry Wives of Windsor, obtained from a play house Copy of that play recently discovered. 1843.
—— A few remarks on the Emendation „Who smothers her with painting" in the play of Cymbeline, discovered by Mr Collier in a corrected Copy of the second Edition of Shakspeare. 8º.
—— - A new Boke about Shakespeare and Stratford on Avon. 4º. London 1850. (75 Copies printed.)
—— Observations on the Shakesperian forgeries at Bridgewater House, illustrative of a facsimile of the spurious letter of H. S. 4º. London 1853. (25 Copies)
—— A Garland of Shakesperiana, recently added to the Library and Museum of O. Halliwell. 4º. 1854. (25 Copies.)
—— Bill of Complaint in Chancery respecting Mr. Shakespeare's Legacy to the Birth Place in Henley Street. 4º. London 1859.
—— Dorastus and Fawnia. The foundation Story of Shakespeare's Winter's Tale. Edit. by Halliwell. 4º. London 1859. (26 Copies printed.)
—— Brief Hand-list of the Records belonging to the Borough of Stratford-on-Avon, showing their general character, and Notes of the few Shakesperian Documents in the same Collection. 12º. London 1862. (50 Copies.)
—— A hand-list of upwards of a Thousand Volumes of Shakesperiana added to the three previous Collections of a similar kind formed by J. O. Halliwell. 4. London 1862. (25 Copies.)

Halliwell, J. O. Dictionary of Old Engl. Plays, existing either in print or manuscript, from the earliest times to the close of the 17th Century. 8°. London 1860.
—— Hand List of the Early English Literature preserved in the Malone Collection in the Bodleian Library. 8°. London 1860 (51 Copies.)
—— Skeleton Hand list of the Early Quarto Editions of the Plays of Shakspeare with Notices of the Old Impressions of the poems. 8°. London 1860 (25 Copies.)
—— Observations on some of the Manuscript emendations on the text of Shakspeare. 8°.
—— Curiosities of modern Shakespeare Criticism. 8°. Lond. 1853.
—— Shakespeare's Will, copied from the Original, in the Prerogative Court, preserving the Interlineations and Facsimiles of the three Autographs of the poet, with a few preliminary Observations. 4°.
—— Notices of Early Editions of Shakespeare. 14 pages. 8°. Only 25 Copies printed 1857.
—— A Hand-List of Books, Manuscripts etc. illustrative of the Life and Writings of Shakespeare, collected between the years 1842 and 1859. Only 30 Copies privately printed 1859.
„This Collection contains upwards of three hundred volumes, entirely relating to Shakespeare."
Halpin, J. A. Oberon's Vision in the Midsumer Night's Dream illustrated by a comparison with Lylie's Endymion. 8. London 1843.
—— The dramatic Unities of Shakespeare etc. 8. Dublin 1849.
Hamilton, E. S. A. The Shakspeare Question: an enquiry into the Genuiness of the M. S. Corrections in Mr. J. Payne Collier's Annotated Shakspeare folio 1632 and of certain Shaksperian Documents, likewise published by Mr. Collier; 8°. London 1860.
—— Strictures on Hamilton's Inquiry by a Scrutator. 8°. 1860.
Hamlet. An Attempt to ascertain whether the Queen were an Accessory, before the Fact, in the Murder of her First Husband. 8°.
—— Some Remarks on the Tragedy of Hamlet Prince of Denmark written by Shakspeare. 8°. London 1736.
—— Slender's Ghost; Hamlet's Soliloquy imitated; a fit of the Spleen in imitation of Shakespeare. 8°. London 1748.
—— Ophelias Airs in Hamlet, arranged by G. Nicks. fol.
Hanmer. Verses to Sir Thomas Hanmer on his Edition of Shakspeare's Works. By a Gentleman of Oxford (W. Collins) folio. London 1743.
—— The Castrated letter of Sir Thomas Hanmer, wherein is discovered the first Rise of the Present Bishop of Gloucester's Quarrel with that Bart., about his Edition of Shakspeare's Plays. 4°. 1763.
—— T. Preface to his Edition of Shakspeare. Oxf. 1744.
Harding. The whole historical dramas of W. Shakespeare, illustrated by an assemblage of portraits of the royal, noble, and other persons mentioned, together, with those of commentators, actors, and views of castles, towns, etc. with short biographical and topographical accounts, 2 vols., 4°. and imperial 8°. London 1793. — 2d. Edition 1811.
Hardinge, George. Another essence of Malone; or, the beauties of Shakespeare's editor. In two parts. 8. London 1801.
—— Miscellaneous Works. London 1818.
Hardy, R. B. Lectures on Shakspeare. 18°. London 1834.
Hardy, T. Duffus. A Review of the Present state of the Shakspearian Controversy. 8°. London 1860.
Hare, J. G. The Victory of Faith, etc. London 1840. (pag 277.)
Hares, R. A Glossary or collection of words, names, and allusions to customs, proverbs etc. which have been thought to require illustration in the works of english authors, particularly Shakespeare and his contemporaries. 8°. London 1823.
Harness, W. The life of Shakspeare, preface to his Edition 1825.
Harris, J. Dramatic Speculations: in his Philos. Inquiries Vol. II.
Harrison, Mr. The Infant Vision of Shakespeare, and other poems. 4°. Lond. 1794.
Hartshorne, C. H. Book Rarities of the University of Cambridge with Notes, 1829. Includes a Collection of Capel's Shakesperiana in Trinity College Library.
Hawkins, F. The Origin of the English Drama. 3 Vols. Oxf. 1773.

Hayward, Th. The British Muse, or a Collection of thoughts of our English poets of the 16th & 17th Centuries, with passages from Shakspeare. 3 Vols. 12°. London 1738.

Hazlitt, Will. Characters of Shakespeare's plays. 1817. 4th Edition, edited by his son. 8. London 1848.

—— Lectures on the dramatic Literature of the age of Elizabeth. 8°. Lond. 1821. 3rd Ed. 1841.

Heath, Charles. A Revisal of Shakespeare's text, wherein the alterations introduced into it by the more modern editors and critics are particularly considered. 8°. London 1765.

—— Shakspeare Gallery. 45 portraits.

—— the Portraits of Shakspeare's Heroines. imp. 8°. 1848. London.

Heron (R. i. e. Pinkerton). Letters on Literature including Remarks on the last Edition of Shakspeare. 1785.

Heywood, Thomas. Fayre Maide of the Exchange, with the merry humors and pleasant passages of the Cripple of Fanchurch. 1637.
  „Contains a curious notice of Shakspeare's poem of Venus and Adonis."

Hifferman, Paul. Dramatic Genius. Essay on Shakspeare. 1772.

Historiographer. The dramatic; or the British Theatre delineated. 12°. London 1735.
  „Criticism on Shakspeare's plays."

Histrionic Topography; or, the Birth Places, Residences and Monuments of distinguished Actors. 8°. London 1818.

Hoe. Wm. Shakspeare. Treasury of Subject Quotations synonymously indexed. 8° London 1863.

Holt, J. An attempte to rescue that aunciente English Poet and Play wrighte, Maistre William Shakespeare, from the many errours falsely charged on him by certaine new fangled wittes, and to let him speak for himself as right well he wotteth, when freede from the many careless mistakings of the heedless first imprinters of his works. 8. London 1749.

—— Remarks on the Tempest; or, an attempt to rescue Shakespeare from the many errors falsely charged on him by his several editors, &c. 8. London 1750.

Home, H. Elements of Criticism. Chap. 2 - 23.

Hornby. Extemporal Verses written at the Birth Place of Shakspeare. 8. s. a.

Howard, H. Visionary Interview at the Shrine of Shakespeare. 4°. Lond. 1756.

Howard, F. Spirit of the Plays of Shakespeare, exhibited in a series of outline Plates illustrative of the story of each play; drawing and engravings by the author with quotations and descriptions. 5 Vols. 8. London 1833—1835.

Hows, J. W. The Shakespearian Reader; a Coll. of the most approved plays of S. with introd. and notes. 12°. New York. 1850.

Huckel, Rev. John. Avon, a poem in three cantos. Birm. 1758. 4°. Lond. 1811. 12°.

Hudson, H. N. Lectures on Shakespeare. 2 Vols. 12. London and New-York 1848.

Hugo, Victor. William Shakspeare. His Life and Works, transl. from the french by A. Baillot. 1864.

Hume, D. History of England. Appendix to James I.

Humphreys, H. N. Shakespeare's Sentiments and Similes. Illuminated etc. 8. London 1851. 1864.

Hunt, Rich. The Bow of Jonathan, with the flower de Luce, in a funeral lamentation upon Robert Lucy of Charlcote in the Country of Warwick. 4to 1757.

Hunter, Jos. Disquisition on the Scene, Origin and Date of Shakespeare's Tempest. 1839. (Only 100 Copies printed.)

—— New Illustrations of the Life, Studies and Writings of Shakspeare. 2 Vols 8o. London 1845.

—— Few words in reply to Mr. Dyce's few Notes on Shakspeare. 8°.

—— Reply to the animadversions of Mr. Dyce on the disquisition on the Tempest. 1863.

—— Henry VIII. adapted for Scholastic Study. 12°. London 1860.

Hurd. Disquisition on the provinces of the drama.

Hurdis, J. M. A. Cursory remarks upon the arrangement of the plays of Shakesp., occasioned by reading Mr. Malone's essay on the chronological order of those celebrated pieces. 8°. London 1792.

Jackson, Wm. Thirty Letters on various Subjects. 12⁰. London 1782, 1795. Cont. Passages in Shak. explained.
Jackson, Z. Shakespeare's genius justified: being restorations and illustrations of 700 passages in Shakespeare's plays, which have [afforded abundant scope for critical animadversion, and hitherto held at defiance the penetration of all Shakespeare's commentators. 8. 1818. 3rd Ed. London 1819.
Jacob, Ed. Lamentable and true tragedie of M. Arden, of Feversham in Kent; with a preface in favour of its being the earliest dramatic work of Shakespeare. 8⁰. London 1770.
Jacob, Giles. The poetical Register, or the Lives of English Dramatick Poets. 2 Vols 8⁰. London 1719—20. "With Shakspeares portrait."
Jameson, Mrs. Characteristics of Women, moral, poetical and historical. Portia, Beatrice, Juliet, Ophelia, Miranda etc. 50 Vignette illustrations. 2 Vols 1833.
—— Shakespeare's female characters. An appendix to Shakespeare's dramatic works. 8⁰. Lond. 1834, 2nd ed. 1840, 3rd ed. 1843.
Jarvis, J. Correct detail of the ceremonies attending the Shakesperian Gala, celebrated at Stratford-upon-Avon, on Monday, Tuesday, and Wednesday, April 23, 24, and 25, 1827; together with some account of Garrick's Jubilee in 1769. 8⁰. Stratford-upon-Avon. 1827.
Ibbot, B. A fit of Spleen, in imitation of Shakspeare. (Dodsley's Collection.)
Jemmat, Catherine. Verses on seeing Mr. Barry perform the parts of Othello, Romeo, Jaffier, etc. 4⁰. London 1766.
Jennens, Charles. The tragedy of King Lear as lately published, vindicated from the abuse of the critical reviewers; and the wonderful genius and abilities of those gentlemen for Criticism set forth, celebrated and extolled. 8⁰. London 1772.
Jephson, J. M. Shakespere, his birthplace, home and grave. A pilgrimage to Stratford on Avon in 1863, with photographic illustrations by E. Edwards. small 4⁰. 1863.
Jerningham, E. The Shakspeare Gallery. A Poem. 4⁰. 1791.
Jervis, Sw. Proposed Emendations to the text of Shakspeare's Plays. 8⁰. Lond. 1860.
Jest Book. The Hundred Merry Tales, or Shakspeare's Jest-Book. 12⁰. Lond. 1831.
—— Specimens of a New Jest Book: also Annotations upon Shakespeare, with various other matters never before published. 12⁰. London. 1810.
Immortality, the, of Shakespeare. A Poem. 4⁰. 1784.
Ingleby, C. M. The Shakspeare fabrications, or the M. S. Notes of the Perkins folio shown to be of recent origin: with an Appendix on the Authorship of Ireland Forgeries. 12⁰. Lond. 1859.
—— Complete View of the Shakespeare Controversy concerning the authenticity and Genuiness of Manuscript matter affecting the works and Biogr. publ. by Collier as the fruits of his researches. 8⁰. Lon. 1861.
Interview. The Interview, or Sir John Falstaff's Ghost; a poem inscribed to David Garrick Esq. 4⁰. London 1766.
Introduction to the School of Shakespeare. 8⁰. s. l. & a.
—— to Shakespeare's pl ys; containing an Essay on Oratory. 8⁰. Lond. 1774.
Johnson, Sam. Miscellaneous Observations on the Tragedy of Macbeth, with Remarks on Sir T[homas] H[anmer's] edition of Shakespeare: to which is affixed Proposals for a new edition of Shakespeare, with a specimen. 12⁰. Lond. 1745.
—— Proposals for printing, by subscription; the dramatic works of W. Shakespeare, corrected and illustrated. 8⁰. Lond. 1756.
Johnson's Dr. preface to his edition of Shakespeare's Plays. 8. Lond. 1765. 1858.
Jones, H. Clifton: a Poem, to which is added an Ode to Shakespeare, in honour of the Jubilee. 4⁰. Bristol 1779.
Jones, G. Tecumseh etc., with Oration on the Life of Shakespeare. 8⁰. 1844.
—— The first Jubilee Orations upon the life, Character and Genius of Shakspeare, pronounced at Stratford 24 April 1836.
Jones, Winter. Observations on the Division of Man's Life into Stages prior to the Seven Ages of Shakespeare. 4⁰. Lond. 1860.
Jordan, J. Welcombe Hills, near Stratford-upon-Avon, a Poem, historical and descriptive. 4⁰. 1777.

Ireland, John. Shakesperiana, selected from the Letters and Poems of the late Mr. John Henderson. 8o. London 1786.
Ireland, Sam. Pict. Views on Avon — with observ on the publ. Buildings and other works of Art in its vicinity. 8o. Lond. 1792.
Ireland, W. H. An authentic account of the Shakespearian Manuscripts. 8o. Lond. 1796.
—— An investigation of Mr. Malone's claim to the character of scholar or critic; being an examination of his "Inquiry into the authenticity of the Shakespeare manuscripts." 8o. London 1797.
—— Vindication of his conduct respecting the publication of the supposed Shakespeare manuscripts; being a preface or introduction to a reply to the critical labours of Mr. Malone. 8o. Lond. 1796.
—— Forgeries: Miscellaneous Papers, Legal Instruments under the hand of Wm. Shakespeare. 8o. Lond. 1796.
—— The confession of W. H. Ireland; containing the particulars of this fabrication of the Shakespeare manuscripts, together with anecdotes and opinions (hitherto unpublished) of many distinguished persons in the literary, poetical, and theatrical world. 8o. Lond. 1805.
Judith, a Sacred Drama, as performed in the church of Stratford-upon-Avon, on occasion of the Jubilee. 4o. Lond. 1769.
Julius Caesar (Shakespeares) rendered into Latin by H. Denison. 8o. 1856.
Kelly, Mich. Hamlet's Letter to Ophelia versified, composed for, and dedicated to Miss Abrams. 8o. 1800.
Kemble and Cooke in Richard the IIIrd. 8o. Lond. 1801.
Kemble. A short Criticism on the Performance of Hamlet by Mr. Kemble. 8o. 1789.
Kemble, John Philip. Macbeth re-considered; an essay intended as an answer to part of the remarks on some of the characters of Shakespeare. 8o. Lond. 1786.
—— Essay on Macbeth and Richard III. An Essay in answer to some remarks on some (by Wm. Whateley) of the Characters of Shakespeare. 8o. Lond. 1817.
Kenny, Th. Life and Genius of Shakespeare. 1864.
Kenrick, W. A review of Dr. Johnson's new edition of Shakespeare. In which the ignorance or inattention of that editor is exposed and the poet defended from the persecution of his commentators. 8o. Lond. 1765.
—— A defence of Mr. Kenrick's Review of Dr. Johnson's Shakespeare; containing a number of curious and ludicrous anecdotes of literary biography. By a friend. 8o. Lond. 1766.
—— Introduction to the school of Shakespeare, held on Wednesday evenings, in the Apollo, at the Devil Tavern, Temple Bar. To which is added a Retort courteous on the Critics, as delivered at the second and third Lectures. 8o. Lond. 1773.
—— Falstaff's Wedding: a Comedy, written in imitation of Shakespeare. 1760.
King Henry the Fourth, being a specimen of Shakespeare's plays, furnished (in imitation of the Waverly Novels) with the manners and costumes of the age in which the drama's plot is laid. 2 Vols. 8o. Lond. 1826.
King Henry the Fifth, Music in, by J. Isaacson. folio. 1858.
King Henry VI. Essay on the Authorship of the three parts of King Henry VI. 8o. Camb. 1859.
King Henry the 8th. Music in, by J. L. Hatton. fol. 1855.
King Lear, history of, revived by Tate. small 8o. 1771.
—— Three Essays on Shakespeare's King Lear by Pupils of the City of London School. 1851.
Kitchiner. Collection of Vocal Music in Shakspeare's Plays from the original M. S. and early printed Copies in the possession of Dr. Kitchiner. 1863.
Knight, Ch. Studies of Shakespeare, forming a Companion Volume to every Edition of the text. 8o. London 1849.
—— Biography of Shakespeare. 8o. Lond. 1843.
—— Old Lamps or New? A plea for the Original Editions of the text of Shakespeare, forming an Introductory Notice to the Stratford Shakespeare. 1853.
Lamb, Ch. Tales from Shakespeare. 2 Vols. 12o. Lond. 1807. Frequently reprinted.
Lamb, Ch. Essay on the Tragedies of Shakespeare, considered with reference to their fitness for Stage Representations. 8o. (In Lamb's Works.)

Lamb, C. Specimens of early dramatic poetry. Lond. 1808.
Landor, W. S. Imaginary Conversations. Shakespeare and Elisabeth. 8o. Lond.
—— Citation and examination of Shakespeare and others before Sir T. Lucy, touching Deer Stealing in 1582. 8o. Lond. 1834.
Langbaine, G. Momus Triumphans, or the Plagiaries of the English Stage exposed in a Catalogue of Plays. (Several Notices of Shakespeare pag. 21 and 22.) 1688.
Langford, J. A. The Shakspeare Tercentenary year, poems in Memoriam. 1864.
Lansdowne. Three Plays, the Jew of Venice altered from Shakspeare. 1713.
—— Lord George, Granville, Works of. 3 Vols. 12o. Lond. 1736.
"Contains Merchant of Venice alterations".
Lardner's Cyclopaedia. The Life of Shakspeare. 1837.
Latham, Revd. H. Sertum Shaksperianum subnexis aliquot aliunde Excerptis Floribus. 12mo. London 1864.
Lennox, Mrs. Ch. Shakespeare illustrated; or the novels and histories on which the plays of Shakespeare are founded, collected and translated from the original authors, with critical remarks. 3 Vols. 12o. Lond. 1753 - 54.
Letter from Mr. Desenfans to Mrs. Montague. 8o. Lond. 1777.
—— on Shakspeare's Authorship of the two Noble Kinsmen. 8o. Edinburg 1833.
—— on the Natural history of Insects mentioned in Shakspeare's plays. Woodcuts 1838.
Letters from Snowdon, descriptive of a Tour through the Northern Counties of Wales. 8o. 1770.
This little work contains the earliest tourist's account of Snowdon, and a curious notice of King Lear as acted in Wales.
Lines, adressed to T. Crofton Croker, Esq. F. A. S. by Mrs. Balmanno, on his acquisition of Shakspeare's Gimmel Ring. Woodcuts. 4o. New York 1857.
Linley, W. Dramatic Songs to all Shakspeare's Dramas 2 Vols. fol. 1820.
Literarius, Th. (ps.) A familiar address to the curious in english poetry, more particularly to the readers of Shakespeare. 8o. Lond. 1784.
Literary and graphical illustrations of Shakespeare and the British Drama. Nearly 200 engravings on wood by Harvey and others. 8o. Lond. 1831.
Lloyd, Rob. Shakespeare: an epistle to Mr. Garrick, with an Ode to Genius. 4o. 1760.
Lofft, C. Aphorisms from Shakespeare arranged according to the plays etc. with a preface and notes, numeral references to each subject and a copious Index. 8o. Bury 1812.
Lowndes. Shakspeare and his Commentators, from Lownde's Bibliographer's Manual, portrait by Worthington, only 52 Copies privately printed 1831.
—— Bibliographer's Manual new Edit. Part VIII contains: Shakespeariana by Henry G. Bohn. The most perfect account of all the various Editions and of the single plays of Shakespeare ever published in England. Lond. 1864.
Luders, A. An essay on the character of Henry the Fifth, when Prince of Wales. 8o. Lond. 1813.
Lyndon, C. Concordance of Select Quotations from Shakespeare. 12o. Lond.1850.
Macbeth. Original Music in Macbeth, as composed by Math. Locke, arranged from the score and adapted for the Pianoforte by B. Jacobs n. d. folio.
—— The Introductory Symphony, Airs, Recitations, Dances and Choruses in the Tragedy of Macbeth in score composed by Matthew Locke. First performed about 1674, corrected by Dr. Boyce. folio.
—— ditto, for Pianoforte by Loder, with historical account of the Music by Reinbauld. folio. 1840. Frequently republished by others.
—— Scotch Airs used in Macbeth, in Score, by Sam. Arnold. fol.
—— A key to the Drama; containing the life, character and secret history of Macbeth. 12o. Lond. 1768.
—— Shakspearian Criticism and Acting (Westminster Review, December 1843).
—— and King Richard III. An Essay in Answer to J.B. Kemble. 8o. Lond. 1817.
—— reconsidered, an Essay intended as an answer to part of Whatley's remarks on some of the characters of Shakspeare. 1786.
—— with Introduction and notes by Dalgleish. 12o. Lond. 1662.
—— the tragical history of Macbeth; a new Song 8o. 1815.
Mac Chaff, A. Letter to the Editor of the Glasgow Argus on Collier's new edit. of Shakespeare. 8o. Lond. 1842.
Macdonell, Essay on the Tragedy of Hamlet, with Notes. 1843.

Macdonell. An Essay on the Play of the Tempest. 8º. Lond. 1840.
Macgregor, R. G. Othello's Character. 8º. Lond. 1852.
Mackenzie, H. On Hamlet, in the *"Mirror"* 1780 Nr. 99—100.
Macnight, Thomas. Shakspeare "a prize Essay" on the historical plays of Shakspeare. 8º. 1850.
Madden, Sir Fr. Observations on an autograph of Shakespeare, and the orthography of his name. 8º. Lond. 1838.
Maginn, Dr. On Farmer's Essay on the learning of Shakspeare. (Frazer's Magazine 1839.)
—— Shakspeare Papers; or, pictures grave and gay. 8º. 1859.
Malone's Caveat against Booksellers, respecting an edition of Shakespeare attributed to him. 8º.
Malone's Hand-list of Early Engl. Literat. see Halliwell.
Malone, Edm. Another Essence of Malone, or, the beauties of a Shakespeare editor. 8º. Lond. 1801.
—— Enquiry into the Conduct of Edmond Malone Esq. concerning the manuscript Papers of John Aubrey, in the Ashmolean Museum. Oxf. 8º. Lond. 1797.
—— The Life of Shakespeare. With an Essay on the phraseology and metre of the Poet and his Contemporaries by Boswell. 8º. Lond. 1821.
—— Chronology of Shakespeare's plays. 18º. Lond. s. a.
—— A supplement to the edition of Shakespeare's plays published in 1778; containing additional observations by several of the former commentators, to which are subjoined, the Genuine Poems of the same Author, and seven plays that have been ascribed to him, with notes by the editor and others. 2 vols. 8º. Lond. 1780.
—— Letter to Dr. Farmer relative to the edition of Shakespeare published in 1790. 8º. Lond. 1792.
—— Prospectus of an intended edition of Shakespeare, in 15 vols. Royal-8. 4º. Lond. 1792.
—— A dissertation on the three parts of Henry VI. 8º. Lond. 1792.
—— Proposals of an intended edition of Shakespeare in 20 Vols. Royal-8. Fol. Lond. 1795.
—— An inquiry into the authenticity of certain miscellaneous papers and legal instruments, published Dec. 24. 1795 and attributed to Shakespeare, Queen Elizabeth and Henry, Earl of Southampton, illustrated by fac-similes of the genuine handwriting of that nobleman and of her majesty, a new fac-simile of the handwriting of Shakespeare never before exhibited, and other authentic documents. 8º. Lond. 1796.
—— Appendix to the above tract. 8. Lond. 1809.
—— A Second Appendix to Mr. Malone's Supplement. Lond. 1783.
—— Preface to his Edition of Shakespeare. 1790.
—— Historical account of the rise and progress of the English Stage and of the economy and usages of the ancient theatres in England. 1790. 1800. 1821.
—— An account of the incidents from which the title and part of the story of Shakespeare's Tempest were derived, and its true date ascertained. 8º. Lond. 1808. 60 Copies printed.
Man and wife; or the Shakespeare Jubilee, a comedy in 3 acts (by Geor. Colman). 8º. s. l. 1770.
Marsh, J. B. Shakespeare's Riddles, selected by M. 16º. 1862.
—— The Reference Shakespeare, containing 11,600 references compiled by John Marsh, Manchester. 1864.
Mason, J. M. Comments on the last edition of Shakespeare's plays. 8º. Dublin 1785. Lond. 1797.
—— Comments on the plays of Beaumont and Fletcher with an appendix containing some further observations on Shakespeare extended to the late editions of Malone and Steevens. 8º. Lond. 1797.
—— Additional comments on the plays of Shakespeare, extended to the late editions of Malone and Steevens. 8º. Lond. 1798.
—— Comments on the several editions of Shakespeare's plays. 8º. Dublin 1807.
May, Geor. A guide to the Birth-town of Shakespeare and the poet's rural haunts. 12º. Eversham. 1847.
Meadows, Kenny. Etchings illustrative of the plays of Shakespeare, with Quotations. 8º. Lond. 1846.
—— Points of Humour. Lond. 1941—45.

Melmoth, Courtney. The Shadows of Shakespeare, a Monody occasioned by the death of Mr. Garrick. 4o. 1779.
Memoirs of the Shakspeare's Head in Covent Garden by the Ghost of Shakespeare. 2 vols. 12o. 1755.
Merchant of Venice. The Songs composed by Th. A. Arne. fol. 1740.
—— The novel from which the Play of The Merchant of Venice, written by Shakespeare, is taken, translated from the Italian: to which is added, a translation of a novel from the Decamerone of Bocaccio. 8o. Lond. 1755.
Meres, Francis (Maister of Artes of both Universities). Palladis Tamia. Wits Treasury, being the second part of Wits Commonwealth. 12o. Lond. 1598.
  "It contains the earliest notice of Shakespeare's plays."
Merridew. A Catalogue of engraved portraits of Nobility, Gentry etc. connected with the County of Warwick, incl. list of all genuine engravings of Shakespeare. 4o. Coventry 1849.
Merry Tales from Shakspeare. 12o. Lond. 1845.
Michel, Nich. The Shakespeare Festival, or the Birth of the World's poet. An ode. 1864.
Midsummer Night's Dream. Merry conceited Humours of Bottom the Weaver, a Droll composed out of the Comic Scenes of the Midsummer Night's Dream about. A. D. 1646. 12o. Chiswick Press 1860 only 30 Copies printed.
—— Six Songs in Harlequin's Invasion, Cymbeline, and Midsummer Night's dream, by Th. Aylward. (Score.) fol.
—— The Fairies, an Opera, composed by J. C. Smith. fol. 1755.
—— The Music composed by Sir H. Bishop. fol. 1816.
—— The Songs by C. E. Horn. folio.
—— The Songs and Music by Mendelsohn-Bartholdy. fol.
Miscellaneous Observations on the Tragedy of Hamlet, Prince of Denmark, with a preface, containing some general remarks on the writings of Shakespeare. 8o. Lond. 1752.
—— **Papers** and legal instruments under the hand and seal of William Shakespeare: including the tragedy of King Lear and a small fragment of Hamlet from the original Manuscript. With a facsimile. 4o. Lond. 1796.
Mitford's Cursory Notes on Beaumont and Fletcher and Shakespeare. 1856.
Modern characters from Shakespeare, alphabetically arranged. 12o. Lond. 1778.
Moncrieff, T. Shakspeare's Festival; or New Comedy of Errors, a Drama in 2 acts. 18o. Lond. 1830.
Montague, Elizabeth, Mrs. An essay on the writings and genius of Shakespeare compared with the Greek and French dramatic poets. With some remarks upon the misrepresentations of Mons. de Voltaire. 8o. Lond. 1769. Frequently reprinted.
Montemayor. Diana of George of Montemayor, translated out of Spanish into English by Bartholomeus Yong, of the Middle Temple, gentleman. folio. Edm. Bollifant 1598.
  "A portion of the Plot employed by Shakespeare in the Two Gentlemen of Verona, is found in this work."
Monthly Review. 1819, Aug. 1824, Decbr. 1828, May.
Monument. Proposals for erecting a Monument to Shakespeare. 8o. 1837.
Moral Sentences and Sentiments, culled from Shakspeare, compared with Holy Writ. 8o. Lond. 1847.
Morgan, A. A. The mind of Shakespeare, as exhibited in his works. 1860.
Morgann, M. An essay on the dramatic character of Sir J. Falstaff. 8o. Lond. 1777.
Morris, C. An essay towards fixing the true standard of wit and humour, raillerie, satire and ridicule; to which is added an analysis of the characters of a Humorist, Sir John Falstaff, Sir Roger de Coverly and Don Quixote. 8o. Lond. 1744.
Murphy, Arth. The Life of D. Garrick. 2 Vols. 8o. Lond. 1801.
Music. Collection of Vocal Music in Shakespeare's Plays, from the Original MSS. and early printed Copies in the possession of Dr. Kitchiner, arranged for piano by Addison.
—— Dramatic Songs to all Shakespeare's Drames, selected by Linley. 2 Vols. folio.
—— The Shakspeare Vocal Magazine. 50 Songs. Lonsdale 1864.
—— The Shakespeare Album for Pianoforte, 100 favorite Airs by the most eminent Masters. Lonsdale 1862.

3 *

Hare's (Archdeacon). A Glossary; or, a collection of words, phrases, names, and allusions to customs, proverbs, &c., which have been thought to require illustration in the works of English authors, particularly Shakespeare and his contemporaries. 8. London 1822.

Hare's Glossary, enlarged by Halliwell and Wright. 2 Vols. 8o. Lond. 1859.

Heale, J. P. Views of Stratford-upon-Avon church in Warwickshire; containing the monument of the immortal Shakespeare. 8. London 1825.

Heale, H. Literary Remains. London 1830.

Hetl, S. Shakespeare: a critical biography, and an estimate of the Facts, Forgeries &c. which have appeared in remote and recent Literature. 8o. London 1861. 1864.

Heve, Phil. Le. Cursory remarks on some of the ancient English poets, particularly Milton. 8. London 1749.

Nichols, Ph. The celebrated letter of Sir Thomas Hanmer, in the sixth volume of the Biographia Britannica, wherein is discovered the rise of the Bishop of Gloucester's quarrel with the baronet, about his edition of Shakespeare's plays, to which is added an impartial account of the extraordinary means used to suppress the remarkable letter. 8. and fol. London 1763.

Nicholls, Jas. Notes on Shakespeare. 8o. London 1861.

Nicol, G. Letter on Boydell's edition of Shakespeare's works. 4. Lond. 1791.
—— Account of the Origin of the Shakspeare undertaking (Boydell's). 1791.

Nossiter. Letter to Miss Nossiter, occasioned by her first appearance on the Stage, with Remarks on the manner of her playing Juliet. 8o. 1753.

Notes and Queries. Many Articles and References etc. in illustration of Shakespeare.

Oakley, H. Selections from Shakespeare. 8. London 1828.

Observations on the Shaksperian Forgeries at Bridgewater house, facs. only 25 Copies privately printed 1853.
—— on Mr. Kemble in the characters of Cato, Wolsey, and Coriolanus. 8o. London 1817.

Ode on Shakespeare, and testimonies to the genius and merits of Shakspeare. 4o. s. l. et a.

Ode. A lyric Ode on the Fairies, Aerial Beings and Witches of Shakspeare. 1776.
—— on erecting a Statue to Shakspeare. 1827.

Ogden, John. Varieties in verse, including Songs for the celebration of Shakespeare's Birth-day. 8o. 1823. (Privately printed.)

Optick Glasses of Humors; or the Touchstone of a Golden Temperature, front. illustrative of the Merchant of Venice. 12o. 1639.

Original letters, &c. of Sir J. Falstaff; selected from genuine Manuscripts, which have been in the possession of Dame Quickly and her descendants. (by James White.) 12o. London 1797.

Othello. Critical Remarks on Shakspeare's Othello by W. N. Anderson's Bee I. 57—90, 132—51.

Othello in Hell, and the Infant with a Branch of Olives. 12o. Lond. 1848.

Ottley on Fechter's Version of Othello. 1861.

Oulton, W. E. Vortigern under consideration, with general remarks on Mr. J. Boaden's letter to Georg Steevens, Esq., relative to the manuscripts, drawings, seals &c., ascribed to Shakespeare, and in possession of S. Ireland, Esq. 8. Lond. 1796.

Parallel of Shakspeare and Scott. 12o. Lond. 1835.

Parr, Wolstenholme, A. M. The story of the Moor of Venice, translated from the Italian with two essays on Shakespeare, and preliminary observations. 8. Lond. 1795.

Passages, selected by distinguished personages on the great literary trial of Vortigern and Rowena, a Comi-Tragedy; „Whether it be or be not from the immortal pen of Shakespeare." 4 vols. 12o. Lond. 1795—1795. (By Sir Bate Dudley and his Lady.)

Patterson, R. Letters on the natural history of the Insects mentioned in Shakespeare's plays, portraits, and cuts. 18o. Lond. 1838.

Pearce, W. The Haunts of Shakespeare, a poem. 4o. Lond. 1778.

Peck, Fr. M. A. Explanatory and Critical Notes on divers passages of Shakespeare. Printed in his
  „New Memoirs of the life and writings of John Milton." 4º. Lond. 1740.
Percy, Th. Essay on the origin of the English Stage, particularly the historical plays of Shakespeare. 8º. Lond. 1793.
Pericles. The Anglo Saxon Version of the Story of Apollonius of Tyre, upon which is founded the Play of Pericles; with transl. by Thorpe. 8º. Lond. 1834.
Philalethes (Col. F. Webb). Shakespeare's manuscripts in the possession of Mr. Ireland, examined, respecting the internal and external evidences of their authenticity. 8º. Lond. 1796.
Philosophy, the, of Shakspeare, delineating in 750 passages selected from his plays the multiform phases of the human mind. 8º. 1857, 2nd Ed. 1864.
Pilon, Fr. An Essay on the Character of Hamlet, as performed by Mr. Henderson at the Haymarket. 8º. Lond. (1777?) ascribed to Thomas Davies.
Pinks, W. J. Country Trips: a Series of Descriptive Visits to Places of various interesting parts of England. (cont. Shakspeare.) 18º. Lond. 1860.
Pitman, J. R. The school of Shakespeare, or plays, and scenes from Shakspeare illustrated for the use of schools. With glossarial notes selected from the best annotators. 8º. Lond. 1822.
Planché, J. R. The costume of Shakespeare's Historial Tragedies. King John, Henry the Fourth, As you like it, and Hamlet. 64 coloured plates drawn by Kenny Meadows; with biographical and critical notices by Planché. 4 Vols. 1823—25.
—— Costumes of Shakspeare's Comedy As you like it, with notices. 18 plates. 1825.
Plumptre, J. M. A. Observations on Hamlet, and the motives which induced Shakespeare to fix on the story of Amleth. 8º. Cambridge 1796.
—— An appendix to observations on Hamlet; being an attempt to prove that Shakespeare designed that tragedy as an indirect censure on Mary Queen of Scots. 8º. Lond. 1797.
Poole, J. Hamlet Travestie. 1811.
Pope, A. Preface to his Edition of Shakspeare. 1728.
—— Answer to Mr. Pope's Preface to Shakespeare in a letter to a friend by a Strolling Player. 8º. 1729.
Portrait of S. The Stratford Portrait of Shakspeare and the Athenaeum. 1861. Privately printed.
Pownall, Revd. Alf. Shakspeare weighed in an even Balance. 1864.
Prefaces (the and Annotations of the various Commentators on Shakspeare. 2 Vols 8º. Lond. 1805.
Prescott, Kenr. An Essay on the Learning of Shakspeare. 4º. Camb. 1774.
—— Shakespeare. Rara Avis in Terra. 4º. Cambridge 1774.
—— Remarks on Shakspeare. 8º. Lond. 1792.
Price, Th. The Wisdom and Genius of Shakespeare, comprising Moral Philosophy, Delineations of Character, Paintings of Nature and the Passions, with 700 Aphorisms and Miscellaneous Pieces, with select and original Notes and Scriptural References. 8º. Lond.1838. — Second Edition. 1853.
Prior, Sir James. Life of Edmond Malone, Editor of Shakspeare. 8º. Lond. 1846.
Proceedings of the Sheffield Shakspeare Club from 1819 to January 1829.
Prologues. Collection of the most celebrated Prologues spoken at the Theatres of Drury Lane and Lincoln's Inn. By a young Lady. 8º. Lond. 1728.
—— A Collection and Selection of Prologues and Epilogues; commencing with Shakespeare and concluding with Garrick. 8º. 4 Vols. 1779.
Proposals for printing the dramatic works of Shakspeare. Lond. 1756.
Pye, H. J. Comments on the commentators of Shakespeare, with preliminary observations on his genius and writings, and on the labours of those who have endeavoured to elucidate them. 8º. Lond. 1807.
Quarterly Review 1826 No. 70. 1834 Nr. 101.
Quincy, De, Life of Shakspeare. Encycl. Britannica, vol. XX. separate Edit. 12º. 1864.
Rankin, M. L. Philosophy of Shakespeare, extracted from his Plays 8º. Lond. 1841.

Ranters Ranting, the, with the apprehending, examinations and confessions of John Collins, J. Shakespear, Tho. Wiberton and five more which are to answer the next Sessions, and several songs or catches which were sung at their Meetings, large woodcut. 4⁰. London printed by B. Alsop 1650.
Readings from Shakspeare by the Author of Aids to Development. 12⁰. Lond. 1848.
Reed, Lectures on English Literature and on English history as illustrated by Shakspeare. 12⁰. 1860.
Reflections, Critical, on the Old English Dramatic Writers. 8⁰. Lond. 1761.
Relics, Precious; or the Tragedy of Vortigern rehearsed; written in imitation of the Critic. 8⁰. Lond. 1796.
Religious Extracts from Shakspeare. 1843.
——— and Moral Sentences culled from the works of Shakspeare, compared with sacred passages, portrait after Jansen. 1847.
Remarks on Mr. John Kemble's performance of Hamlet and Richard III. (by H. Martin.) 8⁰. Lond. 1802.
——— upon a late edition of Shakespeare; with a long string of emendations borrowed by the celebrated editor from the Oxford edition without acknowledgement. To which is prefixed a defence of the late Sir Thomas Hanmer, Bart. adressed to the Revd. Mr. Warburton, preacher of Lincoln's-Inn. 8⁰. s. l. & a.
——— on some of the Characters of Shakspeare. 8⁰. 1785.
——— on the differences in Shakspeare's versification in different periods of his life, and on the like points of difference in poetry generally. 12⁰. 1857.
Retrospective Review 1823 No. VII pag. 380—88.
Review of the Shakesperian Literature (No. V of the Archaeologist). 8⁰.
Richard III. A Parody on the Text Scene in Richard the 3rd. 8⁰. Lond. 1918.
Richard, W. C. The Shakespeare Calendar, or Wit and Wisdom for every day in the year. 16⁰. New-York 1850.
Richardson, W. A philosophical analysis and illustration of some of Shakespeare's dramatic characters. 8⁰. Lond. 1774. 1780. 1785.
——— Cursory remarks on tragedy, on Shakespeare and on certain French and Italian poets, principally tragedians. 8⁰. Lond. 1774.
——— Essays on Shakespeare's dramatic characters of Richard III., King Lear, and Timon of Athens, with an Essay on the Faults of Shakespeare and additional observations on the character of Hamlet. 12⁰. Lond. 1784. 1797. 1812.
——— Essays on Shakespeare's dramatic characters with an illustration of Shakespeare's representations of national character in that of Fluelen. 8⁰. London 1812.
——— Essays on Shakespeare's Dramatic Character of Sir John Falstaff, and on his Imitation of general characters. 8⁰. Lond. 1789.
——— Proposals for engraving the Telton Portrait of Shakespeare. 8⁰. Lond. 1794.
Riddle, J. E. Illustrations of Aristotle, on men and manners, from the works of Shakespeare. 8⁰. Oxford 1832.
Rider, W. Views in Stratford-upon-Avon and its vicinity, illustrative of the biography of Shakespeare, accompanied with descriptive remarks. Folio. Warwick and Leamington 1828.
Rimbault. Who was Jack Wilson, the singer of the Shakspeare Stage. 1847.
Ritson, J. The Stockton Jubilee, or Shakespeare in all his glory. A choice pageant for Christmas Holidays. 12⁰. Newcastle 1781.
——— Remarks, critical and illustrative, on the text and notes of the last (Steeven's) edition of Shakespeare. 8⁰. Lond. 1783.
——— The Quip Modest; a few words by way of supplement to remarks, critical and illustrative, on the text and notes of the last edition of Shakespeare, occasioned by a republication of that edition; revised and augmented by the editor of Dodslay's old plays. 8⁰. Lond. 1788.
——— Cursory criticisms on the edition of Shakespeare published by Edmond Malone. 8⁰. Lond. 1792.
Robert, C. William Shakespeare. 8⁰. Bruxelles 1844.
Roberts, John. An answer to Mr. Pope's preface to Shakespeare, being a vindication of the old actors who were the publishers and performers of that author's plays. Where the errors of their editions are further accounted

for, and some memoirs of Shakespeare and the Stage history of his time are inserted, which were never before collected and published, by a strolling player. 8º. Lond. 1729.
Robertson, T. Essay on the character of Hamlet. 4º. Lond. 1788.
Rodd, H. On the Chandos Portrait of Shakspeare. Privately printed. 1849.
Roderick. Remarks on Shakspeare. In Edward's Cannons of Criticism.
Roffe, A. Essay on the Ghost-Belief of Shakespeare. (Privately published.) 1851.
Romeo and Juliet, The Dirge in, composed by J. Lampe (Score). folio.
—— ditto by Arne. folio.
Rooney, pamphlet on the discovery of the rare Hamlet. Dublin 1856.
Rout, (the), or Despairing Candidate. A Parody on Shakespeare's King Richard III. fol. Lond. n. d.
Rowe, N. The Tragedy of Jane Shore, written in imitation of Shakespeare's style. 4º. Lond. 1714. 12º. 1723, 28, 33, 35, 51, 74, 87.
Rowe. Prefaces to Shakespeare's plays by Dr. Johnson, Mr. Pope, Mr. Theobald, Sir T. Hanmer, and Dr. Warburton, with some account of the life of Shakespeare. 8º. Lond. 1765.
Rudloff. Shakespeare, Schiller and Goethe, relatively considered. 12º. Lond. 1848.
Rushton, W. L. Shakespeare a Lawyer. 8º. Lond. 1860.
—— Shakespeare's legal maxims. 8º. Lond. 1860.
Rymer, Ths. A short view of tragedy, its original excellency and corruption with some reflections on Shakespeare, and other practioners of the stage. 8º. Lond. 1693.
—— The tragedies of the last age by the practice of the ancients and by the common sense of all ages, in a letter of Fleetwood Shepheard. 8º. Lond. 1678. 1692.
Sand, George. Letter to Mr. Regnier, of the Theatre français, upon his adaptation to the french Stage of Shakespeare's As you like it. 8º. Lond. 1856.
Saviolo (Vincentio) his Practice in two Bookes, the first intreating of the Use of the Rapier and Dagger, the second of Honor and Honorable Quarrels. 4º. Printed by John Wolfe, 1595.
This work is alluded to by Shakespeare in As You Like it.
Scadding, Revr. Dr. Shakespeare, the Seer — the Interpreter. An address delivered before the St. George's Society of Toronto. 24º. Toronto 1864.
Scharf, George. On the principal Portraits of Shakespeare. 1864.
Schlegel, A. W. Lectures on Dramatic Art and Literature, transl. by J. Black. 2 Vols. 8º. Lond. 1818. 1840.
School for Satire; containing "Capell's Ghost, to Edm. Malone, Esq., editor of Shakespeare", a parody. 8º. Lond. 1802.
Scott, W. Essay on the Drama — see his Prose Works and Drake's Memorials.
Scriblerus, Mart. Explanations and emendations of some passages in the text of Shakespeare, and of Beaumont and Fletcher. 8º. Edinburgh 1814.
Severn, Ch. Diary of the Rev. John Ward, A. M. Vicar of Stratford-upon-Avon, extending from 1648 to 1679. 8º. Lond. 1839.
Severn, E. Anne Hathaway; or, Shakespeare in Love. 3 Vols. 1845. See Shaksp. Novels.
Seymour, E. H. Remarks, critical, conjectural and explanatory upon the plays of Shakespeare, resulting from a collection of the early copies with that of Johnson and Steevens, edited by Is. Reed. Together with some valuable extracts from the Manuscripts of the late Right. Hon. John Lord Chedworth. 2 Vols. 8º. Lond. 1805.
—— New Readings of Shakespeare. 4 Vols. 18º. 1841.
Shakespeare Society Publications. Books illustrative of Shakespeare and of the literature of his time. 8º. Lond. 1841—53.
1841.
Memoirs of Edward Alleyn, Founder of Dulwich College. By J. P. Collier.
Gosson's School of Abuse. With Introduction, &c.
Thomas Heywood's Apology for Actors. With Introduction, &c.
The Coventry Mysteries. Edited by J. O. Halliwell, with Introduction and Notes.
Thynn's Pride and Lowliness. With Introduction, Notes, &c.
Patient Grissell. A Comedy, by Dekker, Chettle, and Haughton. With Introduction and Notes, by J. P. Collier.

1842.

Extracts from the Accounts of the Revels at Court in Elizabeth and James's Reighs. With Introduction and Notes by Peter Cunningham.
Ben Johnson's Conversations with Drummond. Introduction, &c. by David Laing.
First Sketch of the Merry Wives of Windsor. The Novels on which it is founded, and an Introduction and Notes by J. O. Halliwell.
Fools and Jesters, with Armin's Nest of Ninnies, &c. Introduction, &c. by J. P. Collier.
The Old Play of Timon. Now first printed. Edited by Rev. A. Dyce.
Nash's Pierce Pennilesse. With Introduction, &c. by J. P. Collier.
Heywood's Edward the Fourth, a Play, in Two Parts. Edited by Barron Field.

1843.

Northbrooke's Treatise. With an Introduction, &c. by J. P. Collier.
The First Sketches of the Second and Third Parts of Henry the Sixth. Edited by J. O. Halliwell.
Oberon's Vision Illustrated. By the Rev. A. J. Halpin.
The Chester Whitsun Plays — Part. I. With Introduction and Notes by Thomas Wright.
The Alleyn Papers, illustrative of the Early English Stage. With Introduction by J. P. Collier.
Inedited Tracts (Honour Triumphant, 1606, and Line of Life 1620), by John Forde, the Dramatist. With Introduction by J. P. Collier.

1844.

Tarlton's Jests and Newes out of Purgatory. With a Life, &c. by J. O. Halliwell.
The True Tragedie of Richard the Third, from a unique Copy, and The Latin Play of Richardus Tertius, from a Manuscript. Edited by Barron Field.
The Ghost of Richard the Third. A Poem. Edited by J. P. Collier.
Sir Thomas More. A Play. Edited by the Rev. A. Dyce.
Vol. I. of "Shakespeare Society's Papers," being a Miscellany of Contributions Illustrative of the Objects of the Society.
The Taming of a Shrew. To which is added, the Woman lapped in Morel's Skin. Edited by Thomas Amyot.

1845.

Illustrations of the Fairy Mythology of Shakespeare. By J. O. Halliwell.
First Part and a portion of the Second Part of Shakespeare's Henry the IVth. From a Unique Contemporary Manuscript. Edited by J. O. Halliwell.
Diary of Philip Henslowe, from 1591 to 1609. From the Original at Dulwich College. Edited by J. P. Collier.
Vol. II. of "The Shakespeare Society's Papers." Consisting of Miscellaneous Contributions.

1846.

The Fair Maid of The Exchange. A Comedy, by Thomas Heywood; and Fortune by Land and Sea, a Tragi-Comedy, by Thomas Heywood and William Rowley. Edited by Barron Field.
The Marriage of Wit and Wisdom. An Ancient Interlude. From the Original Manuscript recently discovered.
Memoirs of the Principal Actors in Shakespeare's Plays. By J. Payne Collier.
Rich's Farewell to Military Profession. From the unique Copy of the first edition of 1581.

1847.

Ralph Roister Doyster, a Comedy, by Nicholas Udall, and the Tragedie of Gorboduc, by Thomas Norton and Thomas Sackville. Edited by W. Durant Cooper.
Part II. of The Chester Whitsun Plays. Edited by Thomas Wright.
Vol. III. of „The Shakespeare Society's Papers." Consisting of Miscellaneous Contributions.

1848.

The Moral Play of Wit and Science. Edited by J. O. Halliwell.
Extracts from the Registers of the Stationers' Company of Works entered for publication between 1557 and 1570, with Notes and Illustrations by J. Payne Collier. Vol. I.
Inigo Jones. A Life of the Architect, by Peter Cunningham. Remarks on some of his Sketches for Masques and Dramas; by J. R. Planché. Five Court Masques; edited from the Original Manuscript of Ben Johnson, John Marston,

&c. by J. P. Collier. Accompanied by Facsimiles of drawings by Inigo Jones, and a Portrait from a Painting by Vandyck.

1849.

Vol. IV. of "The Shakespeare Society's Papers."
Vol. II. of Extracts from the Registers of the Stationers' Company, between the years 1570 and 1587. By J. Payne Collier.
An Engraving of the Chandos Portrait, by permission of the President, the Rt. Hon. Earl of Ellesmere, by S. Cousins, A. R. A.
A dissertation on the imputed Portraits of Shakespeare, as an accompaniment to the Engraving of the Chandos Portrait. By J. Payne Collier.
A Selection from Oldys's Manuscript Notes to Langbaine's Dramatic Poets. By Peter Cunningham.

1850.

The First and Second Parts of the Fair Maid of the West, or a Girl worth Gold. Two Comedies by Thomas Heywood. Edited by J. P. Collier.
The Remarks of M. Karl Simrock, on the Plots of Shakespeare's Plays. With Notes &c. by J. O. Halliwell.
The Royal King, and Loyal Subject (1637) and A Woman Killed with Kindness (1607). Two Plays by Thomas Heywood, ed. by Collier.

1851.

Two histor. plays of the Life and Reign of Queen Elizabeth by Thom. Heywood, ed. by Collier.
The Golden Age (1611) and the Silver Age (1613). Two Plays by Th. Heywood. ed. by Collier.

1852.

John a Kent and John a Cumber, a Comedy by Anthony Munday. Also a view of Sundry Examples, reporting many Strange Murders &c. — A Brief and true report of the Executions of certain traitors at Tyburn (1582) etc. by Munday, edit. by Collier.

1853.

Defence of Poetry, Music and Stage Plays by Thomas Lodge. Also "An Alarm against Userers and Forbonuis Prisceria by Lodge", edit. by Laing.

Shakspeare. An Appendix to Shakespeare's dramatic Works contents: the life of the author; his miscellaneous poems; a critical glossary compiled after Nares, Drake, Ayscough, Hazlitt, Douce, and other, with W. Shakspeare's Portrait taken from the Chandos picture and engraved by C. A. Schwerdtgeburth. Roy.-8o. Leipzig 1826.
—— Shakspearian Anthology; comprising the choicest passages and entire scenes selected from the most correct editions. post 8o. Lond. 1830.
——'s Autobiographical Poems; being his Sonnets clearly developed with his Character drawn chiefly from his Works by C. Armitage Brown. gr. 8o. Lond. 1838. (see Brown.)
—— W., a Biography, with 200 engravings. Roy.-8o. Lond. 1843.
—— containing the traits of his character. s. l. 8o. 1770.
—— William. From the Chandos Portrait in the possession of the Earl of Ellesmere. Engraved by Samuel Cousins. Lond. 1849.
—— Essays, by a Society of Gentlemen at Exeter, comprising many interesting papers on Shakspeare's Characters. 8o.
—— A new Book about Shakspeare and Stratford on Avon, facsimile and woodcuts. 75 Copies privately printed. 1850.
—— Almanack for 1849, and 1850. London.
—— The Legend of Shakspeare's Crab Tree, with a descriptive account, showing its relation to the Poet's traditional history. 4o. Privately printed. 1857.
—— Familiar proverbial and select sayings from Shakspeare by John March. 8o. Manchester 1863.
—— Seven Ages of Man. Sqre. 16o. 1864.
—— Jest Book, being reprints of the Early Jest Books supposed to have been used by Shakspeare. Edited by W. C. Hazlitt. 8o. 1864.
—— Album for the Pianoforte, containing above 100 favorite, ancient and modern airs, illustrative of Shakspeare and his time, including Music in Macbeth, Tempest etc. 4o. 1864.

Shakspeare. Calendar of Wit and Wisdom, for every day in the year. 18⁰. New-York. 1849.
—— Gallery, reproduced in 98 photographs by Booth. 4⁰. 1864.
—— Gallery, containing a select Series of Scenes and Characters on fifty Plates. 8⁰. 1792.
—— Gallery, Catalogue of Pictures in the Shakspeare Gallery. 1791.
——'s Garland; being a collection of new songs, ballads, roundelays, catches, glees, comic serenades, &c., performed at the Jubilee at Stratford-upon-Avon. 8⁰. Lond. 1769.
—— Garland, or the Warwickshire Jubilee, being a Collection of Ballads, etc. as performed in the Great Booth; at Stratford-upon-Avon, composed by Mr. Dibdin, 2 parts. — Queen Mab, or the Fairies Jubilee, a Cantata, composed for the Jubilee, which was held in honour of the immortal Shakespear, Sept. 6 and 7, 1769. — The Mask in Amphytrion, composed by Mr. Dibdin. — The Stratford Jubilee, as sung by Mrs. Lowe, at Finch's Gardens. — The Favourite Songs in the Comic Opera, I Viaggiatori Ridicoli, del Sig. P. Guglielmi.
—— and Honest King George versus Parson Irving and the Puritans; front by G. Cruikshank. 8⁰. 1824.
——'s History of the Times; or, the Original Portraits of that Author adapted to Modern Characters. 1776.
—— Household Words of, illuminated by Stanesby. roy 18⁰. Lond. 1845. 1864.
—— Jest Book, 3 parts. Part I. A C Merry Tales; II. Tales and Quick Answers, very Mery, and Pleasand to Rede; III. Supplement to the Tales and Quicke Answers; Mery Tales, Wittie Questions etc. printed by H. Wykes 1567. edited by S. W. Singer. 250 Copies Chiswick, reprinted 1815.
—— Jests. 8⁰. about 1770.
A quaint and gross collection of anecdotes attributed to Shakspeare. Very rare, usually without title.
—— Jests, or Jubilee Jester. 8°. s. l. 1795.
—— Illustrations of, comprised in two hundred and thirty vignette engravings, by Thompson, from designs by Thurton. Adapted to all Editions. Roy. 8⁰. Leipzig s. a.
—— illustrated by an assemblage of portraits and views, with portraits of Actors, Editors, engraved by Harding. 4⁰. Lond. 1793 - 1800.
—— ditto, 2 Vols. publ. by Jeffreys. Lond. 1811.
—— Illustrations of, by R. Smirke. 4 parts 1821.
—— Imposter. W. S's not an Imposter, by an english Critic (G. H. Townsend). 12⁰. Lond. 1857. (A reply to Smith's was Lord Bacon the Author of Shakspeare's plays.)
—— and Jonson. Dramatic verses. Wit Combats. Auxiliary forces Beaumont and Fletcher, Marston, Decker, Chapman, and Webster. post 8⁰. Lond. 1864.
—— compared with Holy Writ. 1843.
—— Library; a collection of the Romances, Novels, Poems and Histories used by Shakespeare, as the foundation of his Dramas, now first collected and accurately reprinted from the original editions with introductory notices by J. P. Collier. 2 Vols. 8⁰. Lond. 1843.
—— Life of, Glossary, Observations, Prolegomena and Annotations, 18 parts, with cuts from Thurstou's designs. Lond. Bensley 1805.
——'s merry tales. 12⁰. Lond. 1845.
—— a Miscellany. 1802.
—— Monument. First Sitting of the Committee on the proposed Shaks. Monument. Taken in short hand by Z. Craft. Cheltenham 1823.
—— Moral Sentences and Sentiments from Sh. 8⁰. Lond. 1850.
—— Philosophy, delineated in 750 passages, selected from his plays. 8⁰. 1857.
—— Romances; collected and arranged by Shakespeare II. 2 Vols. post 8⁰. Lond. 1825.
—— Seven Ages, illustrated with woodcuts from designs by Mulready, Leslie, Callott, Constable, Wilkie, Landseer, Hilton, etc. 4⁰. 1810.
—— Seven Ages of Life, illustrated 4⁰. 1840.
—— All about Shakspeare illustr. with wood engravings by Thom. Gilks. from Drawings by Fritzcrok. 1864.

Shakspeare, his Birthplace, Home and Grave: a Pilgrimage to Stratford-on-Avon, in the Autumn of 1863. With Photogr. Illustr. by Ernest Edwards. Tercentenary Commem. 8º. 1864.
—'s Character Cards. 1855.
— Corespondence of Lewis, Theobald, Dr. Thirlby and Wm. Warburton (In Nichol's Literary history of 19th. Cent.) 8º. Lond. 1817.
— Shaksperian Criticism. British Quarterly No. 78. April 1864.
— — Lond. Quarterly No. 43. April 1864.
— — Criticism (see Retrospective Review). 1823. No. VII. page 380—88.
— — Criticism (Blackwood's Mag.) Febr. 1835.
—'s Day. A Plea for a Monument. 1864.
— Gazette 1864 published every Thursday at 2. (only a few Nos. appeared.)
—'s House, Life etc. illustrated, see Illustrated Lond. News. 18th Sept. 1847.
— Illustrated; or the Novels and Histories on which the Plays of Shakspeare are founded. 2 Vols 12º. 1753.
— Life. A set of 12 Steroscopic pictures, comprising the most interesting Spots connected with the poet's life. 1864.
— Literature, Review of (Archeologist No V.)
— Pearls of Shakspeare. Brilliant Passages in his plays; illustr. by Meadows. 12º. Lond. 1859.
— The History of Sophia Shakespear. 12º. 1753.
— New Exegesis of Shakspeare and interpretation of his plays on the principle of Races. 8º. Edinb. 1859.
— Portfolio, 96 highly finished illustrations to his Works, by Robert Smirke and Heath. small 4º. Lond. s. a.
— Portfolio: a Series of 100 line engravings from Pictures by Stothard, Smirke, etc., and Portrait. fol. 1864.
— Portrait, photogr. from the Original first folio. Ellis, folio 1864.
—'s Tercentenary Number of Chambers Journal. 1864.
—'s Tercentenary Festival. Official Programme of the Terc. Festival of the Birth. of Shaksp. to be held at Stratford-on-Avon 23. April 1864. 8º.
— Tercentenary Pocket Keepsake and Almanack for 1864. Cassel. 48º.
— versus Harlequin, Pantomimical Drama performed at Drury Lane. 8º. Lond. 1820.
— Ye Comic Shakespeare. With 12 drawings by Wm. Gray. 2 pts. 8º. Lond. 1864.
— Treasury of subject quotations. fr. 8º. 1864.
— Vocal Album, containing selections from the best settings of Shakspeare's poetry for one, 2, 3 and more voices by Arne, Purcell, Leveridge etc. 1864.
— Will of Shakspeare, copied from the Original, with facsimile of the 3 Autographs. 8º. Lond. 1838.
Shaksperian Drolls, from a Rare Book (The Theatre of Ingenuity, 1699) edited by J. O. Halliwell, Esq. 1859.
— — The Droll of the Bouncing Knight or the Robbers Robbed; to which is added the Droll of the Gravemakers, both constructed out of Shakspeare's Plays about A.D. 1647, and acted at Bartholomew and other Fairs, *the impression limited to thirty copies.* square 12º. *Chiswick Press,* 1860.
Shakespearian Museum, with portraits and plates. 4º. Lond. 1794.
Shakesperian Novels:
Shakspeare and his friends by F. Williams. 3 Vol. 8º. 1838.
The Youth of Shakspeare by Williams. 3 Vols. 8º. 1839.
The Secret Passion by R. F. Williams. 3 Vols. 8º. 1844.
Shakspeare the Poet, the Lover, the Actor, the Man, by H. Curling. 3 Vols. 1849.
Anne Hathaway, or Shakspeare in love by E. Severn. 3 Vols. 8º. 1845.
Shakesperiana. Catalogue of all the books, pamphlets, &c. relating to Shakespeare 8º. London. Wilson 1827.
— See Gildon, Wilson, Halliwell, Lowndes, Thimm.
— A Hand-list of upwards of a thousand volumes of Shakesperiana, only 25 Copies printed by Whittingham and Wilkins. small 4º. 1862.
— Literature. Article in Bentley's Quarterly Review No. 3.
Sherlock, M. A fragment on Shakespeare extracted from Advice to a young Poet; and translated from the french. 8º. Lond. 1786.

Sherwin, J., M. D. Vindicatio Shakesperiana; or, supplementary remarks on the editions of Shakespeare, by Reed and others; with occasional illustrations of some obscure and disputed passages. 2 vols. 4º.
(Not printed. MSS. in the Library of the Lit. Inst. of Bath.)
Shirley, W. Edward the Black Prince, attempted after the Manner of Shakespeare. 1750.
Short View of Tragedy, with some reflections on Shakspeare 1693.
Siddons. The life of Mrs. Siddons by Campbell. Lond. 1834.
—— Memoirs of Mrs. Siddons by Boaden. 2 Vols. 8º.
Silvayn, Alex. Orator, handling a hundred severall Discourses in forme of Declamations, Englished by L. P. 4º. Printed by Adam Islip, 1596.
"Containing the Story of part of the plot of the Merchant of Venice."
Simrock, K. On the plots of Shakspeare, and Shakspeare Henry IV. from a contemporary M. S. both edited by J. O. Halliwell. 1853.
Singer, S. W. The Text of Shakespeare vindicated etc. 8º Lond. 1853.
"Against Collier's Notes and Emendations".
Sir John Falstaff's letters, dedicated to Sammy Ireland. 12º. Lond. 1796.
Six old Plays on which Shakespeare founded his Measure for Measure, Comedy of Errors, Taming the Shrew, King John, King Henry IV. and V., King Lear. 2 Vols in one. 8º. Lond. 1770. Nichols. 1779.
Skene, G. The Genius of Shakespeare, a Summer-Dream. 8º. Lond. 1793.
Skottowe, Aug. The life of Shakespeare; enquiries into the originality of his dramatic plots and characters, and essays on the ancient theatres and theatrical usages. 2 Vols. 8º. Lond. 1824.
Smart, B. H. Shakspearian Readings. 12º. Lond. 1839.
Smith, W. Henry. Was Lord Bacon the author of Shakspeare's Plays? A Letter to Lord Ellesmere. 8º. Lond. 1856.
—— Bacon and Shakespeare. An inquiry touching Players, playhouses and play-writers in the days of Elizabeth. To which is appended an abstract of a MS. respecting Tobie Matthew. 12º. Lond. 1857.
Some Remarks on the tragedy of Hamlet, Prince of Denmark, written by W. Shakespeare. 8º. Lond. 1736.
Somerset, C. A. Shakspeare's Early days, a historical Play. 12º. Lond. 1812.
Songs, The, of Shakespeare, illustrated by the Etching Club, folio. 1843. 4º.
—— and Ballads, illustr. by the Etching Club. imp. 4º. Lond. 1853.
—— and Ballads of Shakspeare, illuminated by F. W. Gwilt. Mapleson, printed in colours by T. Sinclair of Philadelphia. 4º.
—— and Sonnets, illustr. by John Gilbert. folio 1861, 8º. 1862.
—— do. by Staunton, illustr. by John Gilbert. 4º. 1864.
Songster's Pocket Book, or Jubilee Concert, a Collection of the Songs which have been sung at the Stratford Jubilee. 12º. Lond. 1770.
Sonnets, the, of Shakespeare (Westminster Review No. 23; July 1857.
Spalding, W. A letter on Shakespeare's authorship of the "Two noble Kinsmen", a drama commonly ascribed to John Fletcher. 8º. Edinburgh 1833.
Speed. Theatrum Imperii Magnae Britanniae. Lond. 1616.
Spirit, the, of the Plays of Shakespeare, exhibited in a Series of outline plates illustrative of the Story of each play, drawn and engraved by Frank Howard. 5 Vols. 8º. Lond. 1838.
Stack, Rich. An Examination of an Essay on the Dramatic Charakter of Sir John Falstaff (Transact. of Irish Academ). Vol. II. 1788.
(Stafford, W.) An examination of certain ordinary complaints. Lond. 1751.
Staunton, How. Memorials of Shakspeare. Comprising the Poet's Will etc., illustr. with photographs; annot. folio. 1864.
—— Songs and Sonnets Stratford-upon-Avon, Sweet William: a painted Engraving of Shakespeare on a Sweet William flower. 4º. 1864.
Steevens, G. Proposals for publishing an Edition of Shakespeare's plays. 8º. 1766.
—— Letter to George Hardinge Esq. on the Subject of a Passage in Mr. Steevens' Preface to his Impression of Shakespeare. 4º. 1777.
—— Preface to his Edition of Shakespeare.
Stephens, G. Shakespeare Story-Teller. Introductory Leaves, or, Outline Sketches, with choice Extracts in the words of the poet himself. 8º.
Strachey, A. Analysis of Shakspeare's Hamlet, being an attempt to find a key to a great Moral problem. Lond. 1849.

Stratford Jubilee, a new comedy, with Scrub's Trip to the Jubilee. s. l. 1769.
—— Illustr. of Stratford-upon-Avon with a life of Shakspeare, and Account of the Jubilee held in 1769. 8º. Stratf. 1827.
—— Act for dividing and Inclosing certain common fields, etc. within the Parish of Old Stratford, otherwise Stratford-upon-Avon. folio. 1774.
"Part of Shakspeare's estate laid in the common fields which enclosed under this Act."
—— -upon-Avon, account of, description of the Mausoleum of Shakespeare. 12º. Stratford 1800.
Studies of Shakespeare, 12º. Lincoln 1809.
Symmons, C. The life of Shakspeare, preface to J. W. Singer's Edit. of Shakespeare's Works. 1826.
Taylor, E. (or **Richardson?**) Cursory remarks on tragedy, on Shakespeare, and on certain French and Italian poets, principally tragedians. 8º. Lond. 1772. 2d. ed. 1774.
Taylor, C. Shakespeare Gallery, containing a select series of scenes and characters with criticisms and remarks. 4º. Lond. 1792.
—— The beauties of Shakespeare, selected from his works, to which are added the principal scenes in the same author. 8º. Lond. 1778.
—— The Bee, or a comparison to the Shakespeare-Gallery. n. d.
Taylor, J. E. The Moor of Venice, Clinthio's Tale and Shakespeare. 8º. Lond. 1855.
Tempest. Angelica, or the Rape of Proteus, carried on from the Tempest of Shakespeare. 12º. Lond. 1822.
—— Lock, Matthew. English Opera, or the Musick in Psyche to which is adjoined the Instrumental Musick in the Tempest. 4º. 1675.
"Rare piece of Shakesperian Music."
—— The Tempest, an Opera, taken from Shakespeare, as it is performed at the Theatre Royal in Drury Lane. 8º. 1756.
—— The Music in the Tempest by Purcell, Arne and Linley. folio. London.
—— an Opera, composed by J. C. Smith. fol.
—— Music, composed by Ar. Sullivan. fol. 1862.
—— Choice Ayres and Dialogues. fol. 1675.
—— Musick, by M. Locke. 4º. 1675.
—— The Masque, composed by W. Boyce (full score). 4º.
—— the, illustrated by Birket, Foster. 4º. Lond. 1860.
—— Outlines of, by Selon. imp. 4º. 1836.
Theobald, L. Shakespeare restored, or a specimen of the many errors, as well committed, as unamended by Mr. Pope, in his late edition of this poet. Designed not only to correct the said edition but to restore the true reading of Shakespeare in all the editions ever yet published. 4º. Lond. 1726.
Theobald's Cave of Poverty, written in imitation of Shakespeare. 8º. n. d.
Thersites literarius, a familiar adress to the readers of Shakspeare. Lond. 1784.
Thimm, Franz. Shakspeariana from 1564 to 1864. A Catalogue of the Shakespeare Literature of England, Germany and France. With historical Introductions. 8º. 1864.
Thompson. Illustrations of Shakespeare in 230 wood-cuts from designs by Thurston. 1825. 1830.
Thornbury, G. W. Shakspeare's England, or a Sketch of our social history during the Reign of Elizabeth. 2 Vols. 8º. Lond. 1856.
Thoughts. Choice thoughts from Shakespeare by the Author of book of familiar Quotations. 12º. 1860.
Tieck, L. The Midsummer Night; or Shakespeare and the fairies, transl. from the German by Miss Rumsey. 12º. Lond. 1854. (Privately pr.)
Tighe (R. R. and J. E. **Davis**). Annals of Windsor, being a history of the Castle and Town. (Includes a Shakesperian chapter.) 2 Vols. 1858.
Time and Truth reconciling the moral and religious world to Shakespeare. 12º. Lond. 1854.
Titus Andronicus, the history of, newly translated from the Italian Copy. Printed by C. Dicey. 12º. 1780.
Tour in Quest of Genealogy, and curious fragments from a M. S. Collection, ascribed to Shakspeare. 8º. 1811.

Traditionary anecdotes of Shakespeare, collected in Warwickshire in the year 1693. Now first printed from the original manuscript of Dowdall, edited by P. Collier. 8º. Lond. 1838.

Treatise on the Passions, so far as they regard the Stage; on the Merit of G-k in Lear, Q-n and B-y opposed in Othello. 8º. Lond. n. d.

Trunculo's Trip to the Jubilee, written by E. Thomson. 4º. Lond. 1769. 1770.

Truth illustrated by Great Authors, nearly 4000 aids to reflection, compiled from Shakspeare and others. 1855.

Tupper, F. Ode for the three hundredth Birthday of Shakespeare. 12º. 1864.

Tweddell. Shakespeare's Times and Contemporaries. 12º. Lond. 1852.

Twelfth Night, Music in, by Sir H. Bishop. fol. 1820.

Twiss, F. A complete verbal index to the plays of Shakespeare; adapted to all editions. Comprehending every substantive, adjective, verb, participle and adverb, used by Shakespeare; with a distinct reference to every individual passage, in which each word occurs. 2 Vols. 8º. Lond. 1805.
    Of an impression of 750 Copies — 542 were destroyed by the fire at Bensley's the printer in 1807.

Two Gentlemen of Verona, Music in, by Sir H. Bishop. fol. 1821.

Tyrwhitt, Th. Observations and conjectures on some passages of Shakespeare. 8º. Oxford 1766. 1769.

Ulrici, H. Shakespeare's Dramatic Art and his relation to Calderon and Goethe. Transl. from the German. 8º. Lond. 1846.

Upton, J. Critical Observations on Shakespeare. 8º. Lond, 1746. — 1748.

Useful Miscellanies, containing the Tragi-Comedy of Joan of Hedington in imitation of Shakespeare. 8º. 1712.

Vega, Lopez de. Romeo and Juliet, a Comedy written originally in Spanish by L. de Vega contemporary with Shakespeare. 8º. Lond. 1770.

Victory, B. History of the theatres of London and Dublin. 3 Vols. 12º. Lond. 1761.

Virgin Queen, a drama attempted as a Sequel to Shakespeare's Tempest (by Waldron). Printed for the Author 1797.

Vortigern, under consideration with general remarks on Mr. James Boaden's letter to George Steevens, Esq. relative to the manuscripts, drawings, seal etc. ascribed to Shakespeare, and in possession of Samuel Ireland Esq. 8º. Lond. 1796.

—— an Historical Tragedy, represented at the Theatre Royal, Drury Lane; and Henry the Second, an Historical Drama, supposed to be written by the Author of Vortigern. 8º. Lond. 1799. reprint. 1832.

Wadd, W. A Medico-Chirurgical Commentary on Shakespeare. (Quart. J. of Science) 1829.

Wade, Th. What does Hamlet mean? a lecture at the Jersey-Mechanic Institute. 8º. 1840.

Walbran, C. J. Dictionary of Shakespeare Quotations. 12º. Lond. 1849.

Waldron, F. G. Free reflections on miscellaneous papers and instruments, under the hand and seal of Shakespeare, in the possession of Samuel Ireland, of Norfolk Street; to which is added: extracts from an unpublished play called the Virgin Queen, written by, or in imitation of Shakespeare. 8º. Lond. 1796.

—— The Shakespearean Miscellany: containing a collection of scarce and valuable tracts, biographical anecdotes of theatrical performers with portraits of ancient and modern actors, scarce and original poetry and curious remains of antiquity. With a concise history of the early English stage. 4º. Lond. 1802. 1804.

—— The Shakspearian Museum. 4º. Lond. 1794.

—— see Virgin Queen.

Walker, W. Sidney. Shakspeare's versification and its apparent irregularities explained by Examples from early and late english writers ed. by W. Nanson Lettsom. 8º. London 1854.

—— A critical examination of the Text of Shakespeare. 3 Vols. 12º. London 1859.

Warburton. A Free and Familiar letter to that great Refiner of Pope and Shakespeare, the Rev. Mr. W. Warburton. 8º. 1750.

—— The Horatian Canons of Friendship with two dedications; the first to

that admirable Critic the Rev. W. Warburton, occasioned by his Dunciad and his Shakspeare; etc. 4°. Lond. 1750.
—— Impartial Remarks upon the Preface of Dr. Warburton. 8°. Lond. 1758.
—— A Supplement to Mr. Warburton's Edition of Shakspeare. see Edwards.
—— Preface to his Edition of Shakspeare.
Ward, J. Diary from 1648 to 1679 ed. by Ch. Severn. Lond. 1839.
Warner, Rich. A glossary to the plays of Shakespeare in which are explained technical terms, words obsolete or uncommon, and common words used in an uncommon sense. 71 Vols. 4°. Mss. in the Brit. Museum.
—— A letter to Dav. Garrick, Esq., concerning a glossary to the plays of Shakespeare on a more extensive plan than has hitherto appeared. To which is annexed a specimen. 8°. London 1768. Mss. in Brit. Museum.
Warton, J. The *Adventurer*. 1753. No. 93. 97. 113. 116. 122.
Warton, T. History of English poetry. Lond. 1774 and 4 Vols. 1824.
Was Shakespeare a Catholic? (Article in the Rambler. 1854. No. 7.)
Webb, Col. F. Shakespeare's Manuscripts in the possession of Mr. Ireland Examined etc. 8° Lond. 1796.
Webb, D. Remarks on the beauty of Poetry. Lond. 1774.
Weston, S. Short notes on Shakespeare, by way of supplement to Johnson, Steevens, Malone, and Douce. 8°. Lond. 1808. Privately printed.
Whalley, Th. An Enquiry into the Learning of Shakespeare, with remarks on several passages of his plays, in a Conversation between Eugenius and Neander. 8°. Lond. 1748.
Whateley, Pet. A. B. Remarks on some of the characters of Shakespeare. 8°. Lond. 1785. — 2d. Edition. 8°. Oxford 1808. — 3d. Edition edited by Archbp. Whateley. 12. Lond. 1839.
Wheler, R. B. History and antiquities of Stratford-upon-Avon; comprising a description of the collegiate church, the life of Shakespeare, &c. 8°. n. d.
—— Historical and descriptive account of the birth-place of Shakespeare. With lithographic illustrations by C. F. Green. 8°. Stratford-upon-Avon 1824.
Wheler Collection, the. A brief Hand List of the Collections respecting the Life and Works of Shakespeare, and the History and Antiquities of Stratford-upon-Avon, formed by the late R. B. Wheler, and now preserved in the Shakespeare Museum at Stratford, *one hundred copies printed small* 4°. Chiswick Press, 1863.
Whincop, Thomas. Scanderbeg, a Tragedy; to which are added a list of all the dramatic authors, and their lives. 8°. Lond. 1747.
"An account of Shakspeare and his portrait".
White, J. Original Letters etc. of Sir John Falstaff, selected from genuine M. S. which have been in the possession of Dame Quickly and her descendants. frontispiece. 1797.
—— Rich. Grant. Shakspeare Scholar, being historical and critical Studies of his Text, Characters, and Commentators, with an Examination of Mr. Collier's folio of 1632. 8° New-York. 1854.
Whiter, Walter. A specimen of a commentary on Shakespeare; containing 1.) Notes on As you like it; 2.) An attempt to explain and illustrate various passages, on a new principle of criticism, derived from Mr. Locke's doctrine of the association of ideas. 8°. Lond. 1794.
Wilke's General View of the stage (including Criticisms on Shakespeare). 1759.
Wilkins, George. Pericles, Prince of Tyre: a Novel. Printed in 1608. Founded upon Shakespeare's Play. Edited by Tycho Mommsen, with a preface, including a brief account of some original Shakespeare Edition extant in Germany and Switzerland, etc. and introduction by Payne Collier. 8°. London 1857.
Williams, R., see Shaksperian Novels.
Willobie (Henry) his Avisa; or the true picture of a modest Maide, and of a chaste and constant Wife. 4°. Lond. 1594.
"Allusions to Shakspeare's Lucrece."
Wilmot. A retrospective Glance at Mr. Fechter's Iago and acting edition of Othello. 8°. Lond. 1862.
Wilson see Shaksperiana.
Wilson. A House for Shakspeare. A proposition for the consideration of the Nation. 8°. Lond. 1848.

Wilson, Th. An Analysis of the Illustrated Shakespeare of Thomas Wilson Esq. Imp.-4º. 1820.
Wise, John R. Shakespeare, his birthplace and its neighbourhood. Illustrated by W. S. Linton. 8º. & 12º. Lond. 1860. 1862. 8" 1864.
—. The Beauties of Shakspeare; a Lecture by John Wise. 8º. 1857.
Wiss James. On the Rudiments of Shakspearian Drama, an inaugural Dissertation at the Univ. of Marburg. 8º. Frankf. 1828.
Wivell, Abr. Account of his portrait of Shakespeare, from the Stratford Bust. 8º. Lond. 1825.
—— An Historical Account of the Monumental Bust of Shakespeare in the church of Stratford-upon-Avon, with critical remarks on the authors who have written on it. 8º. Lond. 1827.
—— A Supplement to the above with 15 add. portraits. 8º. Lond. 1827.
—— An inquiry into the the history, authenticity and characteristics of the Shakespeare portraits, in which the criticisms of Malone, Steevens, Boaden and others are examined, confirmed, or refuted, embracing the Felton, the Chandos, the Duke of Sommersets pictures, the Droeshout print, and the monument of Shakespeare at Stratford. Together with an expose of the spurious pictures and prints. With 8 engravings. 8º. London 1827.
Woodward, G. M. (the caricaturist). Familiar verses from the ghost of Willy Shakespeare to Sammy Ireland. To which is added Prince Robert, an auncient ballad. 8º. Lond. 1796.
Wordsworth (Charles). Shakespeare's Knowledge and use of the Bible. 8". Lond. 1864.
Wright, Thom. The Chester plays, a collection of Mysteries founded upon scriptural objects, and formerly represented by the trades of Chester at Whitsuntide. 8º. Lond. 1843.
Wyatt, Mat. A comparative review of the opinions of Mr. James Boaden (Editor of the Oracle), in February, March, and April, 1795; and of J. Boaden, Esq. (Author of Fontainville Forest, and of a letter to George Steevens, Esq.), in February, 1796, relative to the Shakespeare manuscripts. By a friend to Consistency. 8º. n. d.
Yarrow, John. Shakespeare. A Tercentenary Poem. 8º. 1864.
Young, E. Conjectures on original Composition. Lond. 1750.
Youth of Shakespeare, see Shakesperian Novels.

II.

SKETCH OF THE PROGRESS OF SHAKSPEARIAN CRITICISM,
AND OF THE GRADUAL APPRECIATION OF SHAKSPEARE
IN
GERMANY.

It was the custom of English strolling actors, towards the end of the sixteenth century, to visit Germany, and to give performances of the plays they brought with them, in the larger towns, and at the courts of the petty princes. They acted plays which were of a type and character quite new to a public accustomed to the "Miracle-plays", or "Mysteries", and "Moral-plays"; — a species of performance even now repeatedly witnessed in Germany, in the obscure places of the Catholic South.

The route these actors took was generally that of Holland, to the North of Germany, and along the Rhine, to Frankfort.

No time could have been more favourable for their appreciation, and the consequent introduction of a new species of dramatic representation. There is indeed no period of German literature more barren than that which lies between 1590 and 1610; for in these twenty years scarcely five poetical works were printed; and even these are of doubtful merit. These Shakspearian actors were at first genuine Englishmen, who acted in their mother-tongue; but their plays were afterwards either translated entire, or adaptations were made of them in German; and they were then performed by German companies, under the title of "Englische Komödianten".

We may fairly surmise that Shakspeare was known to the Germans, even during his life time; for German statesmen, savants, and merchants were continually in England; and cannot have altogether abstained from visiting the theatres of London, during the reign of James I. In the year 1614, a young man from Zurich, by name Johann Rudolf Hess, (who afterwards became a member of the Senate), stayed in England; and on his return, brought home, amongst other books, copies of Shakspeare's "Hamlet", and "Romeo and Juliet", and Ben Jonson's "Volpone"; which, together with a copy of George Wilkin's Tale, "Pericles", have been found in the Library of Zurich.

There is a translation extant in Germany* of the Episode from

---

* *Koberstein's* Shakspeare's allmähliches Bekanntwerden in Deutschland und Urtheile über ihn bis zum Jahre 1773.

the "Midsumer Night's Dream", which was published in the middle of the 17th century. It is the well known farce by *Gryphius*, entitled "Absurda Comica oder Herr Peter Squenz". Tieck maintains that it was taken from a composition by R. Cox, who transposed the episode in question; but, whether derived from this work or not, it is, in any case, the first Shakesperian piece which we find to have been adapted for the German language; and it proves that one of Shakspeare's pieces was actually performed in Germany by English actors, before the year 1636. This is not, however, the only one of Shakspeare's dramas which found its way, at that early period, into Germany. The English comedians brought "Romeo", "Hamlet" and the "Merchant of Venice" with them; and most of these were adapted for the German Stage, and performed repeatedly by German actors, in cities, villages, and barns, throughout the whole of the 17th century. In 1670 a work was published, in three volumes, entitled "Schaubühne englischer und französischer Komödianten", which contained pieces recently acted on the English, French and German stages; and this leaves no doubt that "Romeo and Juliet", "Hamlet", and the "Merchant of Venice", were performed by German players in the 17th century. A copy of a German play has been found by E. Devrient*, entitled "Romeo und Julieta", which proves to be an adaptation from Shakspeare; and a translation of "Hamlet" has been discovered in Germany, under the title of "Tragödie: der bestrafte Brudermord oder Prinz Hamlet aus Dänemark", which must have been adapted early in the 18th century.

Daniel Georg Morhof, who published, in 1682, his "Unterricht von der deutschen Sprache und Poesie", said, that John Dryden had written with much erudition on "Dramatica Poesi"; but of the Englishmen whom he mentions therein, viz. Shakspeare, Fletcher, and Beaumont, Morhof candidly confesses that he knows nothing.

The next German author who mentions Shakspeare is *Berthold Feind* in his book entitled "Gedanken.von der Oper", printed in 1708. It is doubtful whether he had absolutely read Shakspeare; but Gervinus seems to think he had. This author sayd: Mr. le Chevalier Temple, in his 'Essai de la poésie', "informs us that some people had absolutely *cried aloud, and had wept whilst hearing read English tragedies of the renowned English tragici, Shakspeare"*. Not long after, we find *Benthem* mentioning Shakspeare, in his "Englischen Schul und Kirchen Staat" (Chapter 29.) in the following very quaint manner: — "William "Shakspear kam zu Stradford in Warwickshire auf die Welt. Seine "Gelehrtheit war sehr schlecht; und daher verwunderte man sich um "desto mehr, dass er ein fürtrefflicher Poeta war. Er hatte einen sinn- "reichen Kopf, voller Scherz und war in Tragoedien und Comoedien so "glücklich, dass er auch einen Heraclitum zum Lachen und einen De- "mocritum zum Weinen bewegen konnte."**

In the "Compendiösen Gelehrten-Lexicon", by Jöcher, published in 1715, there is also a very quaint article on Shakspeare, which somewhat resembles the former, and which we will quote in the original:

---

* Devrient, Geschichte der Schauspielkunst. Vol. I.
** Eschenburg, Ueber Shakspeare. 1757. pag. 199.

— "Shakespear (Wilh.) ein englischer Dramaticus, geboren zu Stratford
"1564, war schlecht auferzogen und verstund kein Latein. Jedoch
"brachte er es in der Poesie sehr hoch. Er hatte ein scherzhafftes
"Gemüthe, kunte aber doch sehr ernsthaft seyn, und excellirte in Tragödien.
"Er hatte viel sinnreiche und subtile Streitigkeiten mit Ben Jonson,
"wiewohl keiner von beyden viel damit gewann. Er starb zu Stratford
"1616, 23. April im 53. Jahre. Seine Schau- und Trauer-Spiele, deren
"er sehr viel geschrieben, sind in VI Theilen 1709 zu London zusam-
"mengedruckt, und werden sehr hoch gehalten."

But, even in the year 1737, Shakspeare's name was so little known in Germany that there is no mention made of him in the second edition of *Gottsched's* "Kritische Dichtkunst", of that date; though in the third edition, published in 1742, he is alluded to several times. Even *Bodmer*, a German critic of great celebrity in his time, only "knew something of an English poet, 'Saspar', or 'Sasper'," — meant for "Shakespeare", and written down (no doubt) after hearing an imperfect pronunciation of the name. Still, this only proves his complete ignorance of the poet.

In the year 1741 was published a translation of *"Julius Caesar"*, by Caspar Wilhelm von Borck, who had been Prussian Ambassador in London. This translation was by no means bad; but it suited *Gottsched*, who was then the critical oracle, to review it in "den Beiträgen zur Deutschen Sprache", one of the chief periodicals of the time, and to speak in very unfavourable terms of the author. He even went so far as to advise the translator to desist from importing any more tragedies of that sort into Germany, and counselled him, to choose better models in future.

Shortly after this notice, an article appeared, in the same Journal, by Johann Elias Schlegel (1718—1749), which compared Shakspeare with Gryphius. This is an important article, regarded as a specimen of early Shaksperian criticism in Germany; and (strange to say!) written by a namesake (no relation, I believe) of the great German translator of Shakspeare half a century later. This *Schlegel* expresses in the article in question a strong predilection for the French school of dramatic writing, and the arrangements of the French Stage; but gives Shakspeare so far his due as to praise him very highly for the skilful developement of his characters. It is surprising to find, however, that he considers Gryphius eminently superior in ideas, to the English dramatist; for the plays of Gryphius are, in good truth, the most "stale, flat, and unprofitable" declamations imaginable; — utterly tasteless and barren! But such criticisms, coming from abroad, must not surprise us; for even *Wieland*, who translated Shakspeare twenty years after, perpetrated the most extraordinary criticisms on this author, pronouncing him, for instance, to be "full of chaff and empty straw"! German literature and criticism were certainly at that time merely in a transitory state; the fashion being, to aim at an uncertain imitation of the prevalent French taste. Gottsched (who had already received a warning), was delighted to review, in his Journal, in 1755, Mrs. Lennox's "Shakspeare illustrated", with the view of showing how poor were the dramatist's powers of invention, and how much use he made of the tales of other writers.

4*

It was at this particular juncture that *Voltaire* wrote, "Shakspeare, "le Corneille de Londres, grand fou d'ailleurs, mais il a des morceaux "admirables". These few lines had, perhaps, more influence than anything else in introducing Shakspeare to the German public generally; whilst they also drew the attention of the French more seriously than before to the works of the great English dramatist. In 1755, Lessing's "Miss Sara Sampson" appeared; and, three years later, his powerful pen was actively wielded in defence of Shakspeare.

The reform of the tasteless criticism which we have indicated was begun in good earnest by Lessing and Nicolai, at Berlin. Nicolai wrote, in 1756, an article in the "Theatralische Bibliothek", entitled "Geschichte der Englischen Schaubühne", in which he completely extinguished Gottsched and his French imitators, and called the special attention of the public to Shakspeare, Beaumont, Fletcher, and Ben Jonson, — great geniuses, he maintained, who had raised the theatre to what it then was. Nicolai had said, in the "Bibliothek der deutschen Wissenschaften", whilst reviewing Gottsched's "Geschichte der deutschen dramatischen Dichtkunst", that "nobody" would deny Gottsched's influence on the German drama. Lessing took up the subject from the opposite point of view, in his "Literaturbriefe"; and replied that he was this "Nobody", and that he denied the influence of Gottsched altogether. He even maintained that Gottsched had done more harm than good, by his criticisms. It was Lessing who said that, judging Shakspeare even by the standard models of the ancients, he was a much greater tragic poet than Corneille. After Sophocles' "Oedipus", he continued, no tragedies in the world had greater power over our passions than "Othello", "Lear", and "Hamlet". In 1762 appeared the first volume of Wieland's translation of Shakspeare, (consisting of 8 Volumes, in all); which was much praised and recommended by Lessing, in his "Dramaturgie". But although Wieland's translation was not bad, the notes which he appended to it, influenced as they were by Pope's then recent criticisms, were remarkably peculiar and curious. He deplored that Shakspeare wrote so much in rhyme, and maintained that he had but a very imperfect knowledge of verse.

Meantime *Lichtenberg*, the clever describer of Hogarth's paintings, and *Sturz*, a talented prose writer, gave minute descriptions of the acting of Garrick, which they had seen in England; and Wieland's perverse criticism on Shakspeare, found an ardent assailant in the young dramatist, H. W. Gerstenberg, the author of the famous tragedy of "Ugolino", who was a complete Shaksperian enthusiast. He attacked Wieland's translation and notes, in an article inserted in the "Briefe über Merkwürdigkeiten der Literatur", in 1766; in which, also, he suggested some remarkable ideas on the genius of Shakspeare. But the Shaksperian movement had already reached those young and enthusiastic writers who were destined to raise German literature to the high pitch of eminence which it soon afterwards attained. Some were then at the University of Goettingen; others at Strasbourg. At the former was Bürger, at the latter Herder, Goethe, and Lenz.

Herder wrote an article on Shakspeare in 1771 in the "Blätter von deutscher Art und Kunst", which was undoubtedly the most advanced in its notions on Shakspeare, of any yet published; for he deprecated altogether the idea of contrasting Shakspeare's dramas with those of Sophocles, or the other Greek dramatists. Wieland's translation was followed, in 1775, by *Eschenburg's;* and, however unsatisfactory this last may have been as a whole its author's actuating motive was, at any rate, sound and laudable. He felt that a prose translation of "Romeo and Juliet" was impossible; and he therefore tried a poetical one, which in spite of all its shortcommings, was really a very laudable performance.*

To introduce so great a genius as Shakspeare to the German public in such a manner as to make him become his own defender, and the winner of his own greatness, — required both a good translator and a good actor. Germany was lucky in finding a Garrick, in the person of F. L. Schröder, who had an able coadjutor in Fleck. The former became remarkable for his representations of Hamlet, Lear, Macbeth and Othello, the four principal characters in which he earned his well-merited laurels. Then we had Iffland's "Lear"; which has, perhaps, never been rivalled, even in England. Through the exertions of these actors it was, that the general public began, at last, to acknowledge the greatness of Shakspeare. We say the *general public:* for the dramas of our poet had already exercised their influence upon all the great German writers. Goethe had attentively read them, even when at Strasbourg; and there is no doubt but that "Goetz von Berlichingen" was the result of those Shakespearian studies. When, however, he wrote his magnificent critique on "Hamlet", in "Wilhelm Meister's Lehrjahre", *it at once stamped Shakspeare as the gratest of dramatic poets.*

Schiller, who had more difficulty with the language, went so far, notwithstanding, as to translate "Macbeth". Voss also brought out *a Shakspearian translation;* but he know Greek far better than English, and it produced but little effect.

At last the Romantic School of Germany took up the great dramatist; and August Wilhelm Schlegel commenced translating some of his plays. It is a curious piece of literary labour, this splendid and really classical translation, which is now known under the title of "Schlegel's und Tieck's Shakspeare"; for it must not be supposed that such a work was finished off-hand, as though by some "deus ex machinâ". By no means. Schlegel translated one half of Shakspeare, and what he has done is done in so masterly a way as to make it a great loss to German literature, that he did not translate the whole. For although A. W. Schlegel has left behind him, many learned and valuable works, he has achieved nothing better or greater, in his whole life, than this wondrously close and correct translation of Shakespeare's dramas.

"There is but one opinion", remarks Delius**; "and that is that "Schlegel's translation, which has made the writings of the foreign poet "a common treasure to the German people, is still, as it was at the "beginning of our century, a piece of inimitable perfection; and we can "only regret that he translated but 17 out of the 36 dramas of "Shakspeare."

---

* Horn, "Shakspeare in Deutschland".
** Delius, "Die Tieck'sche Shakspeare-Kritik".

Tieck, following in his track, published his "*Altenglisches Theater*" translations, with critical and historical introductions. Partial editions of Shakspeare's works were now published, translated by Schlegel and Eschenburg, and by Tieck and Eschenburg. Then came the translations of Voss and his sons. At last (1797 to 1823) appeared the first collected edition, translated by *A. W. Schlegel*, "*ergänzt und erläutert von Ludwig Tieck*". The second part of the 9th volume which finished the work, was not published till 1830; but even this did not contain all the remaining plays of Shakspeare. The first absolutely complete edition came out in 1833, in 9 volumes.

A great many of the plays were translated by Count Wolff von Baudissin*, a very elegant translator; and six were the work of Tieck's daughter, Dorothea. Ludwig Tieck himself did not even translate a single play; but he was the editor and critic of the whole work, and went over all the translations with great care. His corrections indeed were so numerous, that it would be difficult to deny him the credit of having taken a share in the work. There are still, however, many incorrect readings in the revised translations; and it would be well, in many instances, to restore Schlegel's words as they stood at first. Notwithstanding these few drawbacks, Germany possesses in this translation of Shakspeare one which it will be difficult indeed to rival, and which is only second to the original itself; for it reechoes the soul of the poet's language, as no translation has ever done before, in any tongue in the world. In addition to this principal translation, there are many others; — (those, f. i., by Jos. Meyer, Benda, Julius Körner, A. Böttger, and E. Ortlepp), — which are more or less creditably executed.

It is not however through translations only that the Germans have become acquainted with the great bard. They have investigated his original writings themselves, and by the many erudite critiques which they have published thereon, have obtained a prominent place in Shakspearian literature.

It has been our endeavour, in these short and rapid sketches, to let each country speak through its own critics in such a manner as to show how each has progressed in the study and appreciation of Shakspeare. We have accordingly quoted the English Reviewer as an authority for his own country**, which he may be fairly presumed to be; not so however for Germany; for he has scarcely a perception of what the Germans have done for Shakspeare. "To Germany", he says, "Europe "owes much of its relish for Shakspeare. On the other hand, it has "derived from the same source much that is *obscure, fantastic*, and "*bewildering*, — *theories inconsistent with sense or likelihood*, "*interpretations that darken, and fancies that lead astray.*"

This then is the impression he carries away with him from his German studies. Now let us see what Germany has really done, to show her appreciation of Shakspeare's greatness.

---

* The author of "Ben Jonson und seine Schule", a selection of plays from the early English dramatists.
** "Shaksperian Literature", in Bentley's Quarterly Review, No. 3, October 1859.

English criticism on Shakspeare was but mediocre, even to the beginning of the present century. It was unknown in England that *Lessing*, the great German critic, had given Shakspeare his proper place in the literature of the world forty years previously. The German mind, had thus assigned him his rank in the World of Poets, before England herself so much as dreamed of doing so. It was *Lessing* who first declared that Shakspeare was the poet "$\varkappa\alpha\tau'$ $\dot{\varepsilon}\xi o\chi\dot{\eta}\nu$" of the modern world, just as Homer was of Antiquity. And it resulted from such mighty words, uttered by so great a genius, that our dramatist stepped for the first time into his true and rightful position, and was acknowledged on all hands as the brightest planet in the literary universe. And this verdict, thus publicly delivered before the tribunal of Europe, was not arrived at hastily: it was the result of deep study, thorough investigation, complete understanding, and true appreciation of the dramatist. The delivery of this marvellous judgement, — at a time, too, when France was still ridiculing the dramatic giant, and even England was questioning his knowledge, of Latin and Greek, — is the best proof which can be offered of Lessing's own greatness. This, then, the Germans have done for Shakspeare; and since that time the study of the British poet has been such, in Germany, that no other foreign writer ever received the like, nor (in all probability) ever will again.*

The Germans have moreover contributed greatly towards the due appreciation of Shakspeare by other continental nations, which are all more or less influenced by German literature and German learning. When Goethe wrote his article "Shakspeare und kein Ende", he looked, like a seer of old, into the future, and predicted that Shakspearian literature was then only in its infancy; — that the coming investigations and criticisms would create a "Library", of themselves; — but he could scarcely have foreseen how far that aesthetical enquiry would lead which was begun by Lessing and was followed up by Schlegel, in his famous book "Vorlesungen über dramatische Literatur und Kunst", and afterwards by Tieck. It could scarcely have been within his ken that the spirit of German criticism would, as the English Reviewer says, "awaken new "echoes in England, and produce in Coleridge, and mediately in Lamb "and Hazlitt, a succession of commentators as superior to Steevens, "Farmer and Malone as a blade of Damascus steel is to a common "reaping-hook". This sufficiently shows the proud preeminence of German literature, and the influence it exercised on the great minds of England; — and yet we must not forget that the most searching works, — the best commentaries and the most profound criticisms which have been written on Shakspeare in Germany, — are the offspring of the last few years. We may mention particularly *Ulrici's* "über Shakspeare's dramatische Kunst", *Delius'* Shakspearian Criticisms, *Kreysig's* "Vorlesungen über Shakspeare, seine Zeit und seine Werke", and (the last and crowning effect of German criticism) "Gervinus' Shakspeare", a critical and historical work, unmatched in the literature of any country for the power of appreciation and the critical acumen which are brought to bear upon the great author under illustration. Not only does

---

* Lemcke, Shakspeare in seinem Verhältnisse zu Deutschland.

Gervinus give a life of the dramatist, based on the elaborate materials which English literature has provided; but he analyzes each play, investigates its tendencies, follows it in its developement, and examines with the most minute detail every character in it, subordinate as well as principal.

Bodenstedt's excellent translations of Shakspeare's sonnets was the only thing wanting to give a complete Shakspeare to the German race. We must not omit to mention the influence exercised upon Shakspearian studies by the German actors, who, deriving their dramatic education from the literature of Germany, contributed by their art, to imbue the characters of Shakspeare with life and spirit, and who, indeed, made his plays as immortal on the German stage, as *Garrick, Kean, Kemble* and Mrs. *Siddons* had made them on that of England. Germany was especially fortunate in Ludwig Devrient's "Shylock", which can never be surpassed; while other Shakspearian actors, such as Beck, Esslär, Seidelmann, Dessoir, and (as representatives of female characters) Sophie Schröder, Wolf, and Stich, have been worthy rivals of the best of their profession in England.

We close this article with the words uttered by Prof. Lemcke*, at Marburg, on the occasion of the Shakspeare commemoration:

"Man sagt nun wohl: eben desshalb sind wir Deutschen so tief in "das Verständniss Shakspeare's eingedrungen, eben desshalb ist dieser "Dichter ein solcher Liebling unserer Nation geworden, weil seine Nation "der unsrigen stammverwandt, weil der Geist, der uns aus des Dichters "Werken anmuthet, vorherrschend ein germanischer ist. Es heisst, meiner "Ansicht nach, dem deutschen Geiste ein Armuthszeugniss ausstellen, "wenn man jene Stammverwandtschaft als die Brücke betrachten will, "die uns zu Shakspeare geführt hat. Legen wir auch in diesem Falle "einmal unsere sprichwörtlich gewordene Bescheidenheit bei Seite und "sagen wir es offen heraus: nicht die Stammverwandtschaft mit seiner "Nation, nicht die Kundgebungen germanischen Geistes in seinen Dich"tungen sind es, was uns Shakspeare so nahe gebracht, sondern es ist "jene uns Deutschen vor andern Völkern verliehene Göttergabe, vermöge "deren wir den ächten Genius, welcher Nation er auch angehöre, besser "als andere Nationen, besser oft als seine eigene, zu begreifen, seine "Gaben besser zu geniessen und uns anzueignen vermögen. Wir ver"stehen und lieben Shakspeare vermöge desselben deutschen Geistes, "welcher auch den Italienern geholfen hat, ihren Dante zu verstehen, "welcher den Spaniern geholfen hat, ihre Romanzen zu ordnen, und "welcher jetzt noch immer den Franzosen hilft, die Schätze ihrer mittel"alterlichen Literatur zu erforschen. Wir verstehen und lieben Shakspeare "vermöge jener Faustnatur unserer Nation, welche instinktmässig den "Geist wittert, wo die Wagnersaugen anderer Nationen nichts sehen, "als einen schwarzen Pudel, mit einem Worte — wir verstehen und "lieben Shakspeare, weil wir wirklich jenes 'Volk von Denkern' sind, "als welches die anderen Völker uns so oft schon mit schlecht ver"hehltem Unmuth anzuerkennen genöthigt gewesen sind!"

---

*) Lemcke, "Shakspeare in seinem Verhältnisse zu Deutschland".

GERMAN TRANSLATIONS OF SHAKSPEARE'S WORKS.

1762 **Shakespeare, W.**, theatralische Werke. Aus dem Englischen von Chr. Martin Wieland. 8 Bände. gr. 8. Zürich 1762—1766.
1775 —— theatralische Werke. Herausgegeben von J. J. Eschenburg. 13 Bde. gr. 8. Zürich 1775—1782. The 13th Vol. contains the spurious plays.
1778 ——'s Schauspiele, übersetzt von J. J. Eschenburg. Neue verbesserte Auflage. 22 Bände. 8. Strassburg & Mannheim 1778—83.
1780 —— Werke. Herausgegeben von Gabriel Eckert. 22 Bände. 8. Mannheim 1780—88. (reprint of the Zurich Edition.)
1797 ——'s Dramatische Werke, übersetzt von A. W. Schlegel. 9 Vols. 8. Berlin 1797 - 1810. 2. Aufl. 1821—23.
1798 —— Schauspiele, mit kritischen Anhängen versehen von J. J. Eschenburg. Neue ganz umgearbeitete Ausgabe. 12 Bände. gr. 8. Zürich 1798—1806. also in 12 Vols. 8vo.
1809 ——'s von Schlegel noch unübersetzte dramatische Werke, übersetzt von mehreren Verfassern. 3 Theile. gr. 8. Berlin 1809—10.
1810 —— (von Schlegel noch nicht übersetzt) Schauspiele, übersetzt von H. und A. Voss. 3 Theile. gr. 8. Stuttgart 1810—15. Contains: Cymbeline — Macbeth — Winterstale — Coriolanus Antony and Cleopatra — the Merry Wives of Windsor — Comedy of Errors
1812 —— sämmtliche dramatische Werke, übersetzt von Schlegel u. Eschenburg. 20 Bände. 8. Mit Kupfern. Wien 1812.
1818 —— Schauspiele, übersetzt von J. H. Voss und dessen Söhnen H. und A. Voss. Mit Erläuterungen. 9 Bände. gr. 8. Leipzig 1818-29.
1824 —— sämmtliche Schauspiele, frei bearbeitet von Joseph Meyer. Wohlfeile Taschenausgabe. 52 Bündchen mit 52 Kupfern. 12. Gotha 1824—34.
1825 —— dramatische Werke, übersetzt und erläutert von J. W. O. Benda. 19 Bände. 8. Leipzig 1825, 26. also in 16mo.
1826 —— sämmtliche dramatische Werke und Gedichte; übersetzt im Metrum des Originals, in einem Bande, nebst Supplement, enthaltend: Shakespeare's Leben, nebst Anmerkungen und kritischen Erläuterungen. gr. 8. Wien 1826.
1826 —— dramatische Werke, übersetzt von A. W. v. Schlegel, ergänzt und erläutert von Ludwig Tieck. 9 Theile. 8. Berlin 1826—33.
1828 —— sämmtliche dramatische Werke und Gedichte, übersetzt im Metrum des Originals nebst Supplement, enthaltend: Shakespeare's Leben mit Anmerkungen und kritischen Erläuterungen. 43 Bände Taschenformat. Wien 1828 30.
1830 —— dramatische Werke, übersetzt von Philipp Kaufmann. Band 1—4. 8vo. Berlin 1830—36.
1836 ——'s sämmtliche Werke in einem Bande. Im Verein mit Mehreren übersetzt und herausgegeben von Julius Körner. Mit Shakespeare's Bildniss. gr. 4. Schneeberg 1836. 2. Edit. 1838.
1836 —— sämmtliche Werke im Verein mit Mehreren übersetzt. Ein Band. gr. 8. Wien 1836.
1836 —— sämmtliche Werke; übersetzt von Adolph Böttger, H. Döring, L. Hilsenberg etc. 37 Bdchen. 32. Leipzig 1836, 1837.
1837 —— dramatische Werke. Englisch-deutsche Prachtausg. Mit 1000 Scenen und Vignetten, von Gross. Die deutsche Uebersetzung von Alex. Fischer. 2 Vols. imp. 8vo. Stuttgart.

1838	**Shakespeare, W.**, dramatische Werke, übersetzt von E. Ortlepp. 16 Theile. 8. Stuttgart 1838—39. Neue durchaus verbesserte Auflage mit 16 Stahlstichen. 16 Vols. 16mo. 1842.	
1838	—— Werke in einem Bande. Leipzig 1838.	
1839	—— ditto 12 Bände mit Umrissen und dem Portrait Shakespeares in Stahlstich. 16. Leipzig 1839. ?	
1839	—— sämmtliche Werke. 12 Bände, ohne Umrisse. 16. Leipzig 1839.	
1839	—— Schlegel und Tieck's 2te Ausg. 12 Vols. 8. 1839—1841.	
1840	—— in einem Bande. Leipzig 1840.	
1843	—— Schlegel und Tieck's 3te Ausg. 12 Vols. 8. 1843—1849.	
1843	—— Schauspiele, übersetzt und erläutert von A. Keller und M. Rapp. 8 Bände oder 37 Hefte. 16. Stuttgart 1843. 2te Aufl. 1854.	
1848	—— Werke in 37 Vols. 12. Böttger's new Edit. Berlin 1848. amongst the translators of this edition are: Mügge, Ortlepp, Petz, A. Fischer, K. Simrock, Lampadius, A. Böttger etc.	
1849	Familien - Shakespeare. Eine zusammenhängende Auswahl aus Shakespeare's Werken in deutscher metrischer Uebertragung. Mit Einleitungen, erläuternden Anmerkungen und einer Biographie des Dichters von O. L. B. Wolff. Ein Band. kl. 4. Leipzig 1849.	
1851	—— Schlegel und Tieck's, 4te Aufl. 12 Vols. 16. 1851—52.	
——	—— Dramen für weitere Kreise bearbeitet von Dr. E. W. Sievers. 8. Leipzig 1851-52.	
1853	—— Schlegel und Tieck's 5. Aufl. 12 Vols. 8. 1853—54.	
——	—— ditto. 6. Aufl. 9 Vols. 12. 1853 54. (Collier's Text.)	
——	—— Dramen, in deutscher Uebertragung von F. Jenken. 16. 6 Vols. Mainz 1853—55.	
1856	—— Schlegel und Tieck's. 7te Aufl. 12 Vols. 8. 1856—57.	
1859	—— Dramen, übersetzt von C. Heinichen. 12. (not completed.) Bonn 1859.	
1859	—— Böttger, Döring's etc. Ausg. 6. Aufl. 12 Vols. 16. 1859.	
1863-64	—— Schlegel und Tiecks. 8te (6. Octav-)Aufl. 12 Vols. 1863—64.	

TRANSLATION OF SPURIOUS PLAYS.

Altenglisches Theater, oder Supplemente zum Shakespeare, übersetzt und herausgegeben von L. Tieck. 2 Bände. 8. Berlin 1811.
  Inhalt. König Johann von Engelland. — Georg Green, der Flurschütz von Wackefield. — Perikles, Fürst von Tyrus. — Lokrine. - Der lustige Teufel von Edmonton. — Das alte Schauspiel vom König Leir und seinen Töchtern.
Shakspeare's dramatische Werke. — Supplemente. — Uebersetzt von L. Tieck und J. J. Eschenburg. 2 Bände. 8. Wien 1812.
—— Vier Schauspiele, übersetzt von Ludwig Tieck. gr. 8. Stuttgart 1836.
  Inhalt: Eduard III. — Leben und Tod des Thomas Cromwell. - John Oldcastle. — Der Londoner verlorne Sohn.
—— Supplemente zu allen Ausgaben, übersetzt von H. Döring. 2 Vols. 12. Erfurt 1840.
—— Werke, Nachträge. Uebersetzt von E. Ortlepp. 4 Bde. 16. Stuttgart 1840. — Neue Auflage 1842—43.
Arden von Feversham, übersetzt von Ludwig Tieck.
  In his: Vorschule zu Shakespeare 1. Band.
—— übersetzt von H. Döring. 12. Gotha 1833.
—— übersetzt von E. Ortlepp.
  Nachträge zu Shakespeare 3. Band.
—— ein Trauerspiel in 5 Akten von G. Lillo. 8. Leipzig 1778.
Cromwell's, Thomas, Leben und Tod, übersetzt von J. J. Eschenburg. 8. Zürich 1798
—— übersetzt von H. Döring 12. Gotha 1833. — 2. Aufl. 1840.

Cromwell, Thomas, übersetzt von Ludwig Tieck.
    Vier Schauspiele Shakespeare's, 1. Band.
— übersetzt von E. Ortlepp.
    Nachträge zu Shakespeare 1. Band.
Eduard III., ein Schauspiel aus dem Französischen des Herrn Gresset. 8. Wien 1757.
— ein Trauerspiel (nach Shakespeare) von Christian Felix Weisse. 8. Leipzig 1776.
— ein Schauspiel von Shakespeare, übersetzt von Ludwig Tieck.
    Vier Schauspiele Shakespeare's, 1. Band.
— übersetzt von E. Ortlepp.
    Nachträge zu Shakespeare 2. Band.
Die schöne Emma, übersetzt von Ludwig Tieck.
    In Shakespeare's Vorschule 3. Band.
Schön Emma, übersetzt von H. Döring. 32. Gotha 1833. — 1840.
Georg Green, der Flurschütz von Wakefield, übersetzt von Ludwig Tieck.
    Altenglisches Theater 1. Band.
— — der Feldhüter von Wakefield, übersetzt von H. Döring. 12. Gotha 1833. — 2. Auflage 1840
König Johann von Engelland, übersetzt von Ludwig Tieck.
    Altenglisches Theater 1. Band.
Das alte Schauspiel vom **König Leir** und seinen Töchtern, übersetzt von Ludwig Tieck.
    Altenglisches Theater 2. Band.
Lokrine, übersetzt von J. J. Eschenburg.
— übersetzt von Ludwig Tieck.
    Altenglisches Theater 2. Bd.
— übersetzt von H. Döring. 12. Gotha 1833.
— übersetzt von E. Ortlepp.
    Nachträge zu Shakespeare 2. Band.
Der Londoner Verschwender, übersetzt von J. J. Eschenburg. 8. Zürich 1798.
Kinderzucht oder das Testament. Lustspiel in 4 Aufzügen nach "the London prodigal", bearbeitet von F. L. Schröder; im ersten Bande von Schröder's dramatischen Werken. 8. Berlin 1831.
Der Londoner Verschwender, übersetzt von H. Döring. 12. Gotha 1833. 2. Auflage 1840.
Der Londoner verlorne Sohn, übersetzt von Ludwig Tieck.
    Vier Schauspiele Shakespeare's 2. Band.
— übersetzt von E. Ortlepp.
    Nachträge zu Shakespeare 1. Band.
Die Geburt des Merlin, oder das Kind hat seinen Vater gefunden, ein Schauspiel von W. Shakespeare und W. Rowley, übersetzt von L. Tieck.
    Shakespeare's Vorschule 2. Band.
— übersetzt von H. Döring. 12. Gotha 1833. — 2. Aufl. 1840.
— übersetzt von E. Ortlepp.
    Nachträge zu Shakespeare 1. Band.
Sir John Oldcastle, übersetzt von H. Döring. 12. Gotha 1833. — 2. Aufl. 1840.
— - übersetzt von Ludwig Tieck.
    Vier Schauspiele Shakespeare's 2. Band.
— übersetzt von E. Ortlepp.
    Nachtrage zu Shakespeare 1. Band.
Die Puritanerin oder die Wittwe in der Watlingstrasse, übersetzt von J. J. Eschenburg.
— übersetzt von H. Döring. 12. Gotha 1833. — 2. Aufl. 1840.
Der lustige Teufel von Edmonton, übersetzt von Ludwig Tieck.
    Altenglisches Theater 2. Band.
— — übersetzt von H. Döring. 12. Gotha 1833. — 2. Aufl. 1840.
— übersetzt von E. Ortlepp.
    Nachträge zu Shakespeare 2. Band.
Ein Trauerspiel in Yorkshire, übersetzt von J. J. Eschenburg. 8. Zürich 1798.
— übersetzt von H. Döring. 12. Gotha 1833. — 2. Aufl. 1840.
— übersetzt von E. Ortlepp.
    Nachträge zu Shakespeare 1. Band.

ENGLISH REPRINTS PUBLISHED IN GERMANY.

1799 Reed's Edition. Basel. 23 Vols. 8.
1799 Brunswick Edit. With notes by K. F. Wagner. 8 Vols. 8.
1801 . Zürich Edit. 8 Vols. 8.
1804 Steeven's Leipzig Edit. 20 Vols. 12.
1814 Steeven's Vienna Edit. 20 Vols. 12.
1826 With Life by Skottowe. roy. 8. Leipzig 1826.
1828 Singer's Frankfört Ed. 10 Vols. 12mo.
1830 Reed's Johnson and Steevens. imp. 8. Frankfort 1830.
1833 Reeds with suppl. by Tieck. imp. 8.
1833 Singer's 2nd Edit. Halle.
1837 Leipzig Edit. with life by Symmons. 270 engravings.
1839 Berlin Edition. 8 Vols. 32.
1840 Chalmer's Edition. Leipzig. roy. 8
—— —— choiced Plays containing: Romeo and Julia. — Midsummer night's dream. — Julius Caesar. — Macbeth. 8. Halle 1840.
—— Shakespeare's Plays, arranged by Dr. J. Fölsing. 2 Vols. 12. Berlin 1840.
    Contents: Julius Caesar. — The Tempest. — King Richard II. — The merchant of Venice.
—— Shakespeare, W. Plays with historical and grammatical explanatory notes in german by H. S. Pierre. 8 Vols. gr. 12. Frankfort a. M.
1842 Reed's Edit. Leipzig. 2 Vols. 8.
—— Leipzig (Schumann). 8 Vols. 16.
1843 Singer's Edit. Frankfort. 10 Vols. 12.
1843 Collier's Edit. (Tauchnitz.) 7 Vols. 16.
1846 Selected plays for youth. Frankf. 2 Vols. 12.
1853 Collier's Edit. from the folio of 1632. 4. Leipzig 1853.
1854 Shakespeare's, W., Werke, herausgegeben von Dr. N. Delius. Mit englischem Text und deutschen Anmerkungen kritischer und erklärender Art. gr. 8. 7 Vols. Elberfeld 1854, 1860. new Edition 1864.

GERMAN TRANSLATION OF SEPARATE PLAYS.

ALLS WELL THAT ENDS WELL. (Ende gut, Alles gut.)

Ende gut, Alles gut, übersetzt von J. J. Eschenburg.
—— von H. Voss.
—— von G. W. Kessler. 8. Berlin 1809.
—— von J. W. O. Benda.
—— von Wolff Graf von Baudissin.
—— von H. Döring. 12. Gotha 1828.
—— von Phil. Kaufmann. 8. Berlin 1836.
—— von Th. Oelckers. 32. Leipzig 1836.
—— von G. N. Bärmann.
—— von E. Ortlepp.
—— oder: gelohnte Liebesleiden, übersetzt von M. Rapp.

ANTONY AND CLEOPATRA. (Antonius und Cleopatra.)

Antonius und Cleopatra, bearbeitet von C. A. Horn. 8. Leipzig 1797.
—— übersetzt von C. M. Wieland.
—— ein Trauerspiel in 4 Akten, bearbeitet von Ayrenhof. gr. 8. Wien 1801, 1803, 1808. Wien und Leipzig 1813, 1817.
—— von J. H. Voss.
—— von J. W. O. Benda.
—— von Wolff Graf von Baudissin.
—— von H. Döring. 12. Gotha 1830.

Antonius und Cleopatra, übersetzt von W. Lampadius. 32. Leipzig 1836.
— von J. Körner.
— von E. Ortlepp.
— von A. Keller.
— von C. Heinichen. 1861.

AS YOU LIKE IT. (Wie es Euch gefällt.)
Wie es Euch gefällt, von Shakespeare (no name). 8. Mannheim s a.
— von A. W. von Schlegel.
— von C. M. Wieland.
— von J. H. Voss.
— von J. W. O. Benda.
— von H. Döring. 12. Gotha 1830.
— von E. Thein. 32. Leipzig 1836.
— von E. Ortlepp.
— von M. Rapp.

COMEDY OF ERRORS. (Die Irrungen.)
Die Irrungen, ein Lustspiel in fünf Aufzügen von J. F. W. Grossmann. 8. Frankfurt a. M. 1777.
— von C. M. Wieland.
— von Beauregard Pandin (K. F. v. Jarriges). Zwickau 1824.
— von J. W. O. Benda.
— von J. Meyer. 12. Gotha 1825.
— von Wolff Graf von Baudissin.
— von Phil. Kaufmann. 8. Berlin 1836.
— von K. Simrock. 32. Leipzig 1836.
— von H. Voss.
— von E. Ortlepp.
— u. d. T.: Verwechslungsstück; übersetzt von M. Rapp.
— bearbeitet von C. von Holtei. — Bühnenmanuscript.

CORIOLANUS. (Coriolan.)
Coriolan. Trauerspiel nach Shakespeare von J. H. Schlegel. 8. Copenhagen 1760.
— von J. G. Dyk. 8. Leipzig 1785.
— Trauerspiel in 3 Akten von Schink. 8. Leipzig 1790.
— übersetzt von J. J. Eschenburg.
— Trauerspiel in 5 Akten von J. von Collin. gr. 8. Berlin 1804.
— übersetzt von Joh. Falk; u. d. T.: römisches Theater der Engländer und Franzosen. In freien Bearbeitungen nebst Entwickelung der Charaktere und Zurückführung derselben in ihre Quellen bei den Alten, besonders beim Plutarch, Livius und Dionys von Halikarnass. 1. Bd. Altenburg 1811.
— Travestie von Julius von Voss.
In: Travestien und Burlesken zur Darstellung in geselligen Kreisen. 16. Berlin 1812.
— von A. Voss.
— von J. W. O. Benda.
— von Dorothea Tieck.
— von H. Döring. 12. Gotha 1829.
— von L. Petz. 32. Leipzig 1836.
— von E. Ortlepp.
— von A. Keller.
— ohne Angabe des Uebersetzers. 8. Mannheim s. a.
— von Heinichen. Bonn 1858.

CYMBELINE. (Cymbeline.)
Cymbeline, König von Brittannien; ein Trauerspiel nach einem von Shakespeare erfundenen Stoff. Danzig 1772.
— von J. J. Eschenburg.
— von G. W. Kessler. 8. Berlin 1809.
— von A. Voss.
— von J. W. O. Benda.
— von Dorothea Tieck.

Cymbeline, von H. Döring. 12. Gotha 1829.
— von Phil Kaufmann. 8. Berlin 1832.
— für die deutsche Bühne bearb. von Ernst Rommel. 12. Hannover 1860.
— übersetzt von K. Simrock. 32. Leipzig 1836.
— von E. Ortlepp.
— von M. Rapp.
— von A. Bürck. Wien 1851.
— von Heinichen. Bonn 1858.

HAMLET. (Hamlet.)

Hamlet, ein Trauerspiel, abgeändert von Heufeld. 1773 In der Sammlung neuer Wiener Schauspiele.
— Trauerspiel, von Ch. Bock. Hamburg 1777.
— zum Behuf des Hamburger Theaters übersetzt von F. L. Schröder. 8. Hamburg 1778.1781.1795. Neue rechtmässige Ausgabe 1804; zuletzt in F. L. Schröder's dramatischen Werken herausgegeben von E. von Bülow, eingeleitet von Ludwig Tieck. gr. 8. Berlin 1831.
— der neue, worin Piramus und Thisbe als Zwischenspiel gespielt wird. von J. von Mauvillon.
In: Mauvillon, Gesellschaftstheater 2. Bd. 8. Leipzig 1790.
— nebst Brockmanns Bildniss als Hamlet und der zu dem Ballet verfertigten Musik. 3. genau durchgesehene Auflage. 8. Berlin 1795.
— übersetzt von J. J. Eschenburg.
— Prinz von Dänemark; Marionettenspiel von J. F. Schink. 8. 1799.
— von A. W. v. Schlegel. gr. 8. Berlin 1800. 1844. 1850.
— ein Trauerspiel in 5 Akten, von Eschenburg. gr. 8. Zürich 1805.
— für das deutsche Theater bearbeitet von K. Jul. Schütz. gr. 8. Leipzig 1806. 1819.
— Prinz von Dänemark, Karrikatur in 3 Akten. 8 Wien 1807.
— ein Trauerspiel in 6 Aufzügen. Nach Goethe's Andeutungen in Wilhelm Meister und A. W. Schlegel's Uebersetzung für die Bühne bearbeitet von A. Klingemann. 8. Leipzig 1815.
— übersetzt von J H. Voss.
— von J. W. O. Benda.
— von H. Döring. 12. Gotha 1829
— von J. B. Mannhart. Lex.-8. Sulzbach 1830.
— in deutscher Uebertragung. gr. 8. London (Hamburg) 1834.
— übersetzt von K. Simrock. 12. Leipzig 1836.
— von R. J. L. Samson von Himmelstiern. gr. 12. Dorpat 1837.
— von G. N. Bärmann.
— von E. Ortlepp.
— der Däne, übersetzt von M. Rapp.
— - die erste Ausgabe der Tragödie Hamlet. London, gedruckt bei Nicolaus Ling und J. Trundell, 1603. Uebersetzt von A. Ruhe. gr. 8. Inowraclaw (Berlin) 1844.
— grammatisch und sachlich zum Schul- und Privatgebrauch erläutert von J. Hoffa. 8. Braunschweig 1845.
— Prinz von Dänemark, Drama in 5 Aufzügen, übersetzt von v. Hagen. 4. Berlin 1848.
— a tragedy. Mit Sprache und Sachen erläuternden Anmerkungen, für Schüler, höhere Lehranstalten und Freunde des Dichters. gr. 8. Leipzig 1849.
— übersetzt von Dr. A. Jencken. 12. Mainz 1853.
— mit deutschen Anmerkungen, herausgegeben von Dr. Nicolaus Delius.
— deutsch durch F. Köhler. 16. Leipzig 1856.
— deutsch von E. Lobedanz. 16. Leipzig 1857.
— deutsch von Herm. v. Plehwe. 8. 1863.

HENRY THE FOURTH. (König Heinrich der Vierte.) Part 1 and 2.

Heinrich der Vierte, ein Schauspiel in 5 Aufzügen nach Shakespeare, für's deutsche Theater eingerichtet von F. L. Schröder. 8. Wien 1782.
— übersetzt von A. W. von Schlegel.
— von C. M. Wieland.
— von H. Voss. Mit Erläuterungen. gr. 8. Stuttgart 1822.

Heinrich der Vierte, übersetzt von J. W. O. Benda.
— Drama in two Parts. — Mit kritischen, historischen, besonders aber mit erklärenden Noten für den Gebrauch in höheren Lehranstalten, von Fr. E. Feller. gr. S. Leipzig 1830.
Henry the Fourth. 2 Parts. With historical and grammatical explanatory notes in German by J. M. Pierre. 12. Frankfurt a. M. 1833.
Heinrich der Vierte. 2 Theile, übersetzt von Th. Mügge. 32. Leipzig 1836.
—— 2 Theile, übersetzt von H. Döring. 12. Gotha 1829 u. 1834.
—— 2 Theile, übersetzt von Th. Mügge. 32. Leipzig 1836.
—— 2 Theile, übersetzt von G. N. Bärmann.
—— 2 Theile, übersetzt von E. Ortlepp.
—— von Samson von Himelstiern.
—— Trauerspiel von Shakespeare, zur Aufführung am k. k. Hofburgtheater in Wien bearbeitet von H. Laube.
Bühnenmanuscript.

HENRY THE FIFTH. (König Heinrich der Fünfte.)
Heinrich der Fünfte, übersetzt von A. W. von Schlegel.
—— von J. J. Eschenburg.
—— von J. H. Voss.
—— von J. W. O. Benda.
—— von H. Döring. 12. Gotha 1834.
—— von J. Körner.
—— von E. Ortlepp.
—— von A. Keller.
—— von Samson von Himelstiern.

HENRY THE SIXTH. (König Heinrich VI.) 3 parts.
Heinrich VI. 3 Theile, übersetzt von A. W. von Schlegel.
—— 3 Theile, übersetzt von J. J. Eschenburg.
—— 3 Theile, — von A. Voss.
—— 3 Theile, — von J. W. O. Benda.
—— 3 Theile, — von H. Döring. 12. Gotha 1829—34.
—— 3 Theile, — von A. Böttger. 32. Leipzig 1836.
—— 3 Theile, — von E. Ortlepp.
—— 3 Theile, — von A Keller.

HENRY THE EIGHT. (König Heinrich VIII.)
Heinrich VIII., übersetzt von J. J. Eschenburg.
—— — von Wolff Graf v. Baudissin. gr. 8. Hamburg 1818.
—— — von A. Voss.
—— — von J. W. O. Benda.
—— — von H. Döring. 12. Gotha 1829.
—— — von E. Susemihl. 32. Leipzig 1836.
—— — von S. H. Spiker. 8. Berlin 1837.
—— — von G. N. Bärmann.
—— — von E. Ortlepp.
—— — von A. Keller.

JULIUS CAESAR. (Juli Cäsar.
Julius Cäsar, übersetzt von Caspar Wilhelm von Bork, ehemal. Königl. Preuss. Staatsminister. 8. Berlin 1741.
—— Trauerspiel, übersetzt von J. J. Bodmer. 8. Leipzig 1763.
—— oder die Verschwörung des Brutus; ein Trauerspiel in sechs Handlungen von Shakespeare; für die Mannheimer Bühne bearbeitet von Dalberg. gr. 8. Mannheim 1785.
—— übersetzt von A. W. von Schlegel.
—— — von C. M. Wieland.
—— — von J. H. Voss.
—— — von J. W. O. Benda.
—— — von J. Meyer. 12. Gotha 1825.
—— — von L. Petz. 32. Leipzig 1836.
—— — von J. Körner.
—— — von E. Ortlepp.

Julius Cäsar, übersetzt von A. Keller.
— grammatisch und sachlich zum Schul- und Privatgebrauch erläutert von Dr. J. Hoffa. 8. Jena 1848.
— übersetzt von Dr. A. Jencken. 12. Mainz 1854.
— — von Vollbehr. 8. Kiel 1853.
— - von Adolph Kolb. 16. Stuttgart 1861.

KING JOHN. (König Johann.)
König Johann von Shakespeare. 8. Hamburg 1796.
— übersetzt von A. W. von Schlegel.
— — von C. M. Wieland.
— — von J. H. Voss.
— — von J. W. O. Benda.
— — von J. Meyer. 12. Gotha 1826.
— — von E. Susemihl. 32. Leipzig 1836.
— — von J. Körner.
— — von E. Ortlepp.
— — von A. Keller.

KING LEAR. (König Lear.)
König Lear, bearbeitet von F. L. Schröder. 8. Hamburg 1778.
— nach Shakespeare von Bock. 8. Leipzig 1780. 1794.
— übersetzt von C. M. Wieland.
—, — von J. H. Voss dem Sohne. Mit zwei Compositionen von Zelter. gr. 12. Jena 1806.
— — von Heinrich Voss. Mit Erläuterungen. gr. 8. Leipzig 1819.
— — von Beauregard Pandin (K. F. von Jarriges). 16. Zwickau 1824.
— — und für die deutsche Bühne frei bearbeitet von J. B. von Zahlhas. 8. Bremen 1824.
— — von J. W. O. Benda.
— — von Wolff Graf von Baudissin.
— — von J. Meyer. 12. Gotha 1827.
— — von Phil. Kaufmann. 8. Berlin 1830.
King Lear, with historical notes in German by J. P. Pierre. 8. Frankfurt a. M. 1831.
König Lear, deutsch mit einer Abhandlung über dieses Trauerspiel von E. Schick. 8. Leipzig 1833.
— übersetzt von E. Ortlepp.
— Für die Darstellung eingerichtet von C. A. West. gr. 8. Wien 1841.
— übersetzt von M. Rapp.
— — von Jencken. 16. Mainz 1854.

LOVE'S LABOUR LOST. (Verlorne Liebesmühe.)
Verlorne Liebesmüh', unter dem Titel: "Amor Vincit Omnia", ein Stück von Shakespear'n, bearbeitet von Lenz, als Anhang zu den Anmerkungen über's Theater. 8. Leipzig 1774.
— übersetzt von J. J. Eschenburg.
— — von H. Voss.
— — von J. W. O. Benda.
— — von Wolff Graf von Baudissin.
— — von H. Döring. 12. Gotha 1833.
— — von Phil. Kaufmann. 8. Berlin 1836.
— — von E. Susemihl. 32. Leipzig 1836.
— — von G. N. Bärmann.
— — von E. Ortlepp.
— — von M. Rapp.

MACBETH. (Macbeth.)
Macbeth, nach Shakespeare, von Stephanie dem Jüngern.
Sämmtliche Schauspiele Stephanie des Jüngern 2. Theil. gr. 8. Wien 1774.
— für das Prager Theater bearbeitet von J. F. Fischer. 8. Prag 1778.
— ein Trauerspiel von H. L. Wagner. Frankfurt a. M. 1779.

Macbeth. Deutsch bearbeitet von G. A. Bürger. Mit 12 Kupfern von Chodowiecki. 16. Göttingen 1783. 1784.
—— übersetzt von C. M. Wieland.
—— übersetzt von Fr. v. Schiller, zur Vorstellung auf dem Hoftheater zu Weimar eingerichtet. 8. Stuttgart 1801. — 2. Ed. 1810. -- 3. Ed. 1815.
—— übersetzt von J. F. W. Möller. 8. Hannover 1810.
—— — von J. H. Voss.
—— von J. H. Collin. Berlin 1822.
—— übersetzt von J. Meyer. 12. Gotha 1824.
—— — von J. W. O. Benda.
—— — von Dorothea Tieck.
—— zur Darstellung auf den königl. Bühnen in Berlin neu übersetzt von S. H. Spiker. 8. Berlin 1826.
—— heroische Oper in 3 Akten nach Shakespeare, aus dem Französischen des Rouget de Lisle frei bearbeitet von C. M. Heigel. Musik von A. H. Chelard. 12. München 1829.
—— übersetzt von K. Lachmann. 8. Berlin 1829.
—— — von Phil. Kaufmann. 8. Berlin 1830.
—— a Tragedy; sprachlich und sachlich erläutert für Schüler von Dr. C. L. W. Franke. 8. Braunschweig 1833.
—— übersetzt von L. Hilsenberg. 32. Leipzig 1836.
—— — von E. Ortlepp.
—— — von J. Körner.
—— aus der Folioausgabe von 1623 abgedruckt, mit den Varianten der Folioausgaben von 1632, 1664 und 1687 und kritischen Anmerkungen zum Text herausgeg. von N. Delius. gr. 8. Bremen 1841.
—— übersetzt von M. Rapp.
——·von A. Jacob. 8. Berlin 1848.
—— erklärt von Ludwig Herrig. 8. Berlin 1853.

MEASURE FOR MEASURE. (Maass für Maass.)
Gerechtigkeit und Rache, ein Schauspiel nach Shakespeare's Maass für Maass von W. H. Brömel. 8. Leipzig 1785.
Maass für Maass, Schauspiel, übersetzt von F. L. Schröder. 8. Leipzig 1790.
—— übersetzt von C. M. Wieland.
—— — von A. Voss.
—— — von J. W. O. Benda.
—— — von Wolff Graf von Baudissin.
—— — von H. Döring. 12. Gotha 1827.
—— — von E. Ortlepp.
—— u. d. T.: Vergeltungsrecht, übersetzt von M. Rapp.

THE MERCHANT OF VENICE. (Der Kaufmann von Venedig.)
Der Kaufmann von Venedig, oder Liebe und Freundschaft, ein Lustspiel von Shakespeare für das Prager Theater umgearbeitet von F. J. Fischer. 8. Prag 1779.
—— nach Shakespeare, mit einigen Aenderungen von Friedr. Ludw. Schröder. 8. Hamburg no date.
—— 8. Mannheim no date.
—— übersetzt von A. W. von Schlegel.
—— — von C. M. Wieland.
—— — von J. H. Voss. Mit Erläuterungen. 8. Leipzig 1818.
—— — von J. W. O. Benda.
—— nach Johnson's Text, mit krit. histor. Anmerkungen von Lion. 8. Göttingen 1830.
The Merchant of Venice with historical and grammatical explanatory notes in german by J. M. Pierre. 8. Frankfurt a. M. 1831.
Der Kaufmann von Venedig, übersetzt von A. Fischer. 32. Leipzig 1836.
—— Schauspiel in 5 Akten. Mit untergelegtem kritischen Commentar und historischen Erläuterungen und einer Biographie des Dichters von Dr. Eckenstein. 12. Braunschweig 1836.
—— übersetzt von J. Körner.
—— — von E. Ortlepp.

Der Kaufmann von Venedig. Für die Darstellung eingerichtet von C. A. West. gr. 8. Wien 1841.
— englisch-deutsche Prachtausgabe mit 27 Scenen und Vignetten in Holzschnitten. Die deutsche Uebertragung von A Fischer. gr. Lex. 8. Pforzheim 1843.
—— u. d. T.: Venediger Handelsschaft, übersetzt von M. Rapp.
—— von Fr. Wickenhagen. Berlin 1846.

MERRY WIVES OF WINDSOR. (Die lustigen Weiber von Windsor.)
Die lustigen Weiber zu Windsor, bearbeitet unter dem Titel: „Die lustigen Weiber an der Wien" von Pelzel. 8. Wien 1771.
Die lustigen Weiber von Windsor, unter dem Titel: "Gideon von Tromberg, Posse in 3 Akten", bearbeitet von W. H. Brömel. 8. Amsterdam 1785.
—— übersetzt von G. A. Bürger. Kupfer von Chodowiecki. 16. Göttingen 1786.
—— ein Singspiel nach Shakespeare. 12. Mannheim 1795.
—— Mit Kupfern. 12. Leipzig 1795.
—— übersetzt von J. J. Eschenburg.
—— — von K. H. Dippold. 8. Berlin 1809.
—— — von J. H. Voss.
—— — von J. W. O. Benda.
—— — von Wolff Graf v. Baudissin.
—— gr. 8. Königsberg 1826.
—— übersetzt von H. Döring. 12. Gotha 1831.
—— — von Phil. Kaufmann. 8. Berlin 1835.
—— — von K. Simrock. 32. Leipzig 1836.
—— — von E. Ortlepp.
Die boshaften Windsorerinnen, übersetzt von M. Rapp.
Die lustigen Weiber von Windsor, komisch-phantastische Oper in 3 Akten (nach Shakespeare) von Mosenthal. Musik von O Nikolai.

A MIDSUMMER NIGHT'S DREAM. (Ein Sommernachtstraum.)
Peter Squenz, eine Erweiterung des burlesken Trauerspiels "Pyramus und Thisbe" in Shakespeare's Sommernachtstraum, von Andreas Gryphius. 5. Breslau und Leipzig 1698.
Piramus und Thisbe. Duodrama. 8. Halle 1787.
—— musikalisches Duodrama. 8. Wien 1795.
Ein Sommernachtstraum, übersetzt von A. W. von Schlegel.
—— In den "Dramatischen Probe-Schlüssen ins Blaue der Kritik." 2. Band. 8. Glogau 1795.
—— übersetzt von C. M. Wieland.
—— — von J. H. Voss.
—— — von J. W. O. Benda.
—— - - von H. Döring. 12. Gotha 1831.
—— — von A. Fischer. 32. Leipzig 1836.
—— — von E. Ortlepp.
—— — von G. N. Bärmann.
Ein Traum der Johannisnacht, übersetzt von M. Rapp.
Ein Sommernachtstraum, übersetzt von F. W. Wickenhagen. (Both's Bühnenrepertoir.) Berlin 1845.
—— übersetzt von A. Böttger. 16. Leipzig 1845.
—— — von C. Abel. 16. Leipzig 1855.

MUCH ADO ABOUT NOTHING. (Viel Lärmen um Nichts.)
Viel Lärmen um Nichts, übersetzt von C. M. Wieland.
—— übersetzt von G. W. Kessler. 8. Berlin 1809.
—— — von H. Voss.
—— — von J. W. O. Benda.
—— — von Wolff Graf von Baudissin.
—— — von H. Döring. 12. Gotha 1828.
—— — von Phil. Kaufmann. 8. Berlin 1835.
—— — von A. Fischer. 32. Leipzig 1836.
—— — von G. N. Bärmann.
—— — von E. Ortlepp.
—— — von Rapp. — von A. Büttger. — von Karl von Holtei.

OTHELLO. (Othello.)

Othello, Trauerspiel von Shakespeare, aus dem Englischen übersetzt. gr. 8. Frankfurt und Leipzig 1769.
— Trauerspiel in 5 Aufzügen, übersetzt von Ch. H. Schmid. 8. Danzig 1772—77.
— bearbeitet von L. Schubarth. Mit Melodieen vom Zumsteeg. 8. Leipzig 1782. — 2. Aufl. 1802.
— übersetzt von C. M. Wieland.
— der Mohr von Venedig, Posse in 1 Akt. 8. Wien 1806.
— übersetzt von J. H. Voss dem Sohne. Mit 3 Compositionen von Zelter. gr 12. Jena 1806.
— übersetzt von J. Meyer. Gotha 1824.
— — von J. W. O. Benda.
— — von Wolff Graf von Baudissin.
— — von Phil Kaufmann. 8. Berlin 1832.
— heroische Oper in 3 Akten, Musik von Giacomo Rossini.
— übersetzt von E. Ortlepp. 32. Leipzig 1836.
— — von J. Körner.
— für die Darstellung eingerichtet von C. A. West. gr. 8. Wien 1841.
— übersetzt von M. Rapp.
— erklärt von H. Sievers. 8. Berlin 1853.
— nach Shakspeare von Marbach. 12. Leipzig 1864.

PERICLES. (Pericles.)

Pericles, übersetzt von J. J. Eschenburg.
— — von Ludwig Tieck.
— — von J. W. O. Benda.
— — von J. Meyer. 12. Gotha 1826.
— — von H. Döring. 12. Leipzig 1836.
— — von G. N. Bärmann.
— — von E. Ortlepp.
— — von A. Keller.

RICHARD THE SECOND. (König Richard der Zweite.)

König Richard der Zweite, nach Shakespeare für's Prager Theater adoptirt von F. J. Fischer. 8. Prag 1778.
— für die deutsche Bühne von v. Gemmingen. 8. Mannheim 1782.
— übersetzt von A. W. v. Schlegel.
— — von C. M. Wieland.
— — von J. H. Voss.
— — von J. W. O. Benda.
— — von H. Döring. 12. Gotha 1824.
— — von Th. Oelckers. 32. Leipzig 1836.
— — von E. Ortlepp.
— — von A. Keller.
— Heinrich IV. und Heinrich V. Uebersetzt von R. J. L. Samson von Himmelstiern. 2 Bde. gr. 8. Riga 1848.
— 16. Braunschweig 1850.
— nach A. W. v. Schlegel's Uebersetzung für die Bühne eingerichtet von Emil Devrient.

RICHARD THE THIRD. (König Richard der Dritte.)

König Richard der Dritte, ein Trauerspiel (nach Shakespeare) in 5 Aufzügen von Christian Felix Weisse. 8. Leipzig 1776.
— für die Mannheimer Bühne von G. H. Reichsfreiherrn von Gemmingen. gr. 8. Mannheim 1778.
— ein Trauerspiel (nach Shakespeare) von Perchtold. 8. Regensburg 1788.
— übersetzt von A. W. von Schlegel.
— — von J. J. Eschenburg.
— — von H. Voss.
— — von J. W. O. Benda.
— — von H. Döring. 12. Gotha 1834.
— — von E. Thein. 32. Leipzig 1836.

König Richard der Dritte, übersetzt von E. Ortlepp.
—— — von A. Keller.
—— — von J. Körner.

ROMEO AND JULIET. (Romeo und Julia.)

Romeo und Julia, ein Trauerspiel (nach Shakespeare) von Christian Felix Weisse. 8. Leipzig 1776.
—— ein Schauspiel mit Gesang von F. W. Gotter. 8. Leipzig 1779.
—— für's deutsche Theater bearbeitet von Ch. Fr. Bretzner. 8. Leipzig 1796.
—— übersetzt von C. M. Wieland.
—— Quodlibet von Karakteren in 2 Akten. Wien 1808.
—— dramatisches Gedicht (nach Shakespeare) von Julius von Soden. 8. Naumburg 1809.
—— übersetzt von J. H. Voss. Leipzig 1818.
—— — von J. W. O. Benda.
—— — von H. Döring. 12. Gotha 1829.
—— mit erklärenden Noten von Dr. F. E. Feller. 12. Leipzig 1833.
—— übersetzt von E. Ortlepp. 32. Leipzig 1836.
—— — von J. Körner.
Romeo and Juliet, with historical and explanatory notes in german by J. M. Pierre. 12. Frankfurt a. M. 1840.
—— Mit erläuternden Anmerkungen von Ed. Winter. 12. Braunschweig 1840.
Romeo und Julia. Zur Darstellung eingerichtet von C. A. West. gr. 8. Wien 1841.
Romeo und Giulietta, übersetzt von M. Rapp.
Romeo und Julia, grammatisch erläutert von J. Hoffa. 8. Braunschweig 1845.
—— übersetzt von A. W. Schlegel. 16. Berlin 1949.
—— erklärt von Heussi. 8. Berlin 1853.
—— herausgegeben von H. Ulrici. 8. Halle 1853.
—— übersetzt von E. Lobedanz. 16. Leipzig 1855.
—— Eine kritische Ausgabe des überlieferten Doppeltextes, mit vollst. Varia Lectio bis auf Rowe, nebst einer Einleitung über den Werth der Textquellen und den Versbau Shakespeare's von Tycho Mommsen. roy. 8. Oldenburg 1859.

TAMING OF THE SHREW. (Zähmung einer Widerspenstigen.)

Die bezähmte Widerbellerin oder Gessner der Zweite. Lustspiel in 4 Aufzügen (nach Shakespeare) von J. Fr. Schink. gr. 8. München 1783.
—— übersetzt von J. J. Eschenburg.
—— — von A. Voss.
Liebe kann Alles oder die bezähmte Widerspänstige. Lustspiel in 4 Abtheilungen frei nach Shakespeare und Schink von Fr. von Holbein. gr. 8. Pesth 1822.
—— übersetzt von J. W. O. Benda.
Zähmung einer Widerspänstigen, übersetzt von Wolff Graf von Baudissin.
—— übersetzt von H. Döring. 12. Gotha 1830.
—— — von K. Simrock. 32. Leipzig 1836.
—— — von E. Ortlepp.
Die Widerspänstige. Lustspiel in 4 Aufzügen. Mit Benutzung einiger Theile der Uebersetzung des Grafen Baudissin, von Deinhardstein. gr. 8. Wien 1839.
—— u. d. T.: Gebrochner Trutzkopf, ein Lustspiel, nebst dem Fragment: Der versoffne Kesselflicker, übersetzt von M. Rapp.
—— Kunst über alle Künste Ein bös Weib gut zu machen, deutsche Bearb. von Taming of the Shrew, aus dem Jahre 1672. Neu herausg. mit engl. Original und Anmerk. von Reinhold Köhler. 8. Berlin 1864.

TEMPEST. (Der Sturm.)

Der Sturm, eine Oper nach Shakespeare, vom Kammerherrn von Einsiedel in Weimar. (Not printed.) 1787.
—— Ein Schauspiel für das Theater bearbeitet von L. Tieck. Nebst einer Abhandlung über Shakespeare's Behandlung des Wunderbaren. Mit Vignette. 8. Berlin 1796.

Der Sturm, übersetzt von A. W. von Schlegel.
—— übersetzt von C. M. Wieland.
Die Geisterinsel, ein Singspiel von F. W. Gotter. 8. Leipzig 1798.
Der Sturm, oder die bezauberte Insel. Singspiel nach Shakespeare. 8. Cassel 1798.
—— übersetzt von H. Voss.
—— — von J. Meyer. 12. Gotha 1825.
—— — von J. W. O. Benda.
The Tempest, with historical notes in german by J. M. Pierre. 12. Frankfurt a. M. 1833.
Der Sturm, übersetzt von Th. Mügge. 32. Leipzig 1836.
—— — von J. Körner.
—— — von E. Ortlepp.
—— — von M. Rapp.
—— für die Bühne bearbeitet von Franz Dingelstedt. (Bühnenmanuscript.)

TIMON OF ATHENS. (Timon von Athen.)
Timon von Athen von Shakespeare; für's Prager Theater bearbeitet von F. J. Fischer. 8. Prag 1778.
—— übersetzt von C. M. Wieland.
—— — von A. Voss.
—— — von G. Regis. 16. Zwickau 1821.
—— — von J. W. O. Benda.
—— — von Dorothea Tieck.
—— — von J. Meyer. 12. Gotha 1825.
—— — von E. Ortlepp. 32. Leipzig 1836.
—— — von A. Keller.

TITUS ANDRONICUS. (Titus Andronicus.)
Titus Andronicus, übersetzt von J. J. Eschenburg.
—— — von H. Voss.
—— — von J. W. O. Benda.
—— — von Wolff Graf von Baudissin.
—— — von J. Meyer. 12. Gotha 1826.
—— — von Th. Oelckers. 32. Leipzig 1836.
—— — von G. N. Bärmann.
—— — von E. Ortlepp.
—— — von A. Keller.

TROILUS AND CRESSIDA. (Troilus und Cressida.)
Troilus und Cressida, übersetzt von J. J. Eschenburg.
—— — von J. H. Voss.
—— — von J. W. O. Benda.
—— — von Beauregard Pandin (K. F. von Jariges). gr. 12. Berlin 1824.
—— — von Wolff Graf von Baudissin.
—— — von H. Döring. 12. Gotha 1829.
—— — von G. N. Bärmann.
—— — von E. Ortlepp.
—— — von A. Keller.

TWELFTH NIGHT. (Der heilige Dreikönigsabend oder Was ihr wollt.)
Was ihr wollt, übersetzt von A. W. von Schlegel.
—— — von C. M. Wieland.
—— — von J. H. Voss.
—— — von J. W. O. Benda.
—— — von H. Döring. 12. Gotha 1827.
—— — von A. Fischer. 32. Leipzig 1836.
—— — von E. Ortlepp.
—— — von M. Rapp.
—— Viola. Lustspiel in 5 Aufzügen. Nach "Was ihr wollt" von Shakespeare. Für die Bühne bearbeitet von Deinhardstein. gr. 8. Wien 1842.
—— übersetzt von A. Büttger. 16. Leipzig 1849.

TWO GENTLEMEN OF VERONA. (Die beiden Edlen von Verona.)
Die beiden Veroneser, übersetzt von C. M. Wieland.
—— Schauspiel in 4 Akten; nach Shakespeare von Kleedig. 8. Leipzig 1862.
—— übersetzt von H. Voss.
—— — von J. W. O. Benda.
—— — von Dorothea Tieck.
—— — von J. Meyer. 12. Gotha 1827.
—— — von Phil. Kaufmann. 8. Berlin 1835.
—— — von A. Fischer. 32. Leipzig 1836.
—— — von J. Körner.
—— — von E. Ortlepp.
—— u. d. T.: Die Freunde von Oporto, übersetzt von M. Rapp.

WINTER'S TALE. (Ein Wintermärchen.)
Ein Wintermärchen, übersetzt von J. J. Eschenburg.
—— — von L. Krause. 8. Berlin 1810.
—— — von H. Voss.
—— — von J. W. O. Benda.
—— — von Dorothea Tieck.
—— — von H. Döring. 12. Gotha 1830.
—— — von W. Lampadius. 32. Leipzig 1836.
—— — von G. N. Bärmann.
—— — von E. Ortlepp.
Ein Märchen beim Kamin, übersetzt von M. Rapp.
—— übersetzt von C. Abel. 8. Berlin 1854.

POEMS.

Shakespeare's Gedichte, übersetzt von Schumacher und E. von Bauernfeld. 16. Wien 1817. 2. Aufl. 1827.
—— übersetzt von Schneider. 2 Bände. Gotha 1834.
—— übersetzt von Karl Richter.
- — sämmtliche poetische Werke. 3 Bände. Wien 1839.
—— vermischte Gedichte von Ortlepp.
—— sämmtliche Gedichte von E. Wagner. Königsberg 1840.
—— übersetzt von Jordan. Berlin 1861.
Shakespeare's Sonette, übersetzt von K. Lachmann. 12. Berlin 1820.
—— von Fr. Bodenstedt. 8. Berlin 1862. 2. Aufl. 12.
Venus und Adonis. Tarquin und Lukrezia. Zwei Gedichte übersetzt von H. C. Albrecht. gr. 8. Halle 1783.
—— übersetzt von F. Freiligrath. 8. Düsseldorf 1849.
—— übersetzt von J. H. Dambeck. 8. Leipzig 1856.

GERMAN
COMMENTARIES, ESSAYS AND PLATES.

Abecken, R. B. Ueber Shakespeare. Im Taschenbuch: "Urania für 1819". 16. Leipzig 1818.
Abendzeitung 1823, No. 50—55. 1825, No 60. 63. 1826, No. 35—37.
Ahne, W. Shakspeare-Blüthen als Festgabe zur 300jähr. Gedächtnissfeier des grossen brittischen Dichters. 8. Prag 1863.
Alberti, C. E. R. Shakspeare-Album. Des Dichters Welt- und Lebensanschauung aus seinen Werken systematisch geordnet. 16. Berlin 1864.
Alexis, W. Shakspeare als Romanheld. Blätter für Literar. Unterhaltung. 1839. No 233—236.
Alter Ego. Eine Studie zu Shakspeare's Kaufmann. 8. 1862.
Ancillon, F. Zur Vermittlung der Extreme. Berlin 1831. Vol. II. 176—217.
Anmerkungen, alte und neue, zu Shakespeare's dramatischen Werken. Für Alle, welche den Dichter in der Ursprache lesen wollen. 1. Theil. gr. 8. Greifswalde 1825.
Assmann, K. Shakespeare und seine deutschen Uebersetzer. Lit.-linguistische Abhandlung. 4. Liegnitz 1843.
Ast, F. System der Kunstlehre. 1805. p. 293—295.
Ausland, das. September-Nummer 1835.
Bachmann, C. F. Die Kunstwissenschaft. 1811. § 28.
Barnstorff, D. Schlüssel zu Shakspeare's Sonetten. 8. 1861.
Becker's Weltgeschichte. VIII. pag. 404—7.
Bekk, A. William Shakespeare. Eine biographische Studie. 8. München 1864.
Bell, W. Ist Shakespeare in Deutschland gewesen? Mitgetheilt im Morgenblatte Nr. 50, Jahrgang 1853. — Vom Verfasser in deutscher Sprache geschrieben.
Bernhardi, W. Shakespeare's Kaufmann von Venedig. Eine kritische Skizze. Altona 1859.
Betrachtungen über die religiöse Bedeutung Shakespeare's. 8. Heidelberg 1858.
Beyfuss, A. Tieck und Hamlet.
    In: Sibyllinische Blätter aus der neuesten Zeit 1. Heft. gr. 8. Berlin 1826.
Bibliothek der schönen Wissenschaften. 1775, No. 23.
Blankenberg, C. F. Zusätze zu Sulzer's Theorie der schönen Künste. Vol. 3.
Blätter für literar. Unterhaltung. 1841, No. 162—3. 224—5. 1842, Nr. 57. 61. 111. 1844, No. 4—8. etc.
Blümner, H. Von der Idee des Schicksals. Leipzig 1814. pag. 98. 156.
Boas, Dr. E. Gaukeleien der Liebe, Lustspiel in 3 Akten.
    Bühnenmanuscript. Behandelt die Entstehung des Shakespeare'schen Lustspiels: "Was ihr wollt!"
Bode, H. Englische-Kritik.
    Im ersten Hefte von Gödecke's deutscher Wochenschrift für 1851.
Bodenstedt, Fr. Shakespeare's Zeitgenossen und ihre Werke. In Characteristiken und Uebersetzungen. 3. Bde. 8. Berlin 1858.
Börne, Ludwig. Ueber Hamlet von Shakespeare.
    In Börne's gesammelten Schriften 2. Band. 12. Hamburg 1828—40.
Bohtz, A. W. Geschichte der neuern deutschen Poesie. Göttingen 1832. (pag. 27—209.)

Bohlz. A. W, die Idee des Tragischen. Gött. 1836. (pag. 74—76. 237—240.)
—— über das Komische und die Komödie. 1844. (pag. 203—221.)
Bouman, Jahrb. der Wissenschaftl. Kritik. Berlin 1838.
Bouterwek, F. Geschichte der Poesie und Beredsamkeit. Gött. 1809. Bd. 7. pag. 273—290.
Boye, C. J. William Shakespeare, romantisches Schauspiel. 8. Copenhagen 1826.
Bracker, Ulrich. Etwas über Shakespeare.
    In: Der arme Mann vom Tokkenberge, herausgegeben von E. v. Bülow. 16. Leipzig 1852.
Braun v. Braunthal, J. K. Shakespeare. Drama in 3 Acten. Nach L. Tieck's Novelle: "Dichterleben". gr. 8. Wien 1836.
Bredow, G. G. Shakespeare und seine Dramen, aus dem Englischen des Johnson.
—— Herr Peter Squenz, oder Pyramus und Thisbe. Schimpfspiel in zwei Abtheilungen nach Andreas Greif (Gryphius).
    In G. G. Bredow's Schriften, ein Nachlass, herausgegeben von J. G. Kurisch. gr. 8. Breslau 1816.
Breier's Studien zu Shakespeare's Macbeth. Archiv f. N. S. VIII, pag. 231. X, p. 51.
Brummer, B. Der Affe Shakespeare's, oder Leben und Lieben, Lustspiel in 5 Akten. 8. Amberg 1841.
Brun. G. Shakespeare und Schiller's auserlesene Schätze des Geistes. 8. Wien 1788.
Canzler, K. C. Briefe über die Einführung des Englischen Geschmacks in Schauspielen betreffend. 8. Leipzig 1759.
Carové, F. W. Hamlet. Neorama I. Leipzig 1838. pag. 21—32.
Chalmers, A. Shakespeare's Leben. — Charakteristik der Shakespeare'schen Dramen von W. Hazlitt. — 37 Umrisse zu den 37 Shakespeare'schen Dramen und Portrait Shakespeare's in Stahlstich. — Supplement zu Shakespeare in Einem Bande. Lex.-8. Leipzig 1838.
Chasles, Phil. und F. Guizot. William Shakespeare, sein Leben, seine Werke und seine Zeit; ein Commentar zu des Dichters sämmtlichen Werken, herausgegeben von P. H. Sillig. 16. Leipzig 1854.
Clement, K. J. Shakespeare's Sturm, historisch beleuchtet. gr. 8. Leipzig 1846.
Clodius, A. Ueber Shakespeare's Philosophie, besonders im Hamlet.
    In dem Taschenbuche "Urania" für 1820. 16. Leipzig 1819.
Clodius, E. A. H. Hermes, Jahrbuch der Literatur. 1819. No. I.
Cohn, A. Shakspeare in Germany in the sixteenth and seventeenth Century. Berlin and London 1864.
Collier, J. P. Beiträge und Verbesserungen zu Shakespeare's Dramen nach handschriftlichen, in einem Exemplar der Folio-Ausgabe von 1632 befindlichen Aenderungen für den deutschen Text bearbeitet und herausgegeben unter dem Titel: "Ergänzungsband zu Shakespeare's Werken", von Dr. J. Freese. gr. 8. Berlin 1853.
—— Beiträge und Verbesserungen zu Shakespeare's Dramen, nach handschriftlichen, in einem Exemplare der Folio-Ausgabe von 1632 befindlichen Aenderungen für den deutschen Text bearbeitet und herausgegeben von Dr. F. A. Leo. 8. Berlin 1853.
Collin, M. Ueber das histor. Schauspiel; in F. Schlegel's Museum. 1812. II. pag. 193—213.
—— Jahrb. der Literatur. Wien 1822. XX. p. 133. 139—141.
Conversations-Blatt, Berliner, 1828, No. 55—57. 62—64. 128. 138. 139. 141. 170. 180—181.
Conversations-Lexicon, Brockhaus', Artikel "Shakspeare".
Corrodi, Aug. Shakespeare's Lebensweisheit aus seinen Werken gesammelt. 8. Winterthur 1863.
Cynthii (Joanis Baptistae Gyraldi) Novellae, aus dem Italienischen in die hochdeutsche Sprache versetzet. Frankfurt 1614.
    "Shakspeare has had recourse to the hundred Tales of Cynthio in two instances, Cymbeline and Measure for Measure, for the subject of his plays.
Danzel, Th. W. Shakespeare und noch kein Ende.*
    In den Blättern für literarische Unterhaltung, Jahrgang 1850.
Davies. Leben von Garrick, aus dem Englischen 1782. 12. 2 Vols.

Delius, N. Beiträge zur Kritik von Shakespeare's Othello und König Lear. Archiv V. 254.
—— Beiträge zur Kritik des Shakespeare. Archiv d. n. Spr. Bd. 7 u. 13.
—— Die Schlegel-Tieck'sche Shakespeare-Uebersetzung beleuchtet. 8. Bonn 1846.
—— Der Mythus von W. Shakespeare. Eine Kritik der Shakespeare'schen Biographieen. gr. 8. Bonn 1851.
—— Shakespeare-Lexikon. gr. 8. Bonn 1852.
—— Ueber das englische Theaterwesen zu Shakespeare's Zeit, ein Vortrag. gr. 8. Bremen 1853.
—— J. Payne Collier's alte handschriftliche Emendationen zum Shakespeare gewürdigt gr. 8. Bonn 1853.
Dingelstedt, Fr. Studien und Copien nach Shakespeare. 8. Pesth.
Docen, B. J. Altdeutsches Museum. II. pag. 277.
Eckart, Dr. Ludwig. Dramaturgische Studien: I. Vorlesungen über Hamlet. 8. Aarau 1853.
Eckermann, J. P. Beiträge zur Poesie. Stuttgart 1824. p. 17. 19. 87—88.
Eckert, G. An das gelehrte Publikum wegen der Mannheimer Ausgabe der Werke Shakespeare's. 8. Mannheim 1780.
Eichhorn, J. G. Geschichte der Literatur 1807. IV. Band.
—— Literär-Geschichte. 1811. 2. Band.
Ekendahl, D. G. Die höchsten Ideen der Kunst. 1831. pag. 265.
Elze, K. Festrede zur 300jähr. Geburtstagsfeier Shakespeare's in Dessau gehalten. 8. Dessau 1864.
Enk, M. Melpomene, oder vom tragischen Interesse. Wien 1827.
Erhard, A. Möron. Passau 1826. pag. 388—390.
Eschenburg, J. J. Ueber Shakespeare's Leben und Schriften. 8. Zürich 1787. — 2. Auflage 1806.
—— Versuch über Shakespeare's Genie und Schriften, im Vergleich mit den dramatischen Dichtern der Griechen und Franzosen. 8. Leipzig 1787.
—— über den vorgeblichen Fund Shakspeare'scher Handschriften. 8. Leipz. 1797.
—— Deutsches Museum. Januar 1777. p. 40 ff.
Etwas über William Shakespeare.
Im vierten Stücke der Horen für 1796.
Falk, J. Vorrede zu Coriolan. Leipzig 1812.
—— Goethe dargestellt. 1832. pag. 35. 214. 240.
Flir, Alois. Briefe über Shakespeare's Hamlet. 1850.
Feist. Ueber das Verhältniss Hamlet's und Ophelia's. Frankfurt 1859.
Flathe, J. L. F. Shakespeare in seiner Wirklichkeit. 1. Band 1863. 2. Band 1864. Leipzig
Flögel. Geschichte der komischen Literatur. 1787. IV. p. 113—114.
Fontane, Th. Aus England. Studien und Briefe über Londoner Theater. 8. Stuttgart 1860.
Francke, C. L. W. Bemerkungen über Shakespeare. 8. Bernburg 1837.
Frese, J. Ergänzungsband zu allen englischen Ausgaben und zur Schlegel-Tieck'schen Uebersetzung von Shakspeare. 8. Berlin 1853.
Friesen, H. v. Briefe über Shakespeare's Hamlet. Leipzig 1864.
Fritzart, Fr. War Shakespeare ein Geist? Shakespeare war nicht ganz Shakespeare. Oder: Ueber das christliche Prinzip in der romantisch-dramatischen Poesie.
Anregungen, erste Nummer. 8. Heidelberg 1832.
Funck, Z. Iffland als Shylock im Kaufmann von Venedig.
In dessen Erinnerungen aus dem Leben zweier Schauspieler: August Wilhelm Iffland und Ludwig Devrient.
Gans, E. Der Hamlet des Ducis und des Shakspeare. (Vermischte Schriften Vol. 2.) Berlin 1834.
Garrick. Memoiren. — Garrick im Makbeth. — Vertheidigung dieser Tragödie. — Das Shakespeare-Jubiläum.
In: Vor und auf den Bretern, Schauspieler-Memoiren nach Barrière's Bibliothèque des Mémoires deutsch bearbeitet von Ida Frick. 2. Theil. 8. Dresden 1849.
Garrick oder die englischen Schauspieler. Ein Werk über Drama, die Kunst der Vorstellung und das Spiel der Acteurs. (von J. E. Schlegel's Werke.) Kopenhagen 1771.

Garve, C. Abhandlung aus der Bibliothek der schönen Wissenschaften. Leipzig 1802.
—— Ueber die Rollen der Wahnsinnigen in Shakespeare's Schauspielen und über den Charakter Hamlet's insbesondere. (In: Versuche über Gegenst. der Moral. 1796. Vol. II. p. 480.)
Gedenkblatt zu Shakspeare's 300jähr. Geburtsfeier erfunden und lithogr. von Bartsch. Berlin 1864.
Gerstenberg, H. W. von. Etwas über Shakespeare. In dessen vermischten Schriften 3. Band. 8. Altona 1815—17.
Gerth, A. Der Hamlet von Shakspeare. Acht Vorlesungen. 8. Leipzig 1862.
Gervinus, G. G. Shakespeare. 4 Theile. 8. Leipzig 1849—50. — 3. Aufl. 2 Vols. 1862.
Gieseke, K. L. Der travestirte Hamlet, in Knüttelversen mit Arien. 8. Wien 1798.
Pasquil on Schröder's transl. of Hamlet.
Görres, J. Die deutschen Volksbücher. 1807. pag. 296.
Goethe, J. W. von. Wilhelm Meisters Lehrjahre. III, Cap. 11. IV, Cap. 3. 13. 15. V, Cap. 4—11.
—— Ueber Retzsch's Galerie zu Shakespeare's sämmtlichen Werken.
—— Werke. Anmerkungen über Rameau's Neffe.
—— — Aus meinem Leben.
—— — Kunst und Alterthum. III, 3.
—— — Shakespeare als Theaterdichter (Kunst und Alterth.) V, 3.
—— — Shakspeare und kein Ende V, 3.
—— — Vol. XLV, 3". 58—63. 111. 152—154.
—— — Gespräche mit Goethe von Eckermann. Vol. I. pag. 201. 205. 233—235. 251. 327. Vol. II. 80, 153.
Grabbe, Dietr. Chr. Dramatische Dichtungen. Nebst einer Abhandlung über die Shakespeare-Manie. 2 Bände. 8. Frankfurt a. M. 1827.
Greverus, J. P. E. Ueber Shakespeare's Romeo und Julie. Versuch einer Charakteristik. Programm. 4. Oldenburg 1834.
Grohmann, J. C. A. Die Aesthetik als Wissenschaft. 1830. p. 171. 214 fg.
Gruber, J. G. Wieland's Leben. 1816. Vol. I, p. 131—143.
Grüner, Fr. Aphorismen und Scenen aus Shakespeare's Werken. Mit Kupfern. 12. Wien 1809.
Grüner, T. Lebens- und Denkbuch aus Shakespeare's Werken. Carlsruhe 1830.
Grundlinien zu einer Theorie der Schauspielkunst. Leipzig 1797. Ueber Falstaff p. 85—90. Ueber Hamlet p. 93—134.
Gruppe, O. F. Ariadne, die tragische Kunst der Griechen. Leipzig 1831. pag. 733—735.
Gutzkow, Carl. Hamlet in Wittenberg. (Werke, Vol. I.) 1838.
—— Eine Shakspearefeier an der Ilm. Leipzig 1864.
Hagen, v. d. Die Nibelungen. Breslau 1819. p. 5—6. 168. 160. 216.
Hagen, E. A. Shakespeare's erstes Erscheinen auf den Bühnen Deutschlands. 8. Königsberg 1832.
Hagena, die Shakespeare-Studien auf dem oldenburgischen Gymnasium, nebst Berichtigungen der Schlegel'schen Uebersetzung. (Schulprogramm.) gr. 8. Oldenburg 1847.
—— Berichtigungen der Schlegel- und Tieck'schen Uebersetzung des Shakspeare. Archiv für n. Spr. III, p. 357. VI, p. 61.
Heath. Shakespeare's Frauenbilder, eine Sammlung weiblicher Portraits zu den sämmtlichen Schauspielen des Dichters. Nach Originalzeichnungen von den berühmtesten Künstlern Englands gestochen. Lex.-8. Berlin und London 1836—38.
Hebler, R. A. C. Shakespeare's Kaufmann von Venedig, ein Versuch über die sogenannte Idee dieser Komödie. 8. Bern 1854.
Hegel, G. W. Aesthetik. 1838. Vol. III, p. 504—6. 520. 566—579.
Heine, H. Shakespeare's Mädchen und Frauen, mit Erläuterungen. Lex.-8. 45 Portraits in Stahlstich und 14½ Bogen Text. Paris und Leipzig 1839.
Hense, C. C. Vorträge über ausgewählte dramatische Dichtungen Shakespeare's, Schiller's und Goethe's. gr. 8. Halberstadt 1844.
—— Geschichte des Sommernachtstraums. In Herrig's Archiv Vol. X. XI. XII.

Hense, C. C. Die wichtigsten Erscheinungen der neueren und neuesten Shakespeare-Literatur in England und Deutschland. In den "Blättern für literarische Unterhaltung", Jahrg. 1853.
Herder, J. G. v. Werke zur schönen Kunst und Literatur. Stuttgart 1830. Vol. XVI, p. 126. 279. 280. XVII, p. 228-244. XVIII, p. 113. 261. XX, 271—302.
—— Shakespeare, dessen characteristische Schicksalsfabel in Hamlet.
—— Etwas über Shakespeare. In: "Von deutscher Art und Kunst", fliegende Blätter etc. 8. Hamburg 1773.
Hermes, K. H. Ueber Shakespeare's Hamlet und seine Beurtheiler. Stuttg. 1827.
Hermes. Jahrbücher der Literatur. Leipzig 1819. Vol. III, p. 21. 1823. VIII, p. 172. 341. 1826. XIX, p. 177—179.
Hettner, H. Ueber Shakespeare; mit einer Anmerkung: über die Darstellungsweise der Rolle des Hamlet durch Bogumil Dawison und Emil Devrient, von Carl Gutzkow. Im 2. Bande von Gutzkow's Unterhaltungen am häuslichen Heerd. 8. Leipzig 1853—54.
Heussi, Dr. J. Zur Shakespeare-Kritik, nebst einem etymologischen Excurse. Archiv d. n. Spr. IV, p. 172. VI, p. 159. XII, p. 174.
Hiecke, R. H. Shakespeare's Macbeth, erläutert und gewürdigt. gr. 8. Merseburg 1846.
Hilgers. Sind nicht in Shakespeare noch manche Verse wieder herzustellen, welche alle Ausgaben des Dichters in Prosa geben? Programm der höheren Bürger- und Gewerbschule in Aachen. gr. 8. Aachen 1852.
Hoffmann. Studien zu Shakespeare's Hamlet. Archiv d. n. Spr. III, p. 373.
Holtey, K. v. Beiträge zur dram. Kunst und Literatur. Richard III. 1828. April. p. 86—105. Hamlet. May. p. 126—153.
—— Shakspeare in der Heimath, oder die Freunde, Schauspiel in 4 Akten. 8. Schleusingen 1840.
Horn, Fr. Shakespeare's Schauspiele erläutert. 5 Bände. gr. 8. Leipzig 1822—31.
—— Freundliche Schriften. 1817. Vol. I, p. 137—39. II, p. 101—94. 200. 226.
—— Umrisse zur Geschichte der Literatur Deutschlands. 1821. p. 81—89. 206. 209. 211—213.
—— Die Poesie und Beredsamkeit der Deutschen. Leipzig 1829. I, 31. 41. 263. III, 94. 128. 335—40. IV, 131—47. 239—42. 264.
Huber, V. A. Englisches Lesebuch. 1834. Vorrede, p. 28—31.
Hugo, Victor. William Shakespeare. Deutsch von A. Diezmann. 8. Leipzig 1864.
Hülsmann, Ed. Shakspeare. Sein Geist und seine Werke. 8. Leipzig 1800.
Humboldt, W. Briefwechsel mit Schiller. 1831. p. 81. 235.
Jacob, J. G. Ueber Walter Scott. Mainz 1827. p. 106—119.
Jahrbücher der Literatur. Wien 1821. No. XV, p. 106—7. 139—54. 1822. No. XVII, p. 2. 17. 27. 29. No. XIX, p. 65—66. 1828. No. XLIII, p. 1—10 (über Macbeth).
Jameson, Mrs. Shakespeare's weibliche Karaktere, übersetzt von E. Ortlepp. 16. Stuttgart 1840.
—— Shakespeare's Frauengestalten. Charakteristiken. Nach der dritten Auflage aus dem Englischen übertragen von Levin Schücking. 16. Bielefeld 1840.
—— Frauenbilder, oder Charakteristik der vorzüglichsten Frauen in Shakespeare's Dramen. Deutsch von A. Wagner. gr. 8. Leipzig 1834.
—— Shakespeare's female Characters. An appendix to Shakespeare's dramatic Works. 8. Bielefeld 1840.
Ideler und Nolte. Handbuch der Engl. Sprache und Literatur. Berlin 1812. Vol. II.
Iffland, A. W. Meine theatralische Laufbahn. 8. Leipzig 1798.
Erklärt sich gegen die Einführung Shakespeare's in Deutschland.
Immermann, K. Ueber den rasenden Ajax des Sophokles. 1826. p. 61—62. 85—86.
—— Ueber Hamlet. Blätter für liter. Unterh. 1842. No. 111.
Jost, Dr. J. M. Erklärendes Wörterbuch zu Shakespeare's Plays. Für deutsche Leser zur richtigen Auffassung des Wortsinnes und der vielen schwierigen Stellen, so wie der Anspielungen und Wortspiele. 8. Berlin 1830.

Kaulbach, W. Shakespeare-Galerie in Kupferstichen. Imp.-Folio. (Macbeth.
— Tempest. — King John.) Berlin 1855—57.
—— Shakespeare-Album in photograph. Abbildungen. 2. Ausg. 3 pts Folio. München 1862.
—— the same in 12mo. 9 plates. 1863.
Kind, F. Die Muse. Febr. 1822. p. 16—19.
Klotz, C. A. Acta litteraria. IV. 2. p. 183—184.
Knauer, B. Die Könige Shakespeare's. Ein Beitrag zur Rechtsphilosophie. 8. Wien 1863.
Koberstein. Shakespeare's allmähliches Bekanntwerden in Deutschland und Urtheile über ihn bis zum Jahre 1773. (Vermischte Aufsätze.) 1858.
König, H. Williams Dichten und Trachten. Ein Roman. 2 Theile. 8. Hanau 1839. Zweite Auflage:
—— William Shakespeare. Ein Roman. 2 Theile. 8. Leipzig 1850. — 4. Aufl. 1854.
Kösting, Karl. Shakespeare, ein Winternachtstraum. Dramatisches Gedicht. Wiesbaden 1864.
Kreyssig, Fr. Vorlesungen über Shakspeare und seine Zeit und seine Werke. 3 Vols. Berlin 1858.
—— Shakpseare-Anthologie. 12. Hamburg 1864.
—— Ueber die volksthümliche und sittliche Berechtigung des Shakespeare-Cultus. Eine Festrede. Elbingen 1864.
Krug, W. T. Geschmackslehre. Leipzig 1823. p. 163 fg.
Kühne, F. G. Conversations-Blatt. 1828. No. 232—238.
—— Shakespeare als Mensch und Lyriker.
In: "Weibliche und männliche Karaktere". 2 Theile. gr. 12. Leipz. 1838.
Kunstblatt. Leipzig 1817. No. 9. 11. 46. 85. 100. 1818. No. 125. 143. 144.
Lamb's Erzählungen nach Shakespeare. Eine Vorschule dieses Dichters für die deutsche Jugend; nebst einer Lebensgeschichte Shakespeare's von H. Künzel. Mit 3 Stahlstichen und 1 Vignette. gr. 8. Darmstadt 1842.
—— Shakespeare-Erzählungen. Uebersetzt von F. W. Dralle. Mit Shakespeare's Bildniss. br. 8. Stuttgart 1843.
Lange, G. Versuch die Einheit der Iliade zu bestimmen. 1826. p. 15. 37. 74.
Lebens- und Denkbuch aus Shakespeare's sämmtlichen Werken, zusammengestellt von Fr. Grüner. Mit 1 Steindruck. 12. Heidelberg 1830.
Lebrun, C. Shakespeare, Spiel in Versen in einem Aufzuge.
In: "Neue kleine Lustspiele und Possen von C. Lebrun." 8. Mainz 1818.
Lembcke, L. G. Shakspeare in seinem Verhältnisse zu Deutschland. Ein Vortrag. 8. Leipzig 1864.
Lenz, J. M. R. Bemerkungen über das Theater, nebst angehängtem übersetztem Stück Shakespeare's. 8. Leipzig 1774.
—— Ueber die Veränderung des Theaters im Shakespeare.
In Lenz, gesammelte Schriften 2. u. 3. Band. 8. Berlin 1828.
Leo, F. A. Die Delius'sche Kritik der von J. Payne Collier aufgefundenen handschriftlichen Emendationen gewürdigt. 8. Berlin 1853.
Lessing, G. E. Hamburgische Dramaturgie. 2 Theile. 8. Berlin 1794.
—— Literaturbriefe. 1758. 17. Brief.
Lewald, A. Seydelmann als Shylock in Shakespeare's Kaufmann von Venedig.
In: Seydelmann, ein Erinnerungsbuch für seine Freunde. 8. Stuttg. 1841.
Lichtenberg. Briefe aus England (Ueber D. Garricks Darstellung des Hamlet.)
Lichtenstein. Shakespeare und Sophokles. 8. München 1852.
Lindner, A. Wilhelm Shakspeare. Ein Schauspiel in 3 Abtheil. Rudolstadt 1864.
Literatur und Theater-Zeitung. Berlin 1778 u. 1779 (enthaltend Nachrichten über die Auffführung Hamlet's auf deutschen Bühnen).
Lüders, Dr. F. Beiträge zur Erklärung von Shakespeare's Othello. 8. Hamburg 1863.
Luden, H. Grundzüge ästhet. Vorlesungen. Göttingen 1808. § 118.
Macbeth. Zur Erklärung einer Stelle in Shakespeare's Macbeth. Archiv für n. Spr. II, p. 357.
Malsburg, E. F. Calderon's Schauspiele. Leipzig 1819. I, 51. II, S. 9. III, 31.
Marggraf, H. Zur Shakespeare-Literatur.
In: Blätter für literarische Unterhaltung 1841. No. 162. 163.
—— William Shakespeare als Lehrer der Menschheit. Lichtstrahlen aus seinen Werken nebst einer Einleitung. 1861.

Marquard, F. Ueber den Begriff des Hamlet von Shakespeare. Ein Versuch. 8. Berlin 1839.
Mayer, R. Geist Shakespeare's oder Sammlung ausgezeichneter Stellen und Scenen, in der Originalsprache und Uebersetzung nach Schlegel, Schiller, Voss und Eschenburg: Macbeth. Der Sturm. Wie es Euch gefällt. 8. Leipzig 1825.
Mendelsohn-Bartholdy. Musik zum Sommernachtstraum. Folio.
Meyer. Shakespeare als Dramatiker. 1. Stück seiner Uebersetzung. 1825.
—— **A.** Shakespeare's Verletzung der historischen und natürlichen Wahrheit. Ein Vortrag. 8. Hildesheim 1863.
—— **F. L. W.** Friedrich Ludwig Schröder. 8. Hamburg 1823. (Vol. I, p. 290. II, p. 153. Ueber die ersten Aufführungen Hamlet's auf dem Hamburger Theater.)
—— **J.** Das Leben Shakespeare's, nebst einer Literärgeschichte und Beurtheilung seiner dramatischen Werke. Mit Shakespeare's Portrait. 2 Bände. 12. Gotha 1825.
Möbius, P. Die Deutsche Shakespearefeier. Eine Rechtfertigung derselben nach einem im kaufmänn. Verein zu Leipzig gehaltenen Vortrage. 8. Leipzig 1864.
—— Shakespeare als Dichter der Naturwahrheit. Festrede. Leipzig 1864.
Mommsen, Tycho. Marlowe und Shakspeare. 8.
—— Der Perkins-Shakspeare. 8. Berlin 1854.
Mönnich, Dr. W. B. Ueber den Character der Ophelia. 1844. (Album des Lit.-Vereins. Nürnberg.)
Morgenblatt. Briefe über Hamlet. 1812. No. 60—80.
Müllner, A. Vermischte Schriften. 1826. II, p. 313—22. 382.
Mundt, T. Kritische Wälder. Leipzig 1833. pag. 92—94.
Nares. Glossary to Shakspeare, German reprint. gr. 8. Stralsund 1825.
Noire, Dr. L. Hamlet's Character. Zwei Vorträge. 8. Mainz 1856.
Novalis' Schriften. Berlin 1815. II, pag. 186 fg.
Nüsslein, F. A. Lehrbuch der Kunstwissenschaft. 1819. § 402.
Ortlepp, E. Nachträge zu Shakespeare's Werken. Stuttg. 1839. III, 366—423.
Perlen aus Shakespeare nach der Uebersetzung von Schlegel und Tieck. Aneinander gereiht von E. A. 16. Frankfurt a. M. 1848.
Pfizer, G. Shakespeare's Charakteristik. Stuttgart 1839.
Pörschke, K. L. Ueber Shakespeare's Macbeth. 8. Königsberg 1801.
Porto, Luigi da. Geschichte der Liebe und des Todes von Romeo und Julie. Aus dem Italienischen übersetzt von N. Motherby. 8. Königsberg 1828.
Prachtstahlstiche, zwölf, als Titelkupfer zu Shakespeare's sämmtlichen dramatischen Werken in allen Ausgaben. 16. Leipzig 1840.
Pries, J. Fr. Ueber Shakespeare's Hamlet. 8. Rostock 1825.
Prutz, F. Hallische Jahrbücher. 1839. No. 105—106.
Pudor, C. H. Ueber Goethe's Iphigenie. 1832. pag. 52. 86 fg.
Quellen des Shakespeare in Novellen, Märchen und Sagen; herausgegeben von Th. Echtermeyer, L. Hentschel und K. Simrock. 3 Thle. 8. Berlin 1831.
Rau, Herib. William Shakespeare. Culturhistorischer Roman. 4 Bände. 12. Berlin 1864.
Retsch, M. Gallerie zu Shakespeare's dramatischen Werken. In Umrissen erfunden und gestochen. Roy.-4. Leipzig 1828—33.
    Hamlet, 16 Blatt. — Macbeth, 12 Blatt. — Romeo und Julie, 12 Blatt. — König Lear, 13 Blatt. — Der Sturm, 13. Blatt. — Othello, 13 Blatt. — Die lustigen Weiber von Windsor, 13 Blatt. — Heinrich IV., 1. u. 2. Theil, 13 Blatt.
Reinhold: Franck's Taschenbuch dramat. Originalien. 1841. p. 510 fg.
Richardson. Ueber die wichtigsten Charactere Shakespeare's. Aus dem Englischen von Chr. H. Schmid. 8. Leipzig 1776.
Richter, Jean Paul. Vorschule der Aesthetik. 1813. § 1. 11. 12. 22. 25. 64.
Rietmann, J. J. Shakespeare's religiöse und ethische Bedeutung, eine praktische Studie. 8. St. Gallen 1853.
—— Shakspeare und seine Bedeutung. Festrede. 8. St. Gallen 1864.
Rio, A. F. Shakspeare. Aus dem Französ. von K. Zell. 12. 1864. Freiburg.
Robert, Cl. William Shakespeare. Deutsch von Emilie Wille. 8. Leipzig 1844.
Rohrbach, C. Shakspeare's Hamlet erläutert. 8. Berlin 1858.
Rosenkranz, K. Handbuch der Geschichte der Poesie. 1832. Vol. III, p. 288—310.

Rötscher, H. Th. König Lear von Shakespeare. gr. 8. Berlin 1837.
—— Romeo und Julie und der Kaufmann von Venedig, mit besonderer Beziehung auf die Kunst der dramatischen Darstellung entwickelt. 8. Berlin 1842.
—— Cyklus dramatischer Charactere. gr. 8. Berlin 1844.
—— Shakespeare in seinen höchsten Charactergebilden enthüllt und entwickelt. 8. Berlin 1864.
Rötscher's Jahrbuch für dram. Kunst, Heft 4, 1848, cont.: Julius Cäsar von Shakspeare und die Darstellung desselben auf der königl. Bühne zu Berlin.
—— Dramaturgische Blätter, 1. Heft, 1864, cont.: Character-Entwickelung des Bastard Faulconbridge aus König Johann von Shakspeare.
Rousseau, J. B. Kunststudien. München 1834. pag. 40. 143—145.
Ruhl. Outlines to Shakespeare's Othello. 13 Plates genuine original edition. Fol. Frankfurt a. M. 1832.
—— Skizzen zu Shakespeare's dramatischen Werken. Mit Erläuterungen in deutscher, englischer und französischer Sprache. Quer gr. 4. Cassel 1838—40.
    Inhalt: Der Kaufmann von Venedig, 10 Blatt. — Der Sturm, 9 Blatt. — Ein Sommernachtstraum, 6 Blatt. — Romeo und Julie, 6 Blatt. — Was ihr wollt, 12 Blatt.
Schacht, Th. Ueber die Tragödie Antigone nebst einem vergleichenden Blick auf Sophocles und Shakespeare. gr. 12. Darmstadt 1842.
Schauspielerschule, die (über Hamlet). Quedlinburg 1810.
Scherr, J. Geschichte der englischen Literatur (Seite 77—96). 8. Leipzig 1854.
Schick, E. Ueber das Trauerspiel "König Lear" von Shakespeare. Eine Abhandlung. Als Anhang seiner Uebersetzung des Lear.
Schiller, F. Shakspeare's Schatten. (Gedichte.)
—— Ueber naive und sentimentale Dichtung.
—— Briefwechsel zwischen Schiller und Goethe. 1830. III, p. 56—57. 388-389.
Schink, J. F. Ueber Brockmann's Hamlet. gr. 8. Berlin 1778.
—— Shakspeare in der Klemme, oder Wir wollen doch auch den Hamlet spielen. 12. Wien 1780.
—— Prinz Hamlet von Dänemark, Marionettenspiel. Berlin 1799.
Schipper, L. Shakespeare's Hamlet. Aesthetische Erläuterungen des Hamlet, nebst Widerlegung der Goethe'schen und Gervinus'schen Ansichten über die Idee und den Haupthelden des Stückes. 8. Regensburg 1862.
Schlegel, A. W. von. Ueber Shakespeare's Romeo und Julie.
    In dessen kritischen Schriften 1. Theil. gr 8. Berlin 1828.
—— Vorlesungen über dramatische Kunst und Literatur. 3 Bände. 8. Heidelberg 1817.
—— Etwas über Shakespeare, in Schiller's Horen. 1796. IV, 2. p. 57—112.
—— Characteristiken und Kritiken. 1801. Vol. I, 282—317.
—— Aesthetische Schriften. Berlin 1828. I, p. 387—416.
Schlegel, Fr. von. Nachtrag über Shakespeare's ältere dramatische Werke.
    In seinen sämmtlichen Werken 10. Band. gr. 8. Wien 1822—25.
—— Athenaeum. Berlin 1798. I, p. 68 fg. III, p. 82—84.
—— Lessing's Geist. 1810. Vol. II, p. 93 - 94. 175—77.
—— Vorlesungen über die Geschichte der Literatur. Berlin 1815. Vol. II, 137—141.
Schlegel, J. E. Vergleichung Shakespeare's und Andreas Gryph's bei Gelegenheit einer Uebersetzung von Shakespeare's Julius Cäsar.
    Im 5. Bande von J. E. Schlegel's Werken. gr. 8. Kopenhagen 1771. — See Garrick.
Schmidt, Alb. Sacherklärende Anmerkungen zu Shakespeare's Dramen. gr. 12. Leipzig 1842.
Schmidt, Ch. H. Biographie Shakespeare's.
    In: Biographie der Dichter 2. Band. gr. 8. Leipzig 1769—70.
Schmidt, Fr. L. Sammlung der besten Urtheile über Hamlet's Charakter, von Goethe, Herder, Richardson und Lichtenberg. 8. Quedlinburg 1808.
—— Dramaturgische Berichte. Hamburg 1834. p. 4—12. 19—30. 39—76.
Schöll, A. Ueber Shakespeare's Sommernachtstraum. Blätter für Lit. Unterh. 1844. No. 4—8.
(Schreyvogel.) Gesammelte Schriften von T. und K. A. West. Wien 1830. II, 2. p. 238—50.
Schröder's (F. L.) Leben von Meyer. See "Meyer".

Schubart, K. E. Zur Beurtheilung Goethe's. 2 Vols. Breslau 1820.
— Palaeophron und Neoterpe. 1823. I, p. 56. 171. II, p. 183—184.
— Gesammelte Schriften. Hirschberg 1835. p. 195—198.
Schütz, F. W. Karl der Kühne. Trauerspiel. 1821. Vorrede.
Schwartzkopff, Aug. Shakespeare in seiner Bedeutung für die Kirche unserer Tage dargestellt. 2. Aufl. 16. Halle.
Seiffardt, W. Lewald's Theater-Revue. 1835. p. 56 fg.
Selous, H. C. Umrisse zu Shakespeare's Sturm. Leipzig 1837.
Seume, J G. Obolen. II, p. 173—174.
Shakespeare-Album. Des Dichters Welt- und Lebensanschauung, aus seinen Werken systematisch geordnet von C. E. Alberti. Berlin 1864.
—— Album. Costümfiguren aus dem Shakespearefest, veranstaltet am 23. April 1864 von der Künstlergesellschaft "Malkasten" in Düsseldorf, photographirt von Overbeck. 64 Photographien. 8. Düsseldorf 1864.
—— Almanach. Herausgegeben von G. Regis. gr. 16. Berlin 1836.
Inhalt: W. Shakespeare's sämmtliche lyrische Gedichte. (Sonette. Der verliebte Pilger). — Zwischenspiel aus Thomas Middleton's Mayer von Quinborough, mit einem Vorwort. — Einleitung zu W. Shakespeare's lyrischen Gedichten. Anmerkungen zu den Sonetten und zum verliebten Pilger. — Nachtrag.
——'s Bestimmung. Schauspiel in 1 Akt.
In: Deutsches Theater von K. Stein. gr. 8. Berlin 1819.
——'s Denkmal in der Shakespeare-Gallerie zu London, gestochen von E. Schuler. Roy.-Folio. Leipzig.
—— ganze Figur. Nach Raubillac's Statue und den verlässigsten Urbildern in Stahl gestochen von E. Schuler. ½ Imp.-Folio. Mit einer Charakteristik des Dichters von G. Pfizer. Stuttgart 1838.
—— und seine Freunde, oder das goldene Zeitalter des lustigen Englands. Nach dem Englischen von W. Alexis. 3 Theile. gr. 8. Berlin 1839.
—— Gallerie, neue. Die Mädchen und Frauen in Shakespeare's dramatischen Werken. In Bildern und Erläuterungen. 4. Leipzig 1847.
—— Gallerie. Illustrationen zu Shakespeare's dramatischen Werken. 40 chemietypirte Blätter, mit Shakespeare's Portrait und Facsimile. Lex.-8. Leipzig 1849.
—— Gallerie. Nach Zeichnungen von Wilhelm von Kaulbach. gr. Folio. Berlin 1853.
Part I: Macbeth. — Part II: Der Sturm. — Part III: König Johann. 3 plates each.
—— Geist, von G. H. Schütze. 8. Altona 1780.
—— Genius. Eine Sammlung gehaltvoller Stellen, meisterhafter Scenen, und treffender Charakterschilderungen aus dessen Werken. 2 Bändchen. 12. Wien 1821.
—— in Deutschland am Tage seiner Jubelfeier. Ein dramatischer Scherz und — Ernst in einem Vorspiele und zwei Akten. 12. 1864.
—— als Liebhaber. Lustspiel in 1 Akt.
In: "Kurländer, Almanach dramatischer Spiele 8. Band." 12. Wien 1819.
—— Literatur, die, in Deutschland Vollständiger Catalog sämmtlicher in Deutschland erschienenen Uebersetzungen Shakespeare's, sowohl in Gesammt- als Einzelausgaben, aller bezüglichen Erläuterungs- und Ergänzungsschriften, wie endlich aller mit ihm in irgend einer Beziehung stehenden sonstigen literarischen Erscheinungen. Von 1791—1851. 8. Cassel 1852.
—— Literatur bis Mitte 1854. Zusammengestellt und herausgegeben von P. H. Sillig. Ein bibliographischer Versuch. Eingeführt von Dr. H. Ulrici. gr. 8. Leipzig 1854.
—— Portrait mit einem Facsimile seiner Handschrift; gezeichnet und lithographirt von Julius Schieferdecker. Brustbild. Folio. Leipzig.
—— Portrait. Brustbild von Rohrbach (Chandos'-Portrait). Fol. Berlin 1864.
—— Portrait, gemalt von Opitz, gestochen von Coupé. Leipzig.
—— Portrait (Duke of Buckingham's), in Stahl gestochen von Passi zu Wien. Folio.
—— Portrait (in ganzer Figur). Nach dem Gemälde des Prof. Peter Geiger in Wien lithographirt von Feeverle. Pesth 1864.
—— Portrait in ganzer Figur nach Raubillac's Statue gestochen von Schuler. Folio. Halle 1864.

Shakespeare und die englische Literatur 1564—1864. Bruckmann. München 1864.
—— Vorschule. Herausgegeben und mit Vorreden begleitet von L. Tieck. 2 Bände. gr. 8. Leipzig 1823 und 1829.
 Inhalt: Die Sage vom Pater Baco, von R. Green. — Arden von Feversham. — Die Hexen von Lancashire. — Die schöne Emma. — Die Geburt des Merlin.
Siebel, C. Dichtungen zur Shakespearefeier des Künstler-Vereins Malkasten in Düsseldorf. 1864.
Sievers, Dr. E. W. Shakespeare's Dramen für weitere Kreise bearbeitet. 8. Leipzig 1851—1852 und Braunschweig 1853.
 Inhalt: 1) Hamlet. — 2) Julius Caesar. — 3) Lear. — 4) Romeo und Julie. — 5) Othello.
—— Ueber die Grundidee des Shakespeare'schen Dramas Heinrich V. 1. Theil. Archiv der n. Spr. Vol. XI, p. 341.
—— Zur Grundlegung einer neuen Auffassung des Shakespear. Dramas Hamlet. Archiv der n. Spr. VI, p. 41. VIII, 65. 129.
Simrock, K. Shakespeare als Vermittler zweier Nationen. Probeband: Macbeth. gr. 8. Stuttgart 1843.
Skottowe, Aug. W. Shakespeare's Leben. Deutsch bearbeitet von A. Wagner. Mit Shakespeare's Bildniss. 16. Leipzig 1824.
Solger, K. W. F. Erwin; Gespräche über das Schöne. Berlin 1815. II, p. 152—153. 281—285.
—— Nachlass. 1826. I, p. 244—695. II, 556. 569 fg.
—— Vorlesungen über Aesthetik. Leipzig 1829. p. 170—77. 248. 330.
Stahlstiche zu Shakespeare's dramatischen Werken in Einem Bande. 16 Blatt. Lex.-8. Stuttgart 1839.
—— zu Shakespeare's sämmtlichen Werken, nach Zeichnungen von Ludwig Richter in Dresden, gestochen von H. Sager. 12 Blatt. Berlin 1850.
Stahr, A. Shakespeare in Deutschland.
 Im "Literar-historischen Taschenbuch", herausgegeben von R. Prutz. Jahrgang 1843. gr. 8. Leipzig 1843.
Steffens, H. Leipziger Kunstblatt. 1818. No. 125.
—— Von der falschen Theologie. 1823. p. 194.
Stein, K. Der Gesellschafter. 1819. No. 64—67.
Storffrich, D. B. (Pseud. D. Barnstorff.) Psychologische Aufschlüsse über Shakespeare's Hamlet. 8. Bremen 1859.
Sträter. Die Compositionen von Shakespeare's Romeo und Julia. 3 Vorlesungen gehalten zu Bonn. 8. Bonn 1861.
Struve, Dr. E. A. Studien zu Shakespeare's Heinrich IV. gr. 4. Kiel 1851.
Sturm, J. Stenographisches Shakespeare-Album. gr. 8. Dresden 1864.
Susemihl, E. Ueber die neuere Shakspeare-Literatur. Hallische Jahrb. der Literatur 1838. No. 206—9.
Süvern, W. Aeschylos' Sieben gegen Theben. 1797. p. 78. 86—87. 127.
—— Ueber Schiller's Wallenstein. 1800. p. 3—4. 43. 58.
Tausch, Jul. Musik zu Shakspeare's Was ihr wollt. Op. 4. Partitur. Düsseldorf 1863.
Theater, das, zu Düsseldorf. Düsseldorf 1835.
Thrandorff. Ueber Hamlet, Programm des Friedrich-Wilhelm-Gymnasiums 1833.
Tieck, Ludwig. Briefe über Shakespeare. Poet. Journal. Berlin 1800. p. 18—80. 459—472.
—— Alt-Englisches Theater. 1811. Vorrede.
—— Shakspeare's Vorschule. 2 Vols. Vorrede.
—— Kleist's Werke. 1826. Vorrede.
—— Hamlet. — John Kemble. (Dramat. Blätter Vol. II.)
—— Kean als Hamlet. (Kritische Schriften IV, 349,)
—— Ueber Shakespeare's Behandlung des Wunderbaren.
 Als Anhang seiner Uebersetzung des "Sturm".
—— Ueber Shakespeare's Sonette, nebst Proben einer Uebersetzung derselben, in der Penelope für 1826.
—— Das Fest zu Kenilworth, Prolog zum Dichterleben (Shakespeare's) und "Dichterleben". Zwei Novellen. 1828—1848.
—— Dramaturgische Blätter, herausgegeben von Eduard Devrient. 2 Bände. 8. Leipzig 1848.

Titelkupfer zu Shakespeare's dramatischen Werken. 14 Blatt. 16. Stuttgart 1839—40.
Ueber die Bedeutung der Shakespeare'schen Schicksalstragödie, insbesondere entwickelt an Macbeth, Lear und Hamlet.
    In den Wiener Jahrbüchern Band 43.
Uhlmann, J. Shakespeare im 16. Jahrhundert für die englische, Schröder im 18. Jahrhundert für die deutsche Nation. 8. Wien 1783.
Ulrici, H. Ueber Shakespeare's dramatische Kunst und sein Verhältniss zu Calderon und Goethe. gr. 8. Halle 1839. 2. Aufl. 1847. 3. Aufl. 3 Vols. 1868. 6 Thlr.
Vehse, Dr. E. Shakespeare als Protestant, Politiker, Psycholog und Dichter. 2 Bände. 8. Hamburg 1851.
Viehoff. Ueber Goethe's Bearbeitung von Shakespeare's Romeo and Juliet. (Archiv der n. Spr. I, p. 263.)
Vischer, Fr. Shakespeare in seinem Verhältniss zur Poesie, insbesondere zur politischen.
    In: Prutz, literarisches Taschenbuch für 1844. 8. Leipzig.
Vogt, Nicolas. Shakespeare's Beruf und Triumph. 8. Mainz 1792.
Voigtmann. Studien zu Shakspeare's Macbeth.
    In: Herrig's Archiv VIII, p. 233. X, p. 62.
Voltaire. Sendschreiben an die Academie, über Shakespeare; aus dem Französischen mit einer Vorrede von A. Wittenberg. 8. Hamburg 1777.
Voss, H. Hermes. 1819. IV, 371.
—— Briefwechsel. Heidelberg 1838. (Ueber Othello.) III, p. 54—66.
Wachler, L. Handbuch der Geschichte der Literatur. 1824. III, 231—33.
Wagner, A. Das Reich des Scherzes. 1823. p. 28.
—— Jahrbücher der wissenschaftlichen Kritik. Berlin 1830. No. 61—63. 1834, No. 12—14.
Warnekros, H. E. Der Geist Shakespeare's. 2 Theile. 8. Greifswalde 1786.
Weber, W. E. Die Aesthetik aus dem Gesichtspunkte gebildeter Freunde des Schönen. 1834. I, p. 216. 257. 263—65. 345. 357.
Weber, Karl Julius. Das Lustspiel der Engländer. — Shakespeare.
    Im achten Bande von Weber's Demokritos Seite 280—295.
Weichselbauer, C. Dramaturgische Dichtungen. 2 Vols. 1828.
Weisse, C. H. System der Aesthetik. Leipzig 1830. Vol. II, p. 313—521.
—— Kritik des Goetheschen Faust. Leipzig 1837. p. 129—30. 139—40.
Wellman, A. Literaturhistor. Taschenbuch von Prutz. 1845. p. 112—118.
Wessenberg, J. H. Ueber die Sittlichkeit der Bühne. 1525. p. 18—28.
Wille, E. William Shakespeare nach Cl. Robert. Leipzig 1844.
Winterfeld, A. Shakespeare, nach authentischen Quellen und eigenen Forschungen. 12. 1864.
Wölffel, Dr. H. Ueber Shakespeare's Sommernachtstraum.
    Im Album des literarischen Vereins. Nürnberg 1852.
—— Ueber Shakespeare's Hamlet. Album 1853.
——   -   —   Sturm. Album 1854.
——   -   —   König Lear. Album 1855.
——   -   —   Wintermärchen. Album 1860.
——   -   —   Timon. Album 1861.
——   -   —   Kaufmann von Venedig. Album 1862.
——   -   —   Julius Caesar. Album 1863.
——   -   —   Coriolan. Album 1864.
Ziegler, Fr. W. Hamlet's Charakter nach psychologischen und physiologischen Grundsätzen, durch alle Gefühle und Leidenschaften zergliedert. 8. Wien 1803.
Ziel. Erklärung einer Stelle von Shakespeare's Hamlet. Archiv für n. Spr. IV, p. 319.
Zimmermann, T. G. Dramaturgische Blätter für Hamburg. 1821. No. 11. 35. 1822. No. 40—44. 68—77.
—— Neue dramaturgische Blätter. 1827. No. 12. 37. 40. 56.
Zur Shakespeare-Literatur. In den Blättern für literarische Unterhaltung, Februar 1854.

I.

GERMAN SHAKSPEARIANA.

On the 23rd of April 1854 a *"Shakespeare Society"* was formed at Weimar, under the protection of the Grand Duchess of Saxony. It numbers about 200 members, under the Presidency of Professor Dr. H. Ulrici of Halle. This Society publishes every year the *"Jahrbuch der Deutschen Shakespeare Gesellschaft"* the interesting contents of which will be found in the list.

The German admirers of Shakespeare consider him the rival of the Greek Dramatists; and see in him their *Ideal of modern Dramatic Art* — their appreciation of him surpasses that for any other writer; and hence the result that the translation by Schlegel and Tieck, a masterpiece in many ways, is not now considered a perfect translation.

The fact is the Germans have learnt to translate through the medium of Shakespeare, and their progress in this art is shown by the results in the rendering of the great Dramatist's works. It has been frequently remarked that the german language has often been illused by Schlegel and Tieck in favour of Shakespeare's ancient english, and that the verses and the rhyme are often incorrect. Under these circumstances the "Shakespeare Gesellschaft" is revising Schlegel's translation; *Bodenstedt* has undertaken altogether a new version assisted by the most eminent poets and writers of the present day in Germany and it is expected that, as the text of Shakespeare has now been based on the early Editions, the translations will be more in unison with the poetic as well as the prose diction of the Author.

GERMAN.

SUPPLEMENT 1864 TO 1871.

TRANSLATIONS.

1835 Musterstücke aus Shakespeare's Dramen. Englisch und Deutsch. 12. Frankf. 1835.
1854 **Shakespeare's** pseudo Dramen von Delius. Elberfeld 1854.
1865 —— sämmtliche Werke. Deutsche Volks-Ausgabe, herausg v. Moltke. In 1 Band mit 300 Holzschnitten. 1865—66. Shakespeare-Verlag.
1866 —— Passages from Shakspeare. Selected and translated into German by G. Sölling. London 1866. Trübner. 2s 6d.
1867 —— dramatische Werke. In deutschen Uebersetzungen, mit Einleitungen und Erläuterungen, herausgegeben von Fr. Bodenstedt, übersetzt von Gildemeister, Paul Heyse, Kurz, Wilbrandt, Bodenstedt, Freiligrath, Herwegh, Delius. 1871. No. 1 to 36. 9 Vols. 8. Leipzig, Brockhaus.
1867—71 —— Dramatische Werke und Sonnette in neuen Original-Uebersetzungen von Dingelstedt, Jordan, Seeger, Simrock, Viehoff und Gelbcke. 10 Vols. 8. Hildburghausen, Bibl. Inst. 7 Thlr. 15 Sgr.
1867 —— sämmtliche dramatische Werke. Deutsche Volksausgabe mit Einleitungen, von Max Moltke. 12 Vols. 12. Leipzig 1867—68. Gebhardt. 2 Thlr.
1868—71 —— nach Schlegel und Tieck, sorgfältig revidirt und theilweis neu bearbeitet, mit Einleitung und Noten versehen unter Redaction von H. Ulrici, herausgegeben durch die deutsche Shakspeare-Gesellschaft, erscheint in 12 Bänden. Berlin. Reimer. 8 Thlr.
1871 —— Dramatische Werke, für die deutsche Bühne bearbeitet von Wilhelm Oechselhäuser. Band 1—8, à 15 Sgr. Berlin 1871. Asher & Co.

ENGLISH EDITIONS.

1864 **Shakespeare's** Werke, herausg. und erklärt von Delius. Neue Ausgabe. 7 Vols. Elberfeld 1864—1871. 15 Thlr.
1869 —— sämmtliche Werke, englischer Text, berichtigt und erklärt von B. Tschischwitz. Nebst histor. und krit. Einleitungen. I. Hamlet. 8. Halle 1869. Barthel. 1 Thlr.
1858 **Brennecke**, Auswahl aus S's. sämmtlichen Werken. Posen 1858. 10 Sgr.
1859 Shak. Works intended for the use of High Schools, with Notes by Otto Fiebig. 8. Leipzig 1859—61. Graebner. 5 Nrs. publ. (Romeo — J. Caesar — Richard III — Macbeth — King Lear — Merchant of Venice.)
1869 Shakspeare. The tragicall historie of Hamlet, prince of Danmarke by Shakspeare, edited according to the first printed copies with the various readings and critical notes by Stratmann. 8. Crefeld 1869 Gehrich & Co. 1 Thlr.

GERMAN TRANSLATIONS OF SEPARATE PLAYS.

Antony and Cleopatra, übersetzt von Paul Heyse 1867.
—— Auf Grundlage der Tieckschen Uebersetzung neu bearbeitet und für die Bühne eingerichtet von F. A. Leo. Halle 1870. Barthel. 20 Sgr.
—— erläutert von R. Blumhof. 8. Celle 1870. Schulze. ²/₃ Thlr.
—— nach Shak. von Oswald Marbach. (Ein Weltuntergang.)
—— übers. von W. Lampadius. 1866. Reclam.
As you like it., Was ihr wollt, deutsch von Dingelstedt. 1869.
—— — von Gildemeister. 1870. (Brockh.)
Coriolanus nach Shaksp. von Oswald Marbach.
—— frei nach Sh. von Falk. Amsterdam 1812.
—— übersetzt von L. Petz. Reclam.
—— — von H. Viehoff. Hildb.
Cymbeline, für die Bühne bearbeitet von Ernst Rommel. 8. Hannover 1860. Lohse.
—— für die deutsche Bühne bearbeitet von A. von Wollzogen. 12. Leipzig 1872. Carl Cnobloch. 12 Sgr.
—— deutsch von Jordan. Hildb.
—— deutsch von Simrock. Reclam.
Hamlet. Zum Behuf des Hamburger Theaters, übersetzt von F. L. Schröder. 1. Ausgabe mit dem Bildniss von Brockmann als Hamlet. Hamburg 1777.
—— Prinz von Dänemark, ein Trauerspiel in 5 Aufzügen nach Shakespeare. Zum Behuf des Frankfurter Theaters. Frankfurt 1779.
—— (Eine Karrikatur in 3 Aufzügen, mit Gesang in Knittelreimen, von Joachim Perinet, Dichter, Schauspieler. Dem Andenken des 17. May 1803 gewidmet. Wien 1807.
—— deutsch von Ludw. Seeger. 8. Hildb. 1865.
—— englisch und deutsch. Text von 1603 und 1604. Neu übersetzt und erläutert mit Quellen-Varianten Noten — Excurse — Commentar — Literatur- Glossar — von Max Moltke. (In 15 Liefer.) Heft 1—3. 8. Leipzig 1869—71. à 10 Sgr. Moltke.
—— (correct) von Caroline und A. W. von Schlegel. 1. Ausgabe, mit einer Einleitung über Shakespeare auf der deutschen Bühne. Berlin 1800.
—— Trauerspiel in 5 Acten, deutsch von Schlegel für die Wiener Bühne bearbeitet von J. Sonnleithner. Wien 1811.
—— bearbeitet von E. W. Sievers. Leipzig 1851.
—— Trauerspiel, in 3 Aufz. für das Kinder-Theater bearbeitet. Neu-Ruppin.
—— englisch, herausg. von Else. Leipzig 1857. Mayer. 1 Thlr. 10 Sgr.
—— von Bodenstedt. 1870.
—— übersetzt von F. Köhler. Reclam.
Julius Cäsar, correct: Versuch einer gebundenen Uebersetzung des Trauerspiels von dem Tode des Julius Caesar. Aus dem Englischen Werke des Shakspeare. Berlin bei Ambrosius Haude 1741. (Uebersetzt von Caspar Wilhelm von Bork.)
—— Shakspeari Julius Caesar. Ad textum qualem Nicol. Delius constituit, Anglicum in Senarios Latinos transtulit Dr. Th. Jos. Hilgers. 8. Dessau 1871. Reissner. 12 Sgr.
—— nach Shakspeare — (ein Weltuntergang) von Oswald Marbach. Leipzig 1861. 2 Thlr.
—— übersetzt von L. Petz. 16. Leipzig 1865.
—— — von Seeger. Hildburgh.
—— erläutert und mit Wörterbuch von Dr. Bucher. Berlin 1856. 10 Sgr.
—— — von Sievers. 8. Berlin 1855.
—— mit Sprach- und Sachanmerkungen von E. Mayer. Hamburg 1857.
—— erklärt von J. Jancke. Cöln 1861.
King John. Arthur Prinz von England, Trauerspiel in 4 Aufzügen nach Shakespeare's König Johann, frei bearbeitet von Fr. W. Schütz. Aufgeführt auf dem Nat.-Theater zu Altona 1801.
—— übersetzt von Otto Gildemeister. 1867.
King Lear, übersetzt von Dr. E. W. Sievers. 1851.
—— — von Ed. Tiessen. 16. Stettin 1871. Nahmer. 15 Sgr.

King Lear. Der moderne Lear, oder Schmul in der Plaite! Schaugem. in 5 Akten. Aus dem Englischen ins Spanische, und aus dem Spanischen ins Deutsche verarbeitet von Max R. Ing (A. Hopf). Berlin. (Brenneke Cal. 1855.)
— übersetzt von G. Herwegh. 1869.
— with explanatory Annotations by Küchler. Zeitz 1794.
— deutsch von F. Bodenstedt. Berlin 1865. Decker. 15 Sgr.
— Die Ritter oder der neue König Lear. Eine divina Comedia, vulgo Puppenspiel in 5 Aufzügen, nach Aristophanes und Shakspeare. Folio. 1831. (a curious alegorical Comedy privately printed.)
Macbeth (correct): ein Trauerspiel in fünf Aufzügen von Shakespeare. Fürs hiesige Theater adaptirt und herausgegeben von F. J. Fischer. Prag, bey Wolfgang Gerle. 1777.
— (correct): ein Trauerspiel von H. L. Wagner. Frankfurt 1779. (Schiller legte diese Uebersetzung der Seinigen zu Grunde.)
— deutsch von Wilh. Jordan. 8. Hildb. 1865.
— übersetzt von F. Bodenstedt. 8. 1868. Brockh.
— — von K. Simrock. 8. Stuttg. 1842.
— — von F. Jenken. 8. Mainz 1854.
— — von Hilsenberg. Reclam.
— — von Heinichen. 8. Bonn 1861.
— deutsch und italienisch von Carcono. Repert. der Signora Ristori. 8. Hamburg.
Merchant of Venice (correct). 8. Mannheim 1780.
— Kaufmann von Venedig. Komödie in 5 Akten, übersetzt von Krais. 12. Stuttgart 1868. 3 Sgr.
— übersetzt von Bodenstedt. 1868. Brockh.
— Merchant of Venice. Für den Schulgebrauch bearbeitet von Müller. Goslar 1869. 6 Sgr.
Merry Wives of Windsor. Komisches Singspiel Falstaff in 2 Aufzügen. Nach dem Italienischen von C. Herklots. Die Musik von Salieri. Libretto. Berlin 1779.
— übersetzt von Hermann Kurz. Leipzig 1867. Brockh.
Midsummer-Nights Dream. Ein Sommernachtstraum, übersetzt von A. W. von Schlegel, mit 24 Schattenbildern von Paul Konewka. 4. Heidelberg 1869. Bassermann. 5 Thlr.
— ditto. englisch. 4. 1869. Bassermann. 5¹/₃ Thlr.
— übersetzt von Bodenstedt. 1869.
— Absurda Comica. Oder Herr Peter Squentz. Schimpff-Spiel von Andreas Gryphius. 1663.
— Die ländlichen Hochzeitfeste; Lustspiel in 5 Aufzügen. (Aufgeführt in Wien 1773, gedruckt im 7. Bande der Sammlung „Neue Schauspiele". Wien 1773. Der Verfasser von Pauersbach.) Eine Nachbildung des Sommernachtstraums.
— Comische Oper in 3 Acten, nach dem Französischen von Hermann Meinhardt. (Musik von Ambroise Thomas.) Berlin 1854.
Othello, der Mohr, übersetzt von Friedr. Bodenstedt. 1867.
— deutsch von Wilh. Jordan. Hildb. 1868. Bibl. Inst.
— — nach Shakspeare von Oswald Marbach. 12. Leipzig 1864. 1 Thlr.
— Tragische Oper in 3 Aufzügen, nach dem Italienischen von C. Grünbaum. Musik von Joachim Rossini. Libretto 1821.
Richard the Second (correct). König Richard der Zweite, nach Shakespeare für's Prager Theater eingerichtet von F. J. Fischer. 8. Prag 1778. (Nach der Vorrede existirte auch ein Druck vom Jahre 1777, der vollständiger war und aus 5 Akten bestand, während diese Ausgabe nur 3 Akte hat.)
— König Richard der 2., übers. von H. Viehoff. 1867. Bibl. Inst. 6 Sgr.
— übersetzt von Gildemeister. Leipzig 1867.
— für den Schulgebrauch erklärt von Dr. L. Riechelmann. 8. Leipzig 1869. Teubner. 12 Sgr.
— Mit Einleitung und Erklärungen herausgegeben von Dr. Noiré. 16. Mainz 1868. Zabern. 10 Sgr.
— with biographical Sketches, Introductions and explanatory Notes by F. H. Ahn. 12. Treves 1870. Gropp.

Richard the Third. König Richard der Dritte. Zuerst gedruckt: „In Beiträge zum deutschen Theater von Weise. I. Band." Leipzig 1770. Dyck.
—— Richard der III. Trauerspiel von Weise. Für die Schuchische Bühne nachbearbeitet von C. Steinberg. Königsberg 1796.
—— in "Neue Probestücke der Englischen Schaubühne." 3 Vols. Bas. 1788.
—— von Gildemeister. Leipzig 1867.
—— von F. A. Krais. Stuttgart 1869. Hoffmann. 3 Sgr.
—— übersetzt von E. Tiessen. 16. Stettin 1871. Nahmer. ¹/₂ Thlr.
Romeo and Juliet. (In Neue Probestücke der englischen Schaubühne, aus der Ursprache übersetzt von einem Liebhaber des guten Geschmacks.) Basel 1758.
—— von C. F. Weise. 1. Ausgabe 1768, 2. Ausgabe 1769.
—— und Juliette, ein dramatisches Gedicht von Soden, nach della Cortes Geschichte von Verona. 8. Leipzig 1803.
—— with notes by Fiebig. 8. Leipzig 1859.
—— übersetzt von Bodenstedt. Leipzig 1868.
—— deutsch von Jordan. 8. Hildburghausen 1865.
—— — von F. Jenken. Mainz 1854.
—— — von E. W. Sievers. Leipzig 1852.
—— — erklärt von J. Heussi. Berlin 1853.
—— — nach Shak. von Oswald Marbach. 12. Leipzig.
—— im Weimarer Theater, bearbeitet von J. W. Goethe (1824), *see Boas*, Nachträge zu Goethe's Werken. 2 Vols. Leipzig 1841.
—— Drama, in's Deutsche übertragen von G. L. 16. Wien 1870.
Taming of the Shrew (correct). Die bezähmte Widerbellerin oder Gasner der Zweite. Ein Lustspiel in vier Akten. Nach Shakespeare frey bearbeitet von Schink. Aufgeführt auf dem Kurfürstlichen Hoftheater zu München 1783.
—— Kunst über alle Künste, Ein bös Weib gut zu machen. Rapperschweyl bei Henning Lieblern. 1672.
—— übersetzt von G. Herwegh. Leipzig 1870.
Tempest. Der Sturm übersetzt von Fr. Bodenstedt. Leipzig 1870. ¹/₆ Thlr.
—— — von Shaks. Musik von Wilhelm Taubert. Libretto. 8. Berlin n. d.
Timon of Athens (correct). Timon von Athen, ein Schauspiel in dreyen Aufzügen von Shakespeare. Fürs Prager Theater eingerichtet von F. J. Fischer. 8. Prag, bei Wolfgang Gerle 1778.
—— übersetzt von P. Heyse. 1868.
—— Nach der Tieck-Schlegelschen Uebersetzung für die deutsche Bühne bearbeitet von Ferd. Wehl. 1862.
Titus Andronicus. Eine sehr klägliche Tragedia von Tito Andronico und der hoffertigen Kayserin, darinnen denkwürdige Actiones zu befinden. (In Englische Comedien und Tragedien 1620.)
—— übersetzt von Delius. 1870.
Troilus and Cressida. Die Griechen vor Troja (Troilus und Cressida), deutsch, für die moderne Bühne frei bearbeitet von A. A. Bekk. Wien 1856.
—— deutsch von K. Simrock. Hildburghausen 1870.
Two Gentlemen of Verona. Die beiden Veroneser, Schauspiel in 3 Akten nach Shaksp. Schauspiel gleiches Namens bearbeitet von K. R. H. Kleediz. 8. Schneeberg 1802 & Mannheim 1810.
—— die beiden Edelleute von Verona. Tragödie von Ed. Arnd. Berlin 1827.
—— übersetzt von Herwegh. Leipzig 1870.
Winter's Tale. Schauspiel in 4 Aufzügen von Shaksp. für die deutsche Bühne übersetzt und bearb. von Franz Dingelstedt. Musik von Fr. v. Flotow. Bühnen-Manuscript 1859.
—— Hermione, Schauspiel mit Gesang nach Shakspeare's Wintermärchen von F. A. C. Werthes. Stuttgart 1801.

POEMS.

Shakespeare's Gedichte. Deutsch von K. Simrock. 8. Stuttgart 1867. Cotta. 1 Thlr. 24 Sgr.
— Sonette, übersetzt von F. A. Gelbke. Hildburghausen 1867. 8 Sgr.
— Sonette, übersetzt von H. F. von Friesen. 8. Dresden 1869. Burdach. 20 Sgr.
—— Sonette, deutsch von Tschischwitz. '16. Halle 1870. Barthel. 12 Sgr.
—— Sonette, übersetzt von O. Gildemeister. 8. Leipzig 1871. Brockhaus. 24 Sgr.

GERMAN

SHAKSPEARIANA

1865 TO 1871 AND SUPPLEMENTS.

Academie der Grazien. Eine Wochenschrift. 129 Stücke. Halle 1774—80.
   Contains: Charaktere der Desdemona, Vergleich der beiden Trauerspiele Romeo und Julie von Shakspeare und Weise, etc.
Alexis, W. Shakspeare und seine Freunde oder das goldene Zeitalter des lustigen Englands. 3 Vols. Berlin 1839. 4½ Thlr.
Andree, Dr. Richard. Macbethplätze in Schottland. (Nordische Revue von Wolfsohn. Vol. II. 1864. pag. 135—144.)
Anfänge Shaksp. Poesie in Deutschland. (Mag. f. Literatur des Auslandes 1864. No. 33.)
Anmerkungen übers Theater, nebst angeh. übersetzten Stücken Shakspeares. Leipzig 1774.
Asher, D. Zur Charakteristik der Lady Macbeth. (Nord. Revue 1864. Vol. III. Heft 2.)
Augustin, S. Shakspeare Musik. (Morgenblatt 1864, No. 32 und 33.)
Barz, Otto. Shakspeare's Brautnacht. Festspiel und dramatischen Anecdoten zur 100jährigen Jubelfeier. Stettin.
Bekk, Dr. Ad. Shakspeare und Homer. Ein Beitrag zur Literatur und Bühne des engl. Dichters. Wien 1865. Hartleben.
Beiträge zum deutschen Theater. 5 Vols. 8. Leipzig 1763—68. Enthält unter Andern: Eduard III — Richard III — Romeo und Julie, etc.
—— zur krit. Historie der deutschen Sprache, herausg. von der deutschen Gesellschaft in Leipzig. 12 Stücke in 3 Vols. Leipzig 1732—1735.
B(eta), H. Shaksp. Jubiläen in England (1769, 1827, 1830). Mag. für Lit. d. Auslands, 1864. No. 17.
Bendixen, Bemerk. zur Textkritik einiger Stellen in Shaksp. Dramen. Plön 1855. (Programm.)
Ben Jonson und seine Schule, dargest. in einer Auswahl von Lustspielen u. Tragödien, übersetzt und erläutert d. Wolff v. Baudissin. 2 Vols. Leipzig 1836.
(Berly). Musterstücke aus Shaksp., deutsch & englisch. Frankf. 1825. 2 Thlr.
Bernhard, L. Shaksp. und unsere Schulen. Progr. 4. Königsberg 1859.
Bitter. Ueber Gervinus' Händel und Shakspeare. 8. Berlin 1869. W. Müller. 10 Sgr.
Blumhof, Karl. Zur Erläuterung von Antony & Cleopatra. (Herrigs Archiv. Vol. 23.)
Bodenstedt, Fr. Aus Ost und West. 6 Vorlesungen. Berlin 1861. (Enthält: 4. & 5. Vorl. Altenglische Bühne.) 1 Thlr.

Böning, Dr. On Troilus and Cressida. (Programm d. Real-Schule zu Bromberg.) 1861. (Rec. in Herrig's Archiv 1862, Vol. 31.)
Boumann. Ueber die Charactere Malcolms und Macduff's mit besonderer Beziehung auf Worte des Letzteren in Shakspeare's Macbeth (Der Gedanke, Band V. 1864. Heft 2). Berlin. Nicolai.
Brachvogel. Hamlet, Roman. 3 Vols. S. Berlin 1867. Trewendt.
Breier. Studien zu Shakspeare's Macbeth. (Herrig's Archiv Vol. 7 & 10.)
Brennecke, W. Auswahl aus Shakspeare's sämmtlichen dichterischen Werken. Posen 1857.
Britisches Museum, see Eschenburg.
Brodersen, D. Shakspeare oder der beglückte Dichter. Lustspiel in 1 Act. Königsberg 1810.
Brokerhoff's Beurtheilung von Gervinus Shakspeare. 1. Auflage. (Herrig's Archiv. Vol. 7.)
Brunier, Lud. Friedrich Ludwig Schröder, Künstler- und Lebensbild. Leipzig 1864. Weber.
Bucher, S. Julius Caesar erläutert.
Büdinger, Max. König Richard III. von England. Vortrag. Wien 1858. Gerold.
Carriere, Moritz. Wilhelm von Kaulbach's Shakspeare - Gallerie erläutert. I. Heft. Allgemeine Einleitung. Macbeth. II. Shakspeare's Seelenleben und Geistesgeschichte. Der Sturm. III. Sh. und die Poesie der Geschichte. König Johann. 4. Berlin 1856. Nicolai. à 10 Sgr.
—— Ueber das Wesen und die Formen der Poesie. Leipzig 1854. 2 Thlr. 10 Sgr.
—— Die Kunst im Zusammenhang der Culturentwicklung und die Ideale der Menschheit. Band IV (Renaissance und Reformation). 8. Leipzig 1871. Brockhaus. 3 Thlr. 20 Sgr.
Carus, C. G. Ludwig Tieck, Zur Geschichte seiner Vorlesungen in Dresden. 1845.
—— Mnemosyne. Blätter aus Gedenk- und Tagebüchern. Enthält: Princip der Tragödie „Hamlet." Pforzheim 1848. 3 Thlr.
(Castelli) J. F. Romeo und Julie. Quodlibet mit Gesang. Wien 1808.
(Cellius). Beschreibung zweier Reisen so Friedrich, Herzog zu Würtemberg in Engellandt gethan. 4. Tübingen 1603.
Cless, G. Medicinische Blumenlese aus Shakspeare zu eigener und seiner Collegen Kurzweil gesammelt. 1865. Cotta. 12 Sgr.
Coriolanus von Shakspeare, die Delius'sche Ausgabe dieser Tragödie kritisch beleuchtet. 8. Berlin 1861.
Czerwinski, Alb. W. Shakspeare und die beiden ersten berühmten Darsteller seiner Characters. Festgabe. Stettin 1864. Saunier.
Daul, A. Leitsterne im Leben und Lieben der Frauen. Eine Shakspeare-Anthologie. 4 Vols. 16. Leipzig 1869. Matthes. 1½ Thlr.
Dawison's Hamlet. (Morgenblatt 1863, No. 26.)
Delius, N. Die Tieck'sche Shakspeare-Kritik beleuchtet. Bonn 1846. ⅔ Thlr.
Devrient, E. Geschichte des deutschen Theaters. 3 Vols. Leipzig 1845—48. 5⅔ Thlr. Enthält: Auszüge einer Handschrift von „Romeo und Julie" in der Dresdner Bibliothek welche vor 1620 geschrieben.
Devrient, Otto. Zwei Shakspeare-Vorträge. Carlsruhe 1861. Braunsche Buchh. 11 Sgr.
Dingelstedt's Studien und Copien nach Shakspeare. (Morgenblatt 1864, No. 33.)
—— Shakspeare's Königsdramen beim Shakspeare-Jubiläum in Weimar zur Aufführung gebracht durch Dingelstedt. (Morgenblatt 1864, No. 29.)
Döring, A. Shakspeare's Hamlet, seinem Grundgedanken und Inhalte nach erläutert. 8. Hamm 1865. Grote. 12 Sgr.
Ebrard, A. Das Verhältniss Shakspeare's zum Christenthum. Vortrag. 8. Erlangen. Deichert. ⅙ Thlr.
Eckardt, Dr. L. Ueber Shakspeare's Hamlet. Herrig's Archiv, Vol. 31. Heft 1 und 2.
Eddelbüttel, Dr. Remarks on Tiecks translation of Shakespere's Macbeth. First Scene. Schul.-Progr. 8. Hagen 1864.
Eggers, F. Macbeth, romantische Oper. Musik von W. Taubert. Berlin 1858. Schiller's Bearbeitung liegt diesem Libretto zu Grunde.
Einsiedel, F. H. v. Grundlinien zu einer Theorie der Schauspielkunst, nebst Analyse e. kom. u. e. trag. Rolle, Falstaff n. Hamlet. n. S. Leipzig 1797.

Emerson, R. W. Ueber Goethe und Shakspeare. Aus d. Englischen von Grimm. Hannover 1857. 15 Sgr. (Beurtheilt im Morgenblatt von L. S. 1858.)
Engel, J. J. Ideen zu einer Mimik. 2 Vols. Berlin 1785—86. Mit Kupfern von Meil. (Entwickelt die Theorie der Mimik an Hamlet.)
Erfurt. Kritische Bemerkungen über 2 Stellen aus Dramen Shakspeares. Timon of Athens III 4, and Twelfth Night II 5. (Herrig's Archiv, Vol. 31.)
Eschenburg, J. J. Britisches Museum f. d. Deutschen. 6 Vols. 1777–80. Portraits. Enthält Vieles über Shakspeare.
Etwas über Shakspeare (ist von W. Schlegel. Vergl. Schlegel's krit. Schriften). Im vierten Stücke der Horen für 1796.
Feldtmeyer, Eug. Schiller's Wallenstein und S's. Macbeth. Programm. 4. Ostrowo 1865.
Ferwer, Jos. On S's. Troilus and Cressida. (Inaug.-Diss.) 8. Düsseldorf 1869.
Fischer, Kuno. Shakspeare's Characteristik Richards III. 8. Heidelberg 1868. Bassermann. 20 Sgr.
Flathe, J. L. F. König Richard II. Shakspeare in der Wirklichkeit. Supplement. Leipzig 1865. Dycksche Buchh. 12 Sgr.
Flir, A. Briefe aus Innsbruck, Frankfurt und Wien. Geschrieben in d. Jahren 1825—1853. 8. Innsbruck 1865. Wagner. $^2/_3$ Thlr.
Flögel, C. F. Geschichte des Grotesk-Komischen. 8. 1788.
Fontane, Th. & Franz Kugler. In Argo — vide Kugler.
Francke, C. L. W. Probe eines Comment. zu Shakspeare's Hamlet. 4. Bernburg 1848. Programm.
Francke. Antwort auf Hagena's Berichtigungen der Schlegel-Tieckschen Uebersetzung im 6. Bande von Herrig's Archiv.
Frankl, L. A. Ein Shakspeare-Club in Wien. Presse 1864. No. 106.
Franklin, Henry. A few observations on Shakspeare and his Merchant of Venice. (Programm.) Frankf. a. M. 1867.
Frenzel, K. Shakspeare-Studien. Deutsches Museum. 1867. vide Hauff.
Freymann, J. Kritik der Schiller-Shakspeare und Goetheschen Frauencharactere. 16. Giessen 1869. Roth. 1 Thlr.
Friesen, N. Freiherr von. Shakspeare von Gervinus. Ein Wort über dasselbe. Leipzig 1869. Baensch. 20 Sgr.
Fritsche. Prolog zurAufführung von Viel Lärmen um Nichts, an Shakspeare's 300jähriger Jubelfeier in Thorn. 8.
Fritzart. (Correct.) War Shakespeare ein Christ?
Fürstenau, M. Geschichte der Musik und des Theaters am Hofe zu Dresden. (Enthält Notizen über Aufführung Shakspearescher Stücke in Dresden im Jahre 1626.) 2 Vols. 8. Dresden 1861—62. 3 Thlr.
Genée, R. Geschichte der Shakspeareschen Dramen in Deutschland. 8. Leipzig 1870. Engelmann. $2^3/_4$ Thlr.
—— Ein Wendepunkt in der deutschen Shakspeare-Kritik. (Shakspeare-Studien. see Hauff.)
—— Das neueste Jahrbuch der deutschen Shakspeare-Gesellschaft (Deutsches Museum 24, 1867).
—— Shakspeare's Leben und Werke. 8. Hildb. 1871. Bibl. Inst. 20 Sgr.
Gerth, A. Shakspeare hat behufs seines dänischen Prinzen Hamlet die nordische Geschichte des 16. Jahrhunderts studirt. (Archiv für neuere Sprachen, Vol. 36, Abth. I, pag. 53.)
—— Warum hat Shakspeare seinem Lear keinen glücklicheren Ausgang gegeben? 4. Putbus 1849. Schulprogramm.
—— Shaksp. dänischer Prinz Hamlet. (Herrig's Archiv 36, 1.) 1864.
Gervinus, Händel und Shakspeare. 8. Leipzig 1868. Engelmann.
—— ditto vide Bitter.
—— Shakspeare 1. Aufl. beurtheilt. vide Brockerhoff.
Geyer, P. T. Studien über die tragische Kunst. (Die aristotelische Katharsis erklärt und auf Shakspeare und Sophocles angewandt.) Leipzig 1860. T. O. Weigel. 9 Sgr.
Gildemeister, Otto. Lady Macbeth. Bremer Sonntagsblatt 1863, No. 11.
Glaser, A. Geschichte des Theaters zu Braunschweig. Braunschweig 1861. (Enthält Notizen über frühere Aufführung Shakspearescher Stücke in Braunschweig.) Neuhoff & Co. 15 Sgr.
Goethe, J. W. von. Anmerkungen über das Theater, mit angehängtem Stück Shakspeares. Leipzig, 1. Ausgabe 1774.

Goethe, J. W. von. Rede über Shakspeare, in Strassburg gehalten, herausgegeben von Otto Jahn.
Goldene Worte aus Shakspeare's dramatischen Werken. Ausgewählt von Julius Wolff. S. Berlin 1871. Lipperheide. 1 Thlr.
Goltz. Shakspeare's Genius und die Tragödie Hamlet. (Vorlesungen, Vol. II.) Berlin 1869. Janke.
Gottschalk, R. Shakspeare-Studien in Frankreich. (Blätter für Literarische Unterhaltungen, 1865, No. 22.)
Grässer, Karl. Unbiassed remarks on S's. Taming of the Shrew. Programm. 4. Marienwerder 1869.
Grimm, H. Essays. (Unter Andern die Bearbeitung von Shakspeare's Sturm durch Dryden und Davenant.) Hannover 1863.
Grohe, Mel. Salvator Rosa, ein Zeit- und Geistesgenosse Shakspeare's. (Allg. Zeitung 1864, Beilage No. 155.)
Grunert, Karl. (Schauspieler.) Dramaturgische Aufsätze. Abhandlung über Macbeth. (Die Universität zu Tübingen verlieh ihm desshalb den Doctor-Titel.)
Grün, K. Ist Hamlet toll? (In *Orion*, Zeitschrift 1863. I. Band, Heft 5 & 6.) Hoffm. & Campe. Hamburg.
Gumlich, Dr. Ueber Shakspeare. (Programm der Handelsschule Berlin.) 4. 1864.
Gutzkow, K. Vermischte Schriften. 4 Vols. (Aufsatz über Shakespeare's Romeo und Julie.) Leipzig 1842—50.
Hagen (A). Die Shakspeare-Feier des literarischen Kränzchens. Königsberg im April 1864. I. Vortrag: Sittliche Haltung der Frauen in Shakspeare's Dramen. II. Vortrag: Shakspeare in Königsberg.
Hamlet, eine pastorale Studie. (Evang. Kirchenz. von Hengstenberg 1864, No. 40—42.)
— (Recension über) in Stimmen der Zeit. 1861. 17. Heft. pag. 198.
— in Deutschland. (Aufsätze in der Vossischen Zeitung 5 und 6. Juni No. 23 und 24. 1870.)
Harder, A. Die Philosophie W. Shakspeare's in 300 Auszügen aus seinen Dramen. gr. 16. Magdeburg 1869. Heinrichshofen. 24 Sgr.
Hauff, Gustav. Shakspeare-Studien.
    (Im Deutschen Museum von Prutz.)
    I. Hamlet. (1866, 5 und 20.)
    II. König Lear. (1866, No. 20.)
    III. Ein Wendepunkt in der deutschen Shaksp.-Kritik von Rud. Genée. (1866, No. 22 und 23.)
    IV. Macbeth von Hauff. (1867, No. 18.)
    V. Das neueste Jahrbuch der deutschen Shakspeare-Gesellschaft von R. Genée. (1867, No. 24.)
    VI. Hamlet von Karl Köstlin. (3 Artikel 1869, No. 29. 30. 31.)
    VII. Zwei Komödien Shakspeare's von Karl Frenzel. (3 Artikel 1867, No. 45. 46. 47.)
Hebbel, Fr. Shakspeare und seine Zeitgenossen. (3 Artikel, Wiener Zeitung 1859—61.)
Hebler, C. Aufsätze über Shakspeare. 8. Bern 1865. Dalp. 24 Sgr.
— — Ueber die Charactere in Shakspeare's Othello. (Neues Schweizer Museum 1863. III. pag. 78—85.)
Heigel, C. M. Macbeth, her. Oper. Musik von Chelard. München 1829.
Heintze. Parallele zwischen des Sophocles Orestes und Shakspeare's Hamlet. 4. Treptow a. R. 1857. Programm.
Heller, H. T. Zur Kritik, Erklärung und Uebersetzung Shakspeare's. (Herrig's Archiv Vol. 23.)
Helms, G. The english Adjective in the language of Shakspeare. S. Bremen 1868. Kühtmann & Co. ⅓ Thlr.
Henry. Hamlet, grosses Ballet. Wien. o. J.
Hense, C. C. Shakspeare's Sommernachtstraum erläutert. Halle 1851.
— poetische Personificationen in griechischen Dichtungen mit Berücksichtigung lateinischer Dichter und Shakspeare. Programm. Parchim 1864.
— Anmerkungen zu einigen Stellen im Shakspeare. (Herrig's Archiv Vol. 16.)
Herbst. Shakspeare. Eine biographische Skizze. (Altpreussische Monatsschrift 1864.)

Herder. Aus Herder's Nachlass herausg. von Düntzer und Herder. 3 Vols. Frankf. 1856 und 57. (Wichtig zur Kenntniss der Aufnahme Shakespeare's im Goetheschen Kreise.)
Hermes 1819. 1. Stück. 8. Leipzig 1819. Brockhaus. Enthält: 1. Shaksp. Schauspiele von Voss und dessen Söhnen. 2. Shaksp. Romeo und Julia von J. H. Voss.
Herrig. Die Entwicklung des englischen Dramas. (Archiv Vol. I.)
Heussi, Dr. J. W. Shaksp. Hamlet erklärt. Parchim 1868. Heussi's Verl. 1 Thlr.
Hettner. Geschichte der deutschen Literatur im 18. Jahrh. Vol. I. (1648 – 1740.) (Enthält Notizen über die Einführung Shakespeare's in Deutschland.) 8. Braunschweig 1862. Vieweg & Co.
Hick, G. Shakspeare in Southampton, oder die letzten Jahre der grossen Königin. Schauspiel in 5 Acten. Hamburg.
—— Ein Wintermärchen. Epische Dichtungen nach Shakspeare. 12. Cöln 1869.
Hiecke, R. G. Analyse von Shakspeare's Heinrich VI. (Gesammelte Aufsätze von Wendt.) Hamm 1864.
Hilgers. Der dramatische Vers Shakspeare's. 4. Programm. 1. & 2. Abth. Aachen 1869.
Hoffmann. Studien zu Shakspeare's Hamlet. 2. Artikel. (Herrig's Archiv IV. Band.)
Hopf, A. Der moderne Lear. (Brennecke Calender.) 1855.
Horen. Etwas über Shakspeare. see *Etwas.*
Hornstein, Rob. von. Musik zu Shakspeare's „Wie es euch gefällt." 2 Nummern. Stuttgart.
Höhnen, Aug. S's. Passionate Pilgrim. (Inaug.-Diss.) 8. Düsseldorf 1867.
Hugo, F. Shakspeare als Liebender. Darstellung des Princips der Sonetten. (In „Neues Frankfurter Museum, Beiblatt der Zeit" 1861, No. 20.)
Hülsmann. Shakspeare. Sein Geist und seine Werke. 8. Leipzig 1856. O. Wigand. 3. Aufl. 1860. 20 Sgr.
Humbert, Dr. C. Molière, Shakspeare und die deutsche Kritik. 8. Leipzig. Teubner. 3 Thlr.
Hüser. Noch ein Wort über Hamlet's Monolog. (Herrig's Archiv 4. Band.)
Jaenicke. Observations sur Hamlet. (Programm.) 4. Graudenz 1853.
—— ditto. (Programm.) 4. Potsdam 1858.
Jahrbuch der Deutschen Shakspeare-Gesellschaft. 1865 bis 1870.

Inhalt:

Band I (1865). Redigirt von Fr. von Bodenstedt.
Vorwort.
Programm.
Shakespeare in Deutschland. Von August Koberstein.
Ueber Shakespeare's Sonette. Von N. Delius.
Christopher Marlowe und Shakespeare's Verhältniss zu ihm. Von H. Ulrici.
Hamlet in Frankreich. Von Karl Elze.
Shakespeare und Sophokles. Von Adolf Schöll.
Marginalien zum Othello und Macbeth. Von Hans Köster.
Flüchtige Bemerkungen über einige Stücke, welche Shakespeare zugeschrieben werden. Von Hermann Freiherrn von Friesen.
Die neue englische Text-Kritik des Shakespeare. Von F. A. Leo.
Shakespeare ein katholischer Dichter. Von Michael Bernays.
Chapmann in seinem Verhältniss zu Shakespeare. Von Friedrich Bodenstedt.
Bodmer's Sasper. Von Karl Elze.
Mrs. Siddons. Von Friedrich Bodenstedt.
Shakespeare's englische Historien auf der Weimarer Bühne. Von Ludwig Eckardt.
Randglossen. Von William Bell.
Der Schlegel-Tieck'sche Shakespeare. Von Michael Bernays.
Einige Bemerkungen und Nachträge zu Albert Cohn's: „Shakespeare in Germany." Von Reinhold Köhler.
Shakespeare-Bibliographie. Von Albert Cohn.
Hinweisung auf einige neuere Werke.
Denkschrift des Vorstandes der Shakespeare-Gesellschaft an die deutschen Regierungen.
Statistischer Ueberblick.

Band II (1867). Redigirt von Fr. v. Bodenstedt.
: Vorwort.
: Jahresbericht, von Hermann Ulrici. Vorgelegt der General-Versammlung der deutschen Shakespeare-Gesellschaft am 8. Oktober 1865.
: Die Charakterzüge Hamlet's, nachgezeichnet von einem Nichtphilosophen.
: Bemerkungen zu den Altersbestimmungen für einige Stücke von Shakespeare. Von Hermann Freiherrn von Friesen.
: Eduard III., angeblich ein Stück von Shakespeare. Von H. Fr. v. Friesen.
: Die dramatische Einheit im Julius Cäsar. Von Dr. Albert Lindner.
: Shakespeare's Geltung für die Gegenwart. Von Karl Elze.
: Cordelia als tragischer Character. Von W. Oehlmann.
: Die realistische Shakespeare-Kritik und Hamlet. Von Fr. Theodor Vischer.
: Shakespeare und die Tonkunst. Von Friedrich Förster.
: Bemerkungen über symbolische Kunst im Drama mit besonderer Berücksichtigung Shakespeare's. Von Dr. Albert Lindner.
: The Still Lion. An Essay towards the Restoration of Shakespeare's Text. By C. M. Ingleby, LL. D., of Trinity College, Cambridge.
: Ueber einige Shakespeare-Aufführungen in München. Von Friedrich Bodenstedt.
: Ueber die Shakespeare-Aufführungen in Karlsruhe. Von Otto Devrient.
: Ludwig Devrient als König Lear. Von Hermann Ulrici.
: Ueber die Shakespeare-Aufführungen in Meiningen. Von W. Rossmann.
: Ueber die Shakespeare-Aufführungen in Stuttgart.
: Eine Characteristik Hamlet's für Schauspieler. Von W. Rossmann.
: Ueber Shakespeare's Timon of Athens. Von N. Delius.
: Hamlet's „Mortal Soil". Von Karl Elze.
: Zur Shakespeare-Literatur.
: Notizen.
: Shakespeare-Bibliographie 1865 August bis Dezember und 1866 Januar bis Oktober. (Nebst einigen Nachträgen zur Bibliographie in Bd. I. des Jahrbuches.) Zusammengestellt von Albert Cohn.

Band III (1868). Redigirt von K. Elze.
: Vorwort.
: Ueber Shakespeare's Fehler und Mängel. Einleitender Vortrag zum Jahresbericht der deutschen Shakespeare-Gesellschaft für 1865–1866. Von H. Ulrici.
: Jahresbericht für 1865–1866. Abgestattet in der General-Versammlung zu Berlin am 23. April 1867.
: Bericht über die General-Versammlung zu Berlin am 23. April 1867.
: Essay über Richard III. Von Wilh. Oechelhäuser.
: Zum Sommernachtstraum. Von K. Elze.
: Ueber Shakespeare's Pericles, Prince of Tyre. Von N. Delius.
: Die Gemüthsseite des Hamlet-Characters. Von W. Oehlmann.
: Glosse zu einer Stelle aus Shakespeare's Hamlet (Akt III, Scene 2). Von H. Freiherrn von Friesen.
: Die Troilus-Fabel in ihrer literatur-geschichtlichen Entwickelung und die Bedeutung des letzten Aktes von Shakespeare's Troilus und Cressida im Verhältniss zum gesammten Stücke. Von Karl Eitner.
: Shakespeare's Antonius und Kleopatra und Plutarch's Biographie des Antonius. Von Theod. Vatke.
: Zur Shakespeare'schen Textkritik. Ein Sendschreiben an den Herausgeber. Von Dr. Alexander Schmidt.
: Die Einrichtung des Cymbeline für die Bühne. Von Dr. A. Lindner.
: Die Shakespeare-Aufführungen in Meiningen. Von Wilhelm Oechelhäuser.
: Zu Shakespeare's The Taming of the Shrew. Von Reinhold Köhler.
: Literarische Uebersicht.
: Notizen.
: Zuwachs der Bibliothek der deutschen Shakespeare-Gesellschaft seit April 1868.
: Bibliographie. Von A. Cohn.

Band IV (1869). Redigirt von K. Elze.
: Vorwort.
: Jahresbericht für 1867–1868. Abgestattet in der General-Versammlung zu Weimar am 23. April 1868. Von Professor Dr. Ulrici.

Bericht über die General-Versammlung zu Weimar am 23. April 1868.
Dryden und Shakespeare. Von N. Delius.
Shakespeare's Coriolan. Von Heinrich Vichoff.
Shakespeare und Euripides. Eine Parallele. Von Th. Vatke.
Ueber Shakespeare's Sonette. Von H. Freiherrn von Friesen.
Sir William Davenant. Von K. Elze.
Timon von Athen. Ein kritischer Versuch. Von B. Tschischwitz.
Ueber Shakespeare's Macbeth. Von H. Freiherrn von Friesen.
Nachlese. Von Hermann Kurz.
  I. Die Wilderersage.
  II. Zum Sommernachtstraum.
Shakespeare's Bildnisse. Von K. Elze.
Ueber eine neue Bühnenbearbeitung von König Richard III. Von W. Oechelhäuser.
Shakespeare auf dem Wiener Burgtheater. Von Wilhelm Oechelhäuser.
Literarische Uebersicht.
Miscellen.
  I. Die Fechtscene im Hamlet. Von H. Freiherrn von Friesen.
  II. English Actors on the Continent. By A. C. Loffelt.
  III. A German Version of the Novel of Romeo and Juliet. By A. C. Loffelt.
  IV. Glosse zu Shakespeare's Cymbeline, Akt II, Scene 3. Von Julius Martensen.
  V. Zu Schiller's Macbeth. Von Gisbert Freiherrn Vincke.
  VI. Zu Hamlet I, 2. Von Ferdinand Lüders.
Zuwachs der Bibliothek der deutschen Shakespeare - Gesellschaft seit April 1868.
Mitglieder-Verzeichniss der deutschen Shakespeare-Gesellschaft.

Band V (1870). Redigirt von K. Elze.

Jancke, Th. Shakespeare's Julius Cäsar erläutert. Cöln 1860.
Ihne, Dr. Notes and Emendations to Shakespeare's Merchant of Venice. (Herrig's Archiv 31. Band 1862.)
Ilwolf, Franz. Germanistisches aus Shakespeare. (Germania, Zeitschrift von Pfeiffer. 9. Jahrg. 1. Heft.) Wien 1864.
Job. Beitrag zur Erklärung des Hamlet von Shakspeare. 4. Annaberg 1850.
Jung, Alb. Hamlet. Eine Schicksalstragödie. (Herrig's Archiv Vol. 27.)
(Kanngiesser), P. F. Anmerkungen für Alle, welche den Shakspeare in der Ursprache lesen wollen. Greifsw. 1825.
Karpf, Carl. Τὸ τί ἦν εἶναι. Die Idee Shakespeare's und deren Verwirklichung. Sonettenerklärung und Analyse des Dramas Hamlet. (Indirecter Beitrag zur Zeitfrage „Glauben und Wissenschaft.") 8. Hamburg 1870. Mauke & Söhne. 1 Thlr. 10 Sgr.
Kaufmann von Venedig. Ueber den Character des Antonio. (In Fed. Wehl's Schaubühne Mai 1864.)
Kaulbach. Neue Cabinet-Ausgabe des Shakspeare-Album. 9 Blätter in photographischen Abbildungen nach den Handzeichnungen. Berlin. Nicolai. 4 Thlr. 15 Sgr.
Kiessling, Ferd. William Shakespeare's Jugend. Schauspiel in einem Akt. (Den Bühnen gegenüber als Manuscript gedruckt.) Berlin. Mathes.
Kissner, A. Philological and critical remarks concerning some passages of Shakspeare's plays. Bartenstein 1866.
Klanke. On the beauties in Shakespeare's Othello. 4. Landsberg a. d. W. 1854. (Programm.)
Klix, G. A. Andeutungen zum Verständniss von Shakspeare's Hamlet. 4. (Programm.) Glogau 1565.
Klopp, Dr. Andreas Gryphius als Dramatiker. 4. Programm. Osnabrück 1850.
Kneschke, E. Zum Shakspeare-Jubiläum. Illustr. Familien-Journal 1864. No. 16.
Knorr. Shakspeare und sein Zeitalter. Programm der Realschule zu Fraustadt 1860.
Kock, Th. Ueber Shakespeare's Macbeth. Neues Schweizer Museum 1864, Heft 4.

Konewka, Paul. Falstaff und seine Gesellen in 22 Silhouetten. Text von Hermann Kurz. 4. Strassburg 1871. Schauenberg. 2 Thlr.
—— Der Sommernachtstraum. Illustrirt. 4. Strassburg 1871.
Kotzebue in England, oder die Auferweckung der schlummernden Plattheit, eine weinerliche Posse in 5 Akten, nebst einem Prolog, gesprochen von W. Shakspeare. 8. Berlin 1799.
Köstlin, K. Shakspeare-Studien „Hamlet". 3 Artikel. see *Hauff*.
—— Shakspeare und Hamlet. Morgenblatt 1864, No. 25 & 26.
Köstlin, K. Shakspeare, ein Winternachtstraum. Dramatisches Gedicht. 8. Wiesbaden 1864. Niedner. 25 Sgr.
Kreyssig, F. Shakespeare's lyrische Gedichte und ihre neuesten Bearbeiter. Preussisches Jahrbuch 1864, pag. 484—85.
—— Shakspeare - Fragen. Kurze Einführung in das Studium des Dichters, in 6 populären Vorträgen. Leipzig 1871. Luckhardt. 1 Thlr.
Kries. Ueber Hamlet. Programm. Rostock 1825.
Kurländer, F. A. Almanach dramat. Spiele. (Enth. Shakspeare als Liebhaber. Wien 1818.
Kugler, Franz. Shakspeare's Bühne und Kunstform. Beobachtungen vom Metier aus. (In *Argo*, belletr. Jahrbuch 1854.) Dessau.
Kurz, Herm. Die Deutschen in den „lustigen Weibern von Windsor". Internationale Revue Heft I. Wien 1866. 1 Thlr.
—— Zu Shakspeare's Leben und Schaffen. Altes und Neues. München 1868. Merhoff's Verlag. 20 Sgr.
Lamb, Ch. Tales from Shakspeare with a Vocabulary by E. Amthor. 12. 3rd Edit. Leipzig 1864. 18 Sgr.
Laube, Heinr. Das Burgtheater. Ein Beitrag zur deutschen Theatergeschichte. 8. Leipzig 1869. Weber. 3 Thlr.
L***. Othello und der Arzt seiner Ehre. (Herrig's Archiv Vol. 26.)
Leo, F. A. Die Tieck'sche Uebersetzung des Coriolan und ihre Bearbeitung durch Mommsen. (Herrig's Archiv Vol. 28.)
—— Beiträge und Verbesserungen zu Shakspeare's Dramen nach handschriftlichen Aenderungen in einem von Collier aufgefundenen Exemplar der Folio-Ausgabe von 1652. Berlin 1853. Asher & Co. 1 Thlr. 20 Sgr.
—— Shakespeare's Frauen-Ideale. Vortrag. 16. Halle 1868. Barthel. 10 Sgr.
Levinstein, S. Faust und Hamlet. Berlin 1855. Stargardt. 5 Sgr.
Liederfreund, der theatralische, oder Sammlung der Gesängen aus den Opern. Pesth 1818. Enthaltend Arien aus den Parodien Romeo & Juliet und Hamlet.
Löffler, Dr. Karl. Dramatische Charactere. I. Hamlet. Deutsche Schaub. v. Wahl & Buchholz. Heft 10 & 11.) Leipzig 1863. Leiner.
Loën, Freiherr von. Die Shakespeare-Kenntniss im gegenwärtigen Frankreich. (Internationale Revue Heft I. 1866.) Wien.
—— die Shakespeare-Aufführung in Weimar. Wissensch. Beilage zur Leipziger Zeitung 1864, No. 455.
Lud, A. L. William Shakspeare. Eine Festrede. Danzig 1864.
Ludwig, Otto. Shakespeare-Studien. Aus dem Nachlass des Dichters herausg. von Moritz Heydrich. 8. Leipzig 1871. Cnobloch. 2¼ Thlr.
Lustigen, die, Weiber von Windsor. Mit Originalzeichnungen von Rudolf Geisler in Nürnberg. (Buch der Welt, Illustr. Volksblatt No. I, 1871.)
Lützelberger, K. Das deutsche Schauspiel und Jacob Ayrer und sein Verhältniss zu Shakspeare. Nürnberger Album 1867.
—— Jacob Ayrer's Phoenizia und Shakspeare's "Viel Lärmen um Nichts." Nürnberger Album 1868.
Meissner, Alfred. Charaktermasken. (Aufsatz: Die Unschuld der Ophelia.) 3 Vols. 8. Leipzig 1862. Grunow. 4 Thlr. 15 Sgr.
Meissner, Johannes. Untersuchungen über Shakespeare's Sturm. 8. Dessau 1872. Alb. Reissner. 1 Thlr. 10 Sgr.
Moltke, M. Die ältesten und neuesten deutschen Shakspeare-Uebersetzungen untereinander und mit dem englischen Grundtext verglichen. I. (Deutscher Sprachwart 1867, Band II, 14—18.)
Mommsen. T. Besprechung der Deliusschen Hamlet-Ausgabe. In Neue Jahrb. für Philologie und Pädag. Band 72, Heft 2—4. 1854.
—— Pericles. Prince of Tyre. A novel by G. W. printed in 1608, and founded upon Shakspeare's play. Edited by Mommsen with a preface and introduction by J. P. Collier. 8. Oldenburg 1851.

Montague. Versuch über Shakspeare's Genie; see *Eschenburg.*
Morgenblatt. Stuttgart. Cotta.
    1856. S. von Emerson übersetzt und besprochen v. Herm. Grimm, No. 12—14.
  „ H. Grimm, Mittheilung über eine Bearbeitung von Shakspeare's Sturm durch Dryden und Davenant.
    1857. Shakspeare's Coriolan auf der Dresdner Bühne. No. 5.
  „ Shakspeare's Charactere, Portia, Helena, Jago, Mercutio. No. 41,43, 45, 46.
    1858. Shakspeare'sche Charactere von Heinrich Deinhardt. Viola und Olivia, Beatrice. No. 4, 5, 6, 22, 23.
    1859. Shakespeare und Calderon als Tendenzdichter. No. 2.
  „ Shakspeare's Hamlet von H. M. Zaubitz. No. 5 und 6.
    1860. Shakspeare's Hamlet von Karl Silberschlag. No. 46 und 47.
Mosenthal, S. H. Die lustigen Weiber zu Windsor. Komisch-phant. Oper. Musik von O. Nicolai. Berlin 1850.
—— Oper. 8. Wien 1871. Wallishausen. ¼ Thlr.
Möser, Ludwig. A few Observations on Shakspeare's Richard III. (Programm.) Hertford 1869.
Müller, Wilhelm. Herr Peter Squenz, oder die Komödie zu Rumpelskirch. Posse in zwei Abtheilungen nach Andreas Gryphius und Shakspeare, frei bearbeitet. 12. n. date.
Müller. Sur les enfants d'Eduard de Delavigne et sur les rapports de cette tragedie au Richard III. de Shakspeare. *4to.* Fulda 1844. (Programm.)
Müller, Julius. Gedanken über das Verhältniss des Christenthums zur Poesie. (Shakspeare.) Deutsche Zeitschrift f. christl. Wiss. und Literatur 1850. No. 17—19.
Müller, Samsweger. Zum Shakspeare-Jubiläum. (Blätter für liter. Unterhaltung.) 1864. No. 18.
Neller, H. J. Ueber Collier's handschriftliche Verbesserungen Shakspeare's. (Sonntagsbeilage zur Vossischen Zeitung.) 1860.
Neidhardt, A. Shakspeare's Sonette. (Herrig's Archiv 38. Band. Heft 3 & 4. 1865.
Neubauer. Shakespeare-Studien. Herrig's Archiv Vol. 24. 1858.
Neumann, H. Ueber Lear und Ophelia. Ein Vortrag. 8. Breslau 1866. Korn. 3 Sgr.
Nicolai. Die lustigen Weiber von Windsor. Oper im Klavierauszuge.
Oechselhäuser, W. Ueber eine neue Bühnen-Bearbeitung von König Richard dem III. Shakspeare auf dem Wiener Burgtheater. 8. Berlin 1869.
Olla Potrida (herausgegeben von J. F. Reichardt). 1779. Enthält: der Brudermord, oder Prinz Hamlet bestraft, nach einer Handschrift von ca. 1603.
Pabst, J. Die Shakspeare-Feier. Nachspiel zu "Wie es euch gefällt." 8. Dresden 1864.
Petri, M. Zur Einführung Shakspeare's in die christliche Familie. 8. Hannover. Carl Meyer. ⅚ Thlr.
Petz, L. Tetralogie tragischer Meisterwerke der Alten und Neuern, übersetzt und erläutert. (Enthält Shaksp. Lear.) Karschau 1824.
Philipp. On Shakspeare's Julius Caesar. Programm. 4. Berlin 1849.
Platzer, F. Shakspeare's Wintermährchen. (Bremer Sonntagsblatt 1864, No.2.)
Polychorda. Zeitschrift herausg. von A. Bode. 6 Hefte. Penig 1803. (Enthält Shakspeare's Sonette, Klagen eines Liebenden und Der Pilgrim, übersetzt von K.)
Prutz, R. Zur Shakspeare-Feier. Prolog gesprochen auf dem Stadttheater zu Stettin. (Deutsches Museum 1864, No. 17.)
Pyramus und Thisbe. Duodrama. Halle 1787.
Quellen, die, des Shakspeare in Novellen, Märchen und Sagen, mit sachgeschichtlichen Nachweisungen von Karl Simrock. 2. Auflage. 2 Vols. Bonn 1870. Ad. Marcus. 2⅔ Thlr.
Ranke, L. Englische Geschichte vornehmlich im 16. und 17. Jahrhundert. I. Band. (Enth. eine Abhdl. über Shakspeare.) Berlin 1862.
Rapp, M. Studien über das englische Theater. 2 Vols. Tübingen 1862. Laupp.
Reich, Adolph. Shakspeare's Shylock, dargestellt von Bog. Dawison und Sam Phelps. (Berliner Dramaturgie III.) 8. Berlin 1864.
—— der Schwan von Avon. Schauspiel in 5 Acten. (Bühnen-Manuscript.) 1863.
Reichensperger, A. William Shakespeare insbesondere sein Verhältniss zum Mittelalter und zur Gegenwart. 8. Münster 1872. Russell. 6 Sgr.

Riechelmann. Zu Richard II. Shakspeare und Holinshed. Gymn.-Programm. 4. Plauen 1860.
Ring, Max. Shakspeare in Deutschland. (Sonntagsbeilage der Vossischen Zeitung.) 1867.
Ritter, J. G. Beiträge zur Erklärung des Macbeth von Shakspeare. 2 Theile. 4to. Leer 1871. Securius. 8 Sgr.
Rodenberg. Hamlet's Grab. (Vier Wochen in Helsingör.) 8. Berlin 1867. Gerschel. 12 Sgr.
—— Ein Tag in Shakspeare's London. (Gartenlaube 1864, No. 16 & 17.)
Rodenberg. Wm. Shakspeare. Ein Gedenkblatt zu seiner 300jährigen Jubelfeier. (Bazar 1864, No. 20.)
Romeo und Julie. Roman. Erfurt 1801.
Rossmann, W. Vom Gestade der Cyclopen und Sirenen. 8. Leipzig 1869. Grunow. 2 Thlr. (Enth.: pag. 69—70 der tanzende Shakspeare.)
Rötscher. Seydelmann's Leben und Wirken (nebst einer dramaturgischen Abhandlung über den Künstler). 8. Berlin. A. Duncker. 2 Thlr.
—— Kritiken und dramat. Abhandlungen. Leipzig 1859. 1½ Thlr. (Enthält Vieles über Shakspeare.)
—— Der 5. Act des Kaufmann von Venedig. (Recensionen und Mitth. über Theater und Musik 1864, No. 38.)
Rudloff, Dr. W. Ein Erinnerungsblatt zum Andenken an die Jubelfeier 23. April 1864. Danzig.
Rümlin, G. Shakspeare-Studien. 8. Stuttgart 1866. Cotta. 27 Sgr.
Sammlung einiger ausgewählter Stücke der Geschichte. (Vide Beiträge zur Krit. Hist. der deutschen Sprache.)
Saupe, J. Shakespeare's Leben und Entwicklungsgang. 8. Gera. Griesbach. ¼ Thlr.
—— Shakspeare's Hamlet für obere Gymnasialclassen erläutert. (Programm.) Gera 1870.
Schad, Ch. Vom Klingenwald. Zur Jubelfeier. Kitzingen 1864.
Schenkl, K. Das Märchen vom Schneewitchen und Shakspeare's Cymbeline. (Germania von Pfeiffer IX. 1861. Heft 4.) Wien. Gerold.
Schirmer, Adolph. Ein weiblicher Hamlet. Novelle. 12. Wien 1870.
Schindhelm. Abhandlung über Hamlet von Shakspeare. 4. (Programm.) Coburg 1866. Dietz.
Schlegel, A. W. Sämmtliche Werke herausgeg. von Ed. Böcking. 12 Vols. Leipzig 1846. Enthält:
Vol. VI. Vorlesungen über dramatische Kunst und Literatur, darin 25. bis 31. Vorlesung: Shakespeare's Zeitalter und Lebensumstände. — S. der grösste Charakteristiker. — S's. Bildung und künstlerischer Tiefsinn. — Die Echtheit des S'schen Pathos gerechtfertigt. Wortspiele. Sittliche Schonung. Ironie. Vermischung des Komischen und Tragischen. Die Rolle des Narren. S's Sprache und Versbau. — Beurtheilung der einzelnen Stücke S's. — Ueber die angeblich Shakespear'n untergeschobenen Stücke.
Vol. VII. Etwas über William S. bei Gelegenheit Wilhelm Meisters. — Ueber Romeo und Julia.
Vol. X. Recension über Romeo und Julia nach S. frei fürs deutsche Theater bearbeitet.
Vol. XI. Recensionen über Tieck's Bearbeitung von S. Sturm. — Wagner's Shakspeare.
Vol. XII. Abfertigung eines unwissenden Recensenten der Schlegelschen Uebersetzung des Shakespeare.
Schlegel, F. Kritik und Theorie der alten und neuen Poesie. Wien 1822. (Enth.: Ueber Shakspeare's ältere dramatische Werke.)
Schloenbach, A. Hamlet in der Eisenhütte. (Illustr. Familien-Journal 1864, No. 9 & 10.)
Schmalfeld, Dr. Einige Bemerkungen zur Electra des Sophocles mit einem Seitenblick auf Shakspeare's Hamlet. (Programm.) Eisleben 1868.
Schmidt, F. L. Dramaturgische Aphorismen. Hamburg 1820.
Schmidt, Dr. Alex. Voltaire's Verdienste um die Einführung Shakspeare's in Frankreich. 4. (Programm.) Königsberg 1864.
Schneider, K. Zur Shakspearefeier. Bremer Sonntagsblatt 1864, No. 18.

Schöne, F. Zum Gedächtniss Shakspeare's. Rede. Neue Jahrbücher für Philologie und Pädagogik 1864 Vol. 89. Heft 9.
—— Ueber den Character Richards III. Dresden 1856.
Schröder, W. Graf Southampton, der Freund Shakspeare's. Nach englischen Quellen. Illustr. Zeit. 1864, No. 1083.
Schröder, F. L. Dramatische Werke herausg. v. E. v. Bülow, mit Einleit. von L. Tieck. 4 Vols. 8. Berlin 1831. (Hamlet.)
Schüller, Ed. Erläuterung von W. von Kaulbach's Shakespeare-Album. Berlin 1859.
Schwartzkopff, A. Göthe's Faust, Shakspeare's Macbeth und König Lear im Lichte des Evangelii. 3 Vorträge. 8. Schönebeck 1868. Berger. 24 Sgr.
Shakspeare-Album in Photographien nach der Natur, enthaltend die Hauptcharactere S's., sowie sie von den hervorragendsten Mitgliedern des Berliner Hoftheater's dargestellt werden. 48 meisterhaft ausgeführte Costümbilder. 8. Berlin 1862. 13 Thlr.
—— Beruf und Triumph. Mainz 1792.
—— Gallerie. Charactere und Scenen aus Shakespeare's Dramen. Gezeichnet von Max Adamo, Heinr. Hoffmann, Hanns Makart, Friedr. Pecht, Fritz Schwoerer, etc. 36 Blätter in Stahlstich gestochen von Bankel, Goldberg, Raab, Schultheiss. Mit erläuterndem Text von Friedrich Pecht. Prachtausgabe in folio 28 Thlr. 4to. 16 Thlr. 1870. Brockhaus.
—— Gallerie, von Carl von Piloty & Anderen. Lief. I. Imp. folio. Berlin 1871. Grote.
—— Gesellschaft, die, und das Shakspeare-Jahrbuch. Aufsatz in "Unsere Zeit" Nov. 1865.
—— Literatur, zur, Herrig Archiv Vol. 23. (Ueber Dingelstedt, Kreysig, Bodenstedt.)
—— Museum. Zeitschrift für Geschichte und Pflege des Shakespeare-Studiums und Shakspeare-Cultus. Organ für Frage und Antwort, für Rede und Gegenrede in Shakespeare-Sachen. Herausg. von Max Moltke. (Lex.-8. Vol. I. 1870.) Shakspeare-Verlag. Leipzig. 4 Thlr.
—— Musik. 2 Artikel im Morgenblatt 1864, No. 32 & 33.
—— Zum Shakspeare-Jubiläum. (Blätter für Lit. Unterh. 1864. No. 18. Von Emil Müller-Samswegen.
—— Studien eines Realisten. (Morgenblatt 1864, No. 48—52.)
Siewers, Dr. Ueber den sittlichen Ideenkreis des Shakspeare'schen Dramencyclus. Heinrich VI. und Richard III. 1863. (Protest. Morgenblätter 1863, April.)
—— William Shakspeare. Sein Leben und Dichten. Vol. I. Gotha 1866. 2 Thlr. 6 Sgr.
—— Ueber die Grundidee des Shakspeare'schen Othello. Programm. Gotha 1851.
—— Shakspeare's Geistesleben. Herrig's Archiv Vol. 25.
—— Ueber Hamlet. (Rötscher's Jahrbuch f. dramat. Kunst 1849. 1. Heft.)
Simrock, K. Die Quellen des Shakspeare in Novellen, Märchen und Sagen mit sachgesch. Nachweisungen. 2. Aufl. 2 Thle. 8. Bonn 1871. Marcus. $2^{2}/_{3}$ Thlr.
Sonnette. (Artikel im Magazin für Literatur des Auslandes 1861, No. 40.)
Spandau. Zur Kritik des Shaksp. Othello. 4to. 1860.
Stahr, A. Kleine Schriften zur Kritik der Literatur und Kunst. 2 Vols. 8. Oldenburg 1845. (Macbeth, Was ihr wollt.)
—— Zur Shakspeare-Literatur. Nationalzeitung 24. December 1857.
Stark, C. König Lear. Eine psychiatrische Shakspeare-Studie. 16. Stuttgart 1871. Lindemann. 18 Sgr.
Stedefeld, G. F. Hamlet, ein Tendenzdrama Shakespeare's gegen die skeptische und kosmopolitische Weltanschauung des Michael de Montaigne. Mit einem Anhang über Leben und Lehre Montaigne's von R. W. Emerson. Frei übersetzt und mit Anmerkungen begleitet. 8. Berlin 1871. Gebr. Petel. 15 Sgr.
—— die christlich-germanische Weltanschauung in den Werken der Dichterfürsten Wolfram von Eschenbach, Dante und Shakspeare. Mit einem Gruss an die Landsleute im Elsass und Lothringen. 8. Berlin 1871. Gebr. Petel. 15 Sgr.
Stigell, Dr. Shakspeare und die tragische Kunst der Griechen. (Gymnasial-Programm.) Mainz 1863.

Stratmann. Hamlet. Crefeld 1869. Gehrich & Co.
Tetschke. Einleitung zu Shakspeare's Julius Cäsar. Stralsund 1855.
Theater, Englisches (übersetzt und bearbeitet von Ch. H. Schmidt). 7 Vols. Danzig 1772—77. Enthält: Othello von Shaksp. & Kleopatra von Dryden.
Tieck. Kritische Schriften. 4 Vols. 12. Leipzig 1852.
    Vol. I. Die Kupferstiche nach d. Shaksp.-Galerie in London. — Shaksp. Behandlung des Wunderbaren. 1793. — Briefe über Shakspeare 1800. Das altenglische Theater. 1811, 1823, 1828.
    Vol. III. Romeo und Julia. — Lear. — Bemerkungen über einige Charactere in Hamlet. — Nachtrag über Hamlet's Monolog.
    Vol. IV. Lear, Macbeth, Julius Cäsar, Othello. — Ueber das altenglische Theater 1817.
—— Nachgelassene Schriften. Herausg. v. R. Köpke. 2 Vols. Leipzig 1855. (Enthält: Das Buch über Shakspeare.)
Tschischwitz, Benno. Nachklänge germanischer Mythen in den Werken Shakspeare's. 8. Halle 1865. 15 Sgr.
—— Shakspeare's Staat und Königthum. Nachgewiesen an der Lancaster Tetralogie. Halle 1866. 12 Sgr.
—— Shakspeare's Hamlet in seinem Verhältniss zur Gesammtbildung namentlich zur Theologie und Philosophie der Elizabeth-Zeit. 4to. Halle. Barthel. ½ Thlr.
—— Shakspeare-Forschungen I, Hamlet, vorzugsweise nach histor. Gesichtspunkten erläutert. 8. Halle 1868. Barthel. 1½ Thlr.
Ullrich, Titus. Verona und Shakspeare. Eine Reise-Erinnerung. 12.
Vischer, Fr. Th. Kritische Gänge. Neue Folge. (2. Heft, Shakspeare.) Stuttgart 1861.
Vogel, Chr. Zusatz zu Hiller's kritischen Erläuterungen und Uebersetzungen Shakspeare's. Herrig's Archiv Vol. 25.
Voss, J. v. Travestien und Parodien zur Darstellung in kleinen Kreisen. Berlin 1812 (Enthält: Coriolan eine Travestie.)
War Shakspeare Katholik? Drei Artikel. "Histor. polit. Blätter, Band 60." München 1867.
War Shakspeare in Stuttgart? Augsburger Allg. Zeitung 1864, No. 164.
Wintermärchen. Ueber die eigentliche Quelle des Wintermärchens von S. (Magazin für Lit. des Auslandes 1863, No. 33.)
Wirtemberg, Herzog von. Tagebücher 1592 und 1610? (Reiste in England zur Zeit der Königin Elisabeth.)
Wiseman, N. William Shakspeare. 12. Cöln 1865. 7½ Sgr.
Wiss, James. On the Rudiments of the Shakspearian-Drama. 8. Frankfurt 1828. Brönner.
Wollzogen, Alfr. von. Zur Geschichte des englischen Theaters im 17. Jahrh. (Wiener Recens. und Mittheil. 1864, pag. 29—33.)
Zahlhas, J. A. Elisabeth's Tod. Trauerspiel in 5 Aufzügen. 1861. (Als Manuscript gedruckt, darin W. Shakspeare als Rolle.)
Zaubitz. Hamlet; see Morgenblatt.
Zimmermann, W. F. Die Hamlet-Tragödie, in philosophischer Beleuchtung. (2 Feuilletons der Berliner Brille 1870. 4to.)

III.

SKETCH OF THE PROGRESS OF SHAKSPEARIAN CRITICISM,

AND OF THE GRADUAL APPRECIATION OF SHAKSPEARE
IN
F.RANCE.

Voltaire, says Guizot, in his "Shakspeare et son temps", was the first person in France, who spoke of Shakspeare's genius; and although he spoke of it merely as *a barbarous genius,* yet the literary public of France were of opinion that Voltaire had said too much in the dramatist's favour. Indeed they thought it nothing less than profanation, to apply the words "genius" and "glory" to the writer of dramas which they considered to be as crude as they were coarse.

At the present day all controversy regarding Shakspeare's genius and glory has come to an end. A greater question has now arisen; — namely, whether Shakspeare's dramatic power is not infinitely superior to that of Voltaire, Racine, or Corneille.

These words contain the essence of that controversy which originated with Voltaire, and to which the French nation is indebted for the importation of Shakspeare into France.

Dramatic writers, such as Saint-Evremond, Lamotte and Lafosse, knew Shakspeare well. The best account of the way in which he influenced them and the French theatre generally, will be found in *"Albert Lacroix's* histoire de l'influence de Shakspeare sur le théâtre français." How the great dramatist became known to the mass of the French people, may be seen in Guizot's chapter, „Shakspeare en France", which gives a good analysis of the subject.

It was *Voltaire* who wrote, in his "Lettres sur les Anglais",[*] thus: — "En Angleterre Shakspeare créa le théâtre. Il avait un génie "plein de force et de fécondité, de naturel et de sublime; mais sans "la moindre étincelle de bon goût, et sans la moindre connaissance "des règles."

Mrs. Montague's "Essay on the writings and genius of Shakspeare", was specially directed against this Voltairian criticism; but it was a useless effort for French literature could surely correct such criticism

---

[*] Dix-huitième lettre, "de la tragedie". — Voltaire spent two years in London, as an exile, (1726—1728).

much better for itself; just as the Germans had, in similar circumstances, followed *their* own path of inquiry, and determined the value of the dramatist themselves.

The first French translation which appeared was that of *Letourneur*, in 20 Vols. 8º. (1776—83). It had the notes of Warburton, Steevens, and Johnson, and the comments of Eschenburg's German translation; but, carefully as it seems to have been edited, it gave but a faint idea of Shakspeare's genius. Letourneur, says Phil. Chasles*, "usait d'un "procédé que l'ignorance générale lui rendait facile. Sur la trame "anglaise il jetait le coloris et la rhétorique gallo-latins; au lieu de "pénétrer dans les mystères du genie étranger, il les supprimait."

Letourneur was a bold man, in spite of the sarcastic sneers of Voltaire, in spite of the storm the latter tried to create against him, in spite of the adverse judgement of Marmontel, he upheld Shakspeare as the sovereign genius of the stage, placing him above both Corneille and Racine. He attacked the classical system and its narrowness, rejected the rules of unity, counselled an assiduous study of Shakspeare, and finally manifested a desire that his dramas should be acted in Paris. There is no doubt either of Letourneur's talent, or of his thorough appreciation of Shakspeare; and he certainly deserves the highest consideration for having stood so manfully by his author. Besides, with all his faults he has left behind him "une oeuvre utile, "une oeuvre qui joue un grand rôle dans la révolution dramatique: elle "donna un chef au mouvement, elle offrit le modèle d'un genre impar-"faitement connu en France."**

Diderot was one of the first who opposed Voltaire, and spoke of Shakspeare with knowledge and reverence. He wrote (in the Encyclopédie) on the genius of Shakspeare, thus: — "qui n'eut jamais de maître "ni d'égal;" — and he proclaimed that this author was endowed with "talents personnels dans lesquels il surpasse tous les poètes du monde ". . . . et malgré ses défauts, il mérite d'être mis au-dessus de tous "les écrivains dramatiques de l'Europe". So bold an opinion had a wonderful influence on French criticism. Madame de Staël, St. Martin, Benjamin Constant, and Lemercier were more or less roused by it, and new attacks were soon made by d'Alembert, Marmontel, Pallissot, and M. Joseph Chénier.

After Letourneur, and until the epoch of the social revolution in 1789, *Bayle* occupied himself with Shakspeare, speaking of him with great praise; and, by degrees, a purer taste developed itself in many French minds with reference to the writings of the English dramatist. Thus *Lucas*, in his "Histoire du théâtre français", says of him: — "Une seule scène de Shakspeare éclaire plus un artiste, que cette foule "des tragédies où toutes les règles sont obervées scrupuleusement "hors la plus essentielle, qui est d'intéresser et de plaire." But the opposition to Shakspeare did not die out with Voltaire, his disciples and other Voltairian fanatics, who had imbibed his prejudices and antipathies, continued the abuse. *D'Alembert* never admitted the merit of

---

* Phil. Chasles, "Etudes sur Shakspeare"; — le chapitre "des traducteurs de Shakspeare".

** Lacroix, histoire de l'influence. page 200.

the English dramatist; nor was *Marmontel* able to understand him in the least; for he wrote of him; — "Shakspeare n'a jamais connu cette "pitié douce qui pénètre insensiblement, qui se saisit des coeurs et qui, "les pressant par degrés, leur fait goûter le plaisir doux de se soulager "par des larmes". *La Harpe* followed Marmontel in his ignorance; and considered Shakspeare, only as a "gross and mediocre" poet! *Marie-Joseph Chénier*, another disciple of Voltaire, imitated his master's abuse, but his brother, *André Chénier*, who had lived some years in England, became his antagonist and the defender of the dramatist whose pieces he had seen, and whom he had learned to appreciate and admire in that country. With the French Revolution the dispute died out, but during the period of the Empire a real "Shakspearian school" arose in France.

The enthusiastic *Madame de Staël*, who had visited England, and was moreover much influenced by German ideas, has written with great spirit on Shakspeare, in her book "de la Littérature". "Il y a dans "Shakspeare," she says, "des beautés du premier genre (sublimes) et "de tous les pays comme de tous les temps. Shakespeare commence ,'une littérature nouvelle: il est empreint, sans doute, de l'esprit et de ,'la couleur générale des poésies du Nord, mais c'est lui qui a donné "à la littérature des Anglais son impulsion, et à leur art dramatique "son caractère". These were great words, with which the era of Shaksperian appreciation was opened in France; but, not content with this, their writer urged an imitation of the English dramatist, as the only thing which could rescue the French theatre from destruction.

In 1801 *Charles Nodier* published a volume entitled "Pensées de Shakspeare", and gave translations from Schiller and other German dramatists who were full of admiration for Shakspeare, and the book had a considerable, though indirect influence on French writers. But it was in particular Schlegel's work on ancient and modern dramatic art, aided as it was by Mad. de Staël's "Allemagne", which may be said to have raised Shakspeare to that position of eminence in France, which, however clearly it may have been his due, he had not hitherto occupied; from that moment his triumph was complete. Some of the greatest names in French literature now began to acknowledge the power of the English dramatist; and in 1821 a new edition was published of the "Oeuvres complètes de Shakspeare", by *Guizot, Barante,* et *Amedée Pichot*, it was Letourneur's old translation, revised, corrected, and improved. Guizot published also his "Essai sur la vie et les oeuvres de Shakspeare"; and, latterly, "Shakspeare et son temps." *Villemain, Rémusat, Alfred de Vigny*, and (particularly) *Philarète Chasles* wrote both with enthusiasm and with thorough intelligence on Shakspeare and English dramatic art. The last named also made a superior translation of Romeo and Juliet.

Nisard published, in 1837, his "Chefs d'oeuvres de Shakspeare"; and in 1842 two new translations of Shakspeare appeared; the one by Benjamin Laroche, the other by Francisque Michel. It will however be at all times a difficult task to translate Shakspeare into any of the Romanic languages; more particularly French, for there is a want, in the languages derived from the latin, of all those elements which characterise the Teutonic tongues. The voice of nature speaking in her sympathy, to man; the changeful emotions of the human heart; the mysteries, now grandly solemn, and now again almost playful, of the poet's mind; the echo, caught ere yet it dies away, of the fleetest and most transient whispers of the soul; nay, the very innermost movement of thought in the brain; — in the expression of which Shakspeare is so grand a master; — all these are not easily rendered into French. They require a Teutonic tongue.

Edgar Quinet gives us some fine passages on Shakspeare, in his "Génie des religions"; and *George Sand* a poetic study on. Hamlet. *Saint Marc-Girardin* in his "Cours de littérature dramatique", *John Lemoinne* in his volume of Critiques, *Gustave Planche*, *Mennechet*, *Saint-Beuve*, *Jules Janin*, *Alf. Michiels*, *de Lamennais*, *Hippolyte Lucas*, and many others whom we could cite, have also written with no less originality than genius, on the great dramatist.

That the old prejudice against Shakspeare should every now and then revive and shew itself is natural, and will probably continue for some time to come. The last effort in this direction was made by M. Ponsard,* in 1856, in his Discourse in the Institute of France, when he was received as a Member. It would have been unnecessary to notice this discourse, (for it is profitless), were it not for the reply which M. Nisard gave it, and which we may take as an expression of the ideas which prevail at the present moment amongst the French, on that subject. Mr. Nisard replied to the attack on the bard of Avon thus: — "Another point on which I should be somewhat "more liberal than you, is relative to Shakspeare. Of all that you have "expressed so brilliantly I would guard what tends to his glory, and "I would put aside the restrictions to his fame, not as unjust, but "because the truth does no longer require them. Time has elevated "Shakspeare above criticism, probably because it has raised him above "eulogium. The very words 'beauties' and 'defects' belong to a rela- "tive language, out of the pale of which special terms must be sought "if it is desired to define the charm, or to characterize the imper- "fections of these astonishing works. Shakspeare has had the same "destiny as Homer. After that famous quarrel of the ancients and the "moderns in which admirers and opponents — Boileau as well as Perrault "— committed the mistake of representing the author of the *Iliad* as "a literary man working regularly at his desk, the Homer who remains "is a Homer transfigured, presiding over the great choir of men of "genius, and naked, in the midst of personages whose costume indicates "their nation and their age, as if the matter related not to the inhabi- "tant of a country nor to the contemporary of an epoch, but to the genius "itself of poetry. Like Homer, Shakspeare appears to us, in his turn, "in a tranquil and mysterious distance, withdrawing from the curiosity "of erudition, which fatigues itself in seeking out a man where there is "only one of the most wondrous sources of creative poetry. With "Homer, with Shakspeare, we are placed on lofty pinnacles, from which "the eye cannot distinguish anything of what passes below. I do not "ask them for any account of the faults which they may have com-

---

* "Discours prononcés dans la séance publique tenue par l'Académie française pour la reception de M. Ponsard". 1856.

"mitted — Homer in creating a first model of beauty, from which has "emanated the very idea of art and of its rules — and Shakspeare in "not being acquainted with them. Why be astonished that these geniuses "are imperfect? If poetry itself has dictated their verses, it is a human "hand that has written them down."

Two new editions are now (1864) in course of publication, the one is by *Guizot,* the other by *François Victor Hugo.* They bear additional testimony that Shakspeare, by the sheer force of his genius has won the complete (if somewhat tardy) appreciation of the French nation. The last French book on "Shakspeare" is by Victor Hugo, it is a sort of poetic effusion on the dramatist; and sufficiently shows that Shakspeare will always be appreciated by a great and artistic mind.

FRENCH TRANSLATIONS AND REPRINTS OF SHAKSPEARE'S WORKS.

1776—1783 Shakespeare (avec des notes des éditeurs anglais: Warburton, Steevens, Johnson, Mrs. Griffith etc., et des Remarques tirées de la traduction allemande de Shakespeare par M. Eschenbourg), traduit de l'anglais (en prose) par Le Tourneur (le comte de Catuelan et Fontaine-Malherbe). 20 vol. in 8. Paris 1776—83.

1821 William Shakespeare. Oeuvres complètes. Nouv. édition, revue et corr. par F. Guizot (ou plutôt Mad. Guizot, née Dillon), et A. P··· (Pichot), traducteur du Lord Byron, précédée d'une Notice biographique et littéraire sur Shakespeare, par F. Guizot. Paris, Ladvocat, 1821. 13 vol. in 8., avec un portrait.

—— —— La même traduction sur gr. pap. velin.

1822 —— Oeuvres dramatiques de Shakespeare, corrigées et enrichies de notes par M. Avenel. Paris 1822. 12 vol. 18.

1826 —— Chefs d'oeuvres; traduits conformément au texte original en vers blancs, en vers rimés et en prose par feu A. Bruguière, revus par M. Chénédollé. 2 vols. 8. Paris 1826.

1834 —— Oeuvres dramatiques, précédés de notices historiques et littéraires sur sa vie et ses ouvrages par J. A. Havard. gr. 8. Paris 1834.

1834 —— Oeuvres dramatiques trad. de Letourneur. Novelle edit. par Horace Meyer. 2 Vols. roy. 8. Paris 1834—35.

1837 —— Chefs-d'oeuvres (Othello, Hamlet et Macbeth), la traduction française en regard par M. M. Nizard, Lebas et Fouinet. 8. Paris 1837.

1837 —— Chefs-d'oeuvres. Avec des Notes par D. O' Sullivan french and english. 3 Vols. 8. Paris 1837—38.

1838 —— the complete Works; with explanatory and historical notes by the most eminent commentators. Accurately printed from the correct and esteemed edition of Alexander Chalmers in two volumes with nearly 200 wood and steel engravings. 2 Vols. gr. 8. Paris (Baudry) 1838.

1839 —— Oeuvres complètes trad. par F. Michel et précédés de la vie de Shakespeare par Wordsworth (Campbell). 3 Vols. roy. 8. Paris 1839. 2. Edit. 1855.

1839 —— Oeuvres complètes traduits par B. Laroche, avec une introduction par Alex. Dumas. gr. 18. Paris 1838—39.

1840 —— Chefs-d'ouvres de Shakespeare (Cesar et la Tempête) français et anglais par Jay et Mme L. Colet, avec notices critiques par M. Villemain. 8. Paris 1840.

1842—1843 —— Oeuvres, traduits par Benj. Laroche. 6 Vols. 12. Paris 1842—43. Gosselin. 21 fr. 50 c.

1844 —— Oeuves complètes. Traduction nouvelle par Benj. Laroche. 2 Vols. 8. 1844. 20 fr.

1851 —— Oeuvres complètes, traduites par Benjamin Laroche. 6 Vols. 8. Paris 1851. 4. Edit. 1859.

1856 —— Oeuvres complètes, trad. par Benj. Laroche. Edition illustrée de gravures sur bois, gravées par Deghouy, sur les dessins originaux de Felix Barrios. 2 Vols. 4. Paris 1856. Charlieu. 11 fr.

1859	——	Oeuvres trad. par Francisque Michel. 2 Edit. 3 Vols. 8. Paris 1859. Didot. 30 fr.
—	—	même traduction. 4. Edition. 6 Vols. 12. Paris 1859. Charpentier. 21 fr.
1862	——	Oeuvres complètes, traduction de M. Guizot. Nouvelle édition, entièrement revue, avec une étude sur Shakspeare. 8 Vols. 8. 1862.
1862	——	Oeuvres complètes par François Victor Hugo. 12 Vols. 8. 1862.
1864	——	Oeuvres complètes, traduction nouvelle par Benjamin Laroche. 2 Vols. 228 gravures sur bois. 1864.
1865	——	traduction de M. Guizot. 8 Vols. 12. Paris 1865. 28 fr.
—	—	chefs-d'oeuvre de Shakspeare. 3 Vols. 12. Paris 1865. Hachette. 3 fr.
1867	——	Oeuvres, traduites par Emil Montégut avec Gravures. 4 Vols. 8. Paris 1867. Hachette. 20 fr.
1868	——	Oeuvres trad. par Francis Victor Hugo. 18 Vol. 8.
1868	——	Oeuvres choisies. Traduction révue par F. Michel. 3 Vols. 12. Didot. 9 fr.
1868	——	Oeuvres complètes traduit par Emile Montégut. 4. Illustrées. Hachette. 252 Livraisons.
1868	—— —	p. Montégut. 3 Vols. 12. Hachette. 10 fr. 50 c.
1868—1870	——	— p. Montégut. 9 Vols. 8. Paris. Hachette.

FRENCH TRANSLATION OF SEPARATE PLAYS.

ANTONY AND CLEOPATRA.

Antoine et Cléopatre, traduit par de la Place. In: Théâtre anglais par de la Place. 8. Paris 1745—48.

CORIOLANUS.

Coriolane. Expliqué littéralement, traduit en français et annoté par M. C. Flemming ancien professeur d'anglais à l'école polytechnique. 8. Paris 1850.
—— with french notes by A. Brown. Paris 1850.
—— text anglais, notice critique et historique accomp. de notes par O' Sullivan 12. 1841. 1 fr.
—— english. Notes grammaticales et explicatives par M. Corréard. Paris 1844. Hingray. 80 c.

CYMBELINE.

Cymbeline, traduit par de la Place. In: Théâtre anglais par de la Place. 8. Paris 1745—48.

HAMLET.

Hamlet, traduit par de la Place. (Théâtre anglais.) 1745—48.
—— en anglais et en français avec la description du costume, des entrées et sorties, de positions relatives des acteurs et de toute la mise en scène. 18. Paris 1833.
—— Une Scène d'Hamlet, traduit en vers par Jules Lainé. 8. Paris 1836. 28 pages.
—— Tragédie imitée de l'anglais en vers français par M. Ducis. 8. Paris 1769, 1813, 1815, 1817, 1826.
—— Tragédie en cinq actes, conforme aux représentations données à Paris. 16. Paris 1827.
—— traduit par Pierre de Garal 8. Paris 1868. Lemerre. 3 fr.
—— traduit par Ernest Goillemot. 12. Paris. Degorce. 1 fr.
—— english. Avec notes par A. Brown. 18. 1865. Truchy. 1 fr.

Hamlet, traduit en vers français par le Chevalier de Châtelain. 8. Londres 1864. 2 frcs.
—— english, with french notes by O' Sullivan. 12. 1843. Hachette. 1 fr.
—— drame en cinq actes, en vers, trad. par Alex. Dumas et Paul Meurice. 12. Paris 1848. Levy. 1 fr.

HENRY THE SIXTH.
Henri le Sixième. Traduit par de la Place. 1745.

JULIUS CAESAR.
Jules César, traduit par de la Place. (Théâtre anglais.) 8. Paris 1745—48.
—— tragédie de Shakespeare en trois actes trad. en vers blancs par Voltaire. 8. Lausanne 1774.
—— traduit par A. Barbier. 18. Paris 1848.
—— traduit en vers par C. Carlhant. 8. Paris 1856.
—— nouvelle édition, publiée avec une notice, un argument analytique et des notes en français par Fleming. 18. Paris 1867. Hachette. 1 fr. 50 c.
—— english, notes by O' Sullivan. 1841. Hachette.
—— traduit en vers français par le Chevalier de Châtelain. 8. Londres 1866. 2 fr.
—— et la Tempête (la traduction française en regard) par M. Jay et Mme Louise Colet, avec des notes critiq. et historiq. accompagnées de traductions et imitations en prose et en vers de 30 drames du tragique anglais par O' Sullivan, précédées d'un nouvel essai sur Shakspeare par M. Villemain. 8. Paris 1840. 6 fr.

KING JOHN.
Jean sans terre, en 3 actes. 8. Paris 1791.

KING LEAR.
Le roi Lear, tragédie par M. Ducis. 8. Paris 1783.
—— tragédie en cinq actes, conforme aux représentations données à Paris. 1828.
—— traduit par Carlhant. 8. Paris 1847.
—— Scènes de, par Antoine Deschamps. Paris 1841.
—— en vers, par Jules Lacroix. 12. Paris 1868. Levy. 2 fr.
—— drame en 5 actes et douze tableaux, traduit par Devicque et Crisafulli. 12. Paris 1857.

MACBETH.
Macbeth, traduit par de la Place. 1745.
—— par M. Lefèbre. Paris 1783.
—— imité en vers français par Ducis. 8. Paris 1784, 1813, 1817, 1826.
—— conforme aux représentations données à Paris. 18. Paris 1828.
—— imitation libre par Ducange et Anicet Bourgeois. 8. Paris 1829.
—— par Fouinet. 8. Paris 1837.
—— drame en vers, par J. Lacroix. 12. Paris 1863.
—— par Halévy. 12. Paris 1862.
—— reduit en quatre actes, traduit en vers italiens par Carcano, traduction française du texte italien par Raymond-Signouret. (Repertoire de Mde. Ristori.) Paris 1858.
—— traduit en vers par le Chev. de Châtelain. 8. Londres 1870.
—— english, with french notes by O' Sullivan. 1843. Hachette. 1 fr.
—— trad. en vers, d'après Shak. par L. Halevy. 12. Paris 1853.
—— trad. en vers par Emile Deschamps. Levy. 1 fr.
—— et Romeo et Juliette, trad. en vers français; préface, notes et commentaires par Emile Deschamps. 8. Paris 1844. Cormon. 6 fr.

THE MERCHANT OF VENICE.
Le Marchand de Venice, comédie en 5 actes et en Prose, traduit de l'anglais. 8. Londres (Paris) 1768.
—— Comédie en 3 actes et en vers, imitée de Shakespeare par M. Laroche. 8. Paris 1830.

Le Marchand de Venise. Shylock, drame en 3 actes imité de Shakespeare par M. Dulac et Alboize. 8. Paris 1830.
—— traduit par Alfr. de Vigny. Paris 1829 et 1839.
—— traduit par Léon Daffry de La Monnoie. 8. Paris 1867. Hachette. 2 fr.
—— english, with french notes by O' Sullivan. 12. Paris 1844. Hachette. 1 fr.

MERRY WIVES OF WINDSOR.

Les femmes de bonne humeur de Windsor, traduit par de la Place. (Théâtre anglais.) 8. Paris 1745—48.
A trompeur trompeuses et demi, comédie en 3 actes, imité des commères de Windsor par M. Portelance. 8. Mannheim 1759.
Les commères de Windsor, traduites en français par Letourneur. 8. Paris 1776.
L'Amand loup-garron ou Mr. Rodomont, pièce comique en 4 actes et en prose, imité de l'anglais des commères de Windsor par Callot d'Herbois. 8. Douai 1777. Paris 1780.

OTHELLO.

Othello, traduit par de la Place. (Théâtre anglais.) 1745.
—— le More de Venise, tragédie anglaise du théâtre de Shakespeare en 5 actes et en vers; précédé d'un discours préliminaire par M. Douin. 8. Amsterdam et Paris 1773.
—— drame en 5 actes et en vers, imité de Shakespeare par M. Butini. 8. Genève 1785.
—— pantomime entremêlée de dialogues en prose; en 3 actes, imitée de la tragédie anglais par M. Cuveller. 8. Paris 1818.
—— opéra en 3 actes et en prose d'après les drames anglaises, français et italien, paroles de Mr. Castil-Blaze. 8. Paris 1823.
—— arrangée pour la scène française en vers par Ducis. 8. Paris 1793. 1817. 1826.
—— tragédie en 5 actes, conforme aux représentations données à Paris. 18. Paris 1827.
—— Melodrame en 5 actes, par Vic. Ducange et Bourgeois. Paris 1829.
—— le More de Venise; tragédie, traduite de Shakespeare en vers français par le Comte Alfred de Vigny. 8. Paris 1830. Brux. 1834.
—— traduction française par Nizard. 8. Paris 1837.
—— traduction italienne de Giulio Carcano. (Texte ital.-français en regard.) 8. Paris 1857. Levy. 2 fr.
—— english, with french notes by O' Sullivan. 12. Paris 1844. Hachette. 1 fr.
—— trad. par Le Bas. Paris 1837.
—— trad. par B. Laroche. Paris 1843.
—— traduction en vers français par le Chevalier de Châtelain. 8. London 1871.

RICHARD THE THIRD.

Richard III., traduit par de la Place. (Théâtre anglais.) 8. Paris 1745—48.
—— tragédie en 5 actes conforme aux représentations données à Paris. 18. Paris 1828.
—— traduit en vers par C. Carlhant. 8. Paris 1856.
—— english, with french notes by O' Sullivan. 18. 1844. 1 fr.

ROMEO AND JULIET.

Romeo et Juliette. Drame en 5 actes, en vers libres. 8. Paris 1777.
Romeo et Julie adaptée à la scène française, en vers par Ducis. 8. Paris 1772.
—— tragédie imitée de Shakespeare par M. Ducis. 8. Paris 1772, 1778, 1813.
—— traduit par St. Pecatier. 8. Paris 1854.
—— Sinfonie Dramatique par H. Berlioz. 8. Paris 1835.
—— et Juliette, traduction en vers français par Emile Deschamps. 12. Paris 1863. Amyot.
—— english, with french notes by O' Sullivan. 12. 1844. 1 fr.

THE TEMPEST.

La Tempête, traduction en vers français par le Chevalier de Châtelain. 8. Londres 1867. 2 fr.
—— english, with french notes by O' Sullivan. 12. 1844.

TIMON OF ATHENS.

Timon d'Athènes; trad. par de la Place. (Théâtre anglais.) Paris 1745—48.
—— en prose; imitation de Shakespeare par L. P. Mercier. 8. Paris 1794.
—— traduit littéralement en vers par Arthur Fleury. 12. 1860.
—— suivi de l'Intermezzo poëme par Heinrich Heine. Traduction en vers par E. Perrot de Chazelles. 8. Paris 1865. Garnier. 4 fr.
—— english, with french notes by O' Sullivan. 12. 1844. 1 fr.
—— Comédie en 3 actes et en vers, imitée de Shaksp. 8. Paris 1844.

POEMS.

Poëmes et Sonnets traduit en vers par Ernest Lafont. 8. Paris 1856.
Les Sonnets de Shakespeare trad. par F. Victor Hugo. 12. Paris 1857.
—— par L. de Wailly (Revue des deux M.).

FRENCH
COMMENTARIES, ESSAYS AND PLATES.

Apologie de Shakespeare. Paris 1777.
Arnauld. Revue de Paris 1830. XI, p. 193—196.
Avenel. Revue encyclop. 1831. Janv. 132—137.
Barante, A. G. Sur Hamlet. (Melanges.) Paris 1824.
Barbier. De Shakespeare. Revue des Revues. Jan. 1837.
Bayle, H. (Stendahl.) Shakespeare et Racine. Etudes sur le Romantisme. 8. Paris 1854.
Belloc, L. S. Revue encyclop. Septbr. 1830, pag. 688.
Bergman. La Vie et les oeuvres de Shakespeare. Lecture dans la Société littéraire de Strasbourg. Strasb. 1864.
Biographie Universelle, Article "Shakspeare".
Blair, H. Lectures ou rhétor. et belles lettres, lect. 46—47.
Bourcharlat, J. L. Cours de littérature. Paris 1826. I, pag. 18—85.
Broglie (Duc de). Sur Othello, traduit en vers français par A. de Vigny, et sur l'état de l'art dramatique en France en 1830. "Revue française". January 1830.
Bruno. Etudes Shakespeariennes. 1. Série 1855. Paris 1856.
Buchon, J. A. De Shakspeare. Revue encycl. Juillet 1821.
Chasles, Ph. Panurge, Falstaff et Sanche, Revue de Paris 1829. II, 224—34.
—— Des drames merveilleux et phantastiques de Shakspeare, Revue de Paris VIII, 190—212. X, 17—26. 245—257. XII, 164—165.
—— Henry VIII. Revue de Paris 1831. V, 181-97. VI, 17—38. 1842. II, 126—132.
—— Etudes sur le Théâtre Espagnol et Anglais (Revue de Paris) 1835.
—— Etudes sur W. Shakespeare. Marie Stuart et l'Arétin. Le Drame, les Moeurs et la Religion au XVI. Siècle. 8. Paris 1851.
—— Sur Richard II. (Dict. de la Conversation et de la Lecture. Vol. 49. Paris 1838.)
—— Hints for the Elucidation of Shakspeare Sonnets. (Athenaeum 1862, No. 1787.)
—— Shakspeare. (Etudes Contemporaines, Théâtre, Musique, et Voyages.) 8. Paris 1867. Amyot.
Chatelain, le Chevalier de. Le Monument d'un français à Shakspeare. 8. London 1867.
Chateaubriand, F. A. Melanges littér. 1801. p. 51—82.
—— Essai sur la littér. anglaise. Paris 1836. I, p. 223—310.
Chaulin, N. P. Précis des pièces dramatiques de Shakspeare. 8. Paris 1829.
Chauvet. Revue encycl. Octbr. 1826 p. 89-97. Novbr. p. 389.
Chénier, J. M. Oeuvres posth. d'André Chénier. Paris 1826. p. 347.
Contemporains de Shakespeare. Beaumont et Fletcher, trad. par Ernest Lafond, avec une notice sur la vie de ces deux poètes. 8. Paris 1865. 6 fr.
Coquerel, Ch. Histoire de la littérature anglaise.
Courdaveaux, V. Etudes sur la littér. ancienne et moderne, Theocrite, Tibulle, Properce, Ovide etc. et Shakspeare. 8. Paris 1867. Durant.
Dabas, J. Ch. A propos de Shakspeare ou le nouveau livre de Victor Hugo. 8. Bordeaux 1864.
Dargaud, M. Historie d'Elisabeth d'Angleterre 1866. (Chapitre sur Shakspeare.)

De Laplace. Théâtre anglais. Paris 1745.
— Lettres sur le théâtre anglais. 2 Vols. 1752.
Delavigne, C. Discours à l'Académie franç. 1824.
Delécluze. Romeo et Juliette. Paris 1827.
— Othello. Revue de Paris 1829. IX, pag. 148—165. X, p. 59—77.
Delille, J. L'Imagination. Chant V.
Deschampes, E. Études franç. et étrangères. Paris 1828. p. 28—59.
— Préface, notes de sa trad. de Macbeth et Romeo. 1844.
Diderot, D. Mémoires, corrésp. et lettres inédits. Paris 1831. IV, p. 38.
Discours sur Shakespeare et sur Mons. de Voltaire. Par Joseph Baretti. London 1777.
Ducuing. Shakespeare et notre Repertoirc. (La Revue Nouvelle, 7. Jan. 1846.)
Dumas, A. Revue des deux Mondes. 1833. IV, p 615—17.
— Etude sur Hamlet et sur W. Shakspeare. 4. Paris 1867. Levy.
Dupin, Ch. Lettre a My Lady Morgan, sur Racine et Shakespeare. Paris 1818.
Duport, M. P. Essais littéraires sur Shakespeare ou analyse raisonnée, scène par scène, de toutes les pièces de cet auteur. 2 Vols. 8. Paris 1828.
Duval, A. Shakespeare et Addison, mis en comparaison ou imitation en Vers des Monologues de Hamlet et de Caton. 8. s. l. 1786.
— Shakespeare amoureux ou la pièce à l'étude. Comédie en un acte. 8. Paris 1804.
Encyclopédie Moderne. Article Shakespeare. 1832.
Essai sur la littérature romantique. Paris 1825. pag. 120—220.
Fouinet, B. Bibliothèque Anglo-français par O' Sullivan.
Fragment sur Shakespeare, tiré des Conseils à un jeune Poëte; traduit de l'italien par M. Sherlock. 8. London 1870.
Fremy-Arnould. Les moeurs de notre temps. (Chapitre les Théâtres. 12. Paris 1861. 3 fr.
Gallerie de Shakspeare. (Outlines to Hamlet — Romeo & J. — Midsummer — Macbeth.) Paris 1828.
— de femmes de Shakspeare. 2 Vols. 8. Paris.
Genlis, Mde de. Mémoires du 18ième Siècle. Vol. IX, p. 242—247.
Geoffroy. Cours de littérat. dramatique. 2. Ed. Paris 1825. IV, p. 1—290.
Girardin. Cours de la littérature dramatique. 3 Vols. Paris 1852. (Vol. I. Hamlet. Lear. Vol. 3. La Pastorale dans Shakspeare. Romeo & Juliette.)
Gordon. Shakspeare et nous-mêmes, traduit de l'Anglais. Caen 1864.
Globe, le. Recueil phil. et littéraire. (Othello.) 1828. No. 61.
Guizot, F. Shakespeare et son temps. Etude littéraire. 8. Paris 1852.
Harriot, John. Napoléon, drame politique et historique en imitation de Macbeth de Shakespeare. 8. Paris 1834.
Hugo, Victor. Littérature et philosophie. Paris 1834. Préface.
— Marie Tudor. Préface.
— William Shakespeare. 8. Paris 1864.
Illustrations of Shakspeare's Works. 105 Engravings on Steel and Wood. Paris 1839.
Jaij, A. Conversion d'un romantique. Paris 1830.
Janin, Jules. Critique Portraits et Caractères contemporains. 12. Paris. Hetzel. (Critique des passions dans le Drame moderne.) 1865. 3 fr. 50 c.
Journal littéraire. 1717. pag. 202—212.
Ketterer. Hamlet. Opéra d'Ambroise Thomas. Fantaisie par Piano. Op. 230. Paris.
König, Henri. William Shakespeare, traduit de l'Allemand. 6 Vols. 12. Bruxelles 1861.
Lacroix, A. De l'Influence de Shakespeare sur le Théâtre française jusqu'à nos jours. 8. Bruxelles 1855.
Laharpe, de. Lycée ou Cours de Littérature, see Index to that work.
Lamartine, Alph. Shakspeare et son oeuvre. 8. Paris 1864.
Lamb. Shakspeare Contes dramatiques, ou légendes populaires traduits par Borghers, introd. par P. Chasles. 20 gravures & 24 vignettes sur bois. gr. 8. Paris 1841. Baudry. 15 fr.
Laroche, B. Notice sur W. Shakespeare. Introduct. to his translation.
Le Blanc, Abbé. Lettres concernant le gouvernement, la politique et les moeurs des Anglais. 3 Vols. (lettre 39. et 77.) 8. Amsterdam 1749.
Legouve, E. La Vie de Shakespeare. Revue universelle. Brux. 1834. III, 99—104.

Lemercier, N. L. Cours analytique de littér. Paris 1817. I, 122. 196. 267—396.
Lemoine, J. Etudes critiques et bibliographiques. (Shaksp. — Goethe & Mirabeau.) 8. Paris 1852. Levy. 3 fr.
Lerminier. Revue univers. 1832. XIV, p. 171.
Letourneur. Préface de sa traduction. 1776.
Lettre de Monsieur de Voltaire à l'académie française, lue dans cette Académie à la solemnité de la St. Louis le 25 Aug. 1776.
Magnin, C. Les Origines du théâtre moderne. I. Paris 1838.
—— Causeries et médit. hist. et littér. 1843. II. 73—270.
Martine, M. Examen des tragiques anciens et modernes. Paris 1834. II, p. 235—307. III, p. 1—131.
Marmontel, J. F. Eléments de littérature 1786. "Essai sur le goût".
Maynard, L. de. Revue de Paris 1834. August and Septbr.
Mémorial de Shakespeare, traduit par Borghers avec beaucoup de gravures. 8. Paris 1842. (See Lamb.)
Menechet. Biblioth. anglo-franç. par O' Sullivan.
Meurice, Théâtre (Etudes et Copies). Hamlet, Fallstaff, paroles d'après Shakspeare. 8. Paris 1864. 2 fr. 50 c.
Mézières, A. Prédécesseurs et contemporains de Shakspeare. Paris 1863. 2nd Edit. 12. 1864.
—— Shakspeare, ses oeuvres et ses critiques. 8. Paris 1861. 12. Paris 1865.
—— Contemporains de Shakespeare. 8. 1863. 2nd Edition sous le title: Contemporains et successeurs de S. 12. 1864.
Michel-Ange en rapport avec Shakespeare. 8. London 1802.
Michel, Francisque. Etudes de Philologie comparée sur l'Argot (Glossary of the Cant and Slang used by Shakspeare). 8. Paris 1856.
Montague, E. Essai sur le génie dramatique de Shakespeare. Traduit de l'anglais. S. Paris 1778.
Moulin, J. Notice de la Collection Shakespearienne formée par M. J. Moulin. 1862.
Nisard, M. D. Etudes sur les poètes latins. Brux. 1834. II, 257—293.
Nodier, Ch. Pensées de Shakespeare, extraits de ses ouvrages. 8. Besançon 1801.
—— Melanges de littér. et de critique. Paris 1820. I, 363 380.
Nottelle, L. Etude Fantaisiste sur Shakespeare. 12. Londres 1865. Simpkin. 2s 6d.
O' Sullivan. Gallerie des femmes de Shakspeare. Paris 1843.
—— Bibliothèque anglo-française 1844.
d'Outrepont, C. Promenades d'un solitaire. Paris 1828. p. 77—98.
Pecatier, A. Roméo et Juliette ou amours et infortune de deux amants. 18. Paris 1854.
Pensées de Shakspeare, suivies de quelques de ses Tragédies. 18. Paris 1822.
Perrin, M. Contes moraux tirés des tragédies de Shakespeare. 12. Paris 1783.
Pichot, A. Gallerie des personnages de Shakspeare reproduits dans les principales scènes des ces pières. 80 gravures. 8. Paris 1843. Baudry. 22 fr.
Prarond, E. Etudes sur Shakspeare. 1853.
Prevost (l'Abbé). In his periodical "le Pour et le Contre" (1733—1740) many articles on Shakspeare.
Quénot, J. P. Leçons de Rhétorique de Blair. Paris 1821. III, 311—12.
Revue de Paris. (Ed. de Bruxelles) 1829. VIII, p. 49—58. IX, 49—58 Othello.
Revue universelle. Brux. 1533. No. 21, p. 56—72. 1835. No. 18, p. 181—86.
Reymond, W. Corneille, Shakespeare et Goethe. Etude sur l'influence anglo-germanique en France au 19ième Siecle. 8. Berlin 1864.
Rivarol. Discours 1785, frequent allusions to Shakspeare and the English Drama.
Rio, A. F. Shakespeare. Paris 1864.
Roger, E. Beautés morales de Shakespeare. Paris 1843.
Rosier et de Leuven, Le Songe d'une nuit d'été. Opera-Comique en 3 actes. Musique de Ambroise Thomas 1850.
Saint-Evremont. Oeuvres. Paris 1699. pag. 245. 260.
Sainte-Beuve, C. A. Tableau histor. de la poésie franç. au 16ième Siècle Paris 1828. p. 331. 351. 362 et s.
—— Critiques et portraits littér. Brux. 1832. I, 98. 100. 136—217.

Sand, G. Gallerie de femmes de Shakespeare par O' Sullivau.
Shakespearian Gems, in French and English Settings, from the plays of the Bard of Avon, arranged for Schools and Students by Le Chevalier de Chatelain. London 1868. Tegg. 3s 6d.
Sherlock, M. Fragment sur Shakespeare, tiré des Conseils à un jeune poëte. 8. London 1790.
Staël, Mde. De la littérature. 1804. I, Chap. 13. 14. II, Ch. 5.
—— De l'Allemagne. 1814. II, Chap. 15.
Stendahl. Racine et Shakspeare. 1854.
Taine, N. Le Théâtre anglais de la renaissance. (Revue germanique 1 April, 1 Mai 1863.)
—— sur Shakspeare. (Revue des deux Mondes.)
Thomas, Ambroise. Hamlet. Opera en cinq actes; Paroles de Mrs. Michel Carré et Jules Barbier.
Tastu, Mad. A. Shakespeare. Poësies. Paris 1827. pag. 295—326.
Villemain, A. E. Essai littéraire sur Shakespeare. (In his Nouveaux Melanges.) Paris 1827.
—— Cours de littérat. 1829. Leç. V et VI.
—— Journal des Savans. Avril 1837. p. 215—225.
Villetard, Edm. Jules César et William Shakespeare. Etude sur les hommes providentiels. Paris 1865. Dentu. 1 fr.
Voltaire. Lettres sur les Anglais. 1755. Lett. 18. 19.
—— Du théâtre Anglais. 1761.
—— Observ. sur J. César de Shakespeare. 1764.
—— Préf. des commentaires sur Medée et le Cid.
—— Dict. philosoph. article "Art dramatique".
—— - see "Lettre".

ITALIAN TRANSLATIONS.*

Shakspeare, tragedie di, recate in versi italiani da M. Leoni. 8 Vol. 8. Pisa e Firenze 1814—15.
—— da M. Leoni. 14 Vols. 8. Verona 1819—22.
—— Teatro completo, voltato in prosa italiano, da Carlo Rusconi. Edition 1, 2, 3, 4. 7 Vols. 12. Torino 1858—59. Edit. I. Padova 1831. II, 1837. III. 1839.
—— Teatro scelto, tradotto da Giulio Carcano. 3 Vols. 12. Firenze 1857 —59. Monnier.
—— Coriolanus. 8. Firenze 1834.
—— — tradotto da Valetta. 8. Firenze 1843.
—— Hamlet. Amleto Tragedia di Ducis, tradotta in versi sciolti. 8. Venez. 1774.
—— Julius Caesar; recata in Italiano da Ignazio Valetta. Firenze 1829.
—— Macbeth. Macbetto trad. da Giuseppe Nicolini. Bresia 1830.
—— — trad. in versi da Frye. 12. Mantua 1827.
—— Merchant of Venice. Il Mercante di Venezia; versione di P. Santi. 16. Milano 1849.
—— Othello, il Moro di Venezie da Leoni. Verona 1821.
—— — da Ignazio Valetta. Firenze 1830.
—— — da Soncini. Milano 1830.
—— — anonimo. Milano 1834.
—— Romeo and Juliet, trad. anonimo. Roma 1826.
—— — trad. da Gaetano Barbiere. Milano 1831.
—— — trad. di Orlando Garbarini. 18. Milano 1847.
—— — Opera "I Capuleti ed I Montecchi". Opera seria in duo atti.

* Lownde's Manual ed. by Henry Bohn, gives a very complete list of these foreign Translations, but I have preferred to mention only those that have gone through my hands.

Shakespeare. Tempest. La Tempesta & I due Gentiluomini di Verona, trad. da Ch. Pasqualigo. 1870.
Montague. Saggio sugli scritti e sul genio di Shaksp. 8. Firenze 1828.
Saggi di Eloquenza estratti del Teatro di Shaksp. Milano 1811.

SPANIHS TRANSLATIONS.

Romeo y Julieta. Historias tragicas exemplares saradas de las obras del Bandelo. 12. Salamanca 1859. (mentioned by Lowndes.)
Hamlet, traducida por Inarco Celenio (pseudonyme of Moratin). 4. Madrid 1795. 8. 1798. (These Editions are extremely rare.)
Zumel, D. Ensig. Guillermo Shakspeare. Drama en cuarto actos. 8. Granada Zamora 1853.

PORTUGUSE TRANSLATIONS.

Othello, ou o Mouro de Venezia, imitação de Shaksp. pelo Lius Aug. Rebello da Silva. 8· Lisboa 1856. (a scarce book.)

DANISH TRANSLATIONS.

Shakspear's Skuespiel oversatte paa Dansk efter de Engleske Originalr af N. Rosenfeldt. 2 Vols. Kiøb. 1790 & 1791.
—— Tragiske Vaerker, oversatte af Peter Foersom, Kongelig Skuespiller. Kiøbenhaven 1807—16. Vol. 1 to 4. Vol. 5 to 9 by P. F. Wulff. 1818—1825.
—— Second Edition. 11 Vols. 8. udgivne af Offe Höyer. 1845—1850.
—— Third Edition af S. Beyer only 5 parts have been published of this Edition 1859—1860.
—— Lystspil oversatte ved Simon Meisling. Første Deel. Kiøbenh. 1810 (no more published, 'the volume contains: „Stormen — og Kiøbmanden i Venedig."
—— New Translations published by Lembke. 25 parts published Kiøb. 1870.
—— All's Well. Kongens Læge. Romantisk Lystspil i 5 Acter. Efter Shakspeare bearb. af S. Beyer. 12. Kiøb. 1850.
—— As you like it. Livet i Skoven. Romantisk Lystspil i 4 Acter. En Bearbeidelse af Shakspeare ved S. Beyer. 12. Kiøb. 1850.
—— Coriolanus. Efter Shakspeare. 12. Christiania 1818.
—— Hamlet. Prinz af Dannemark. Tragoedie af Shaksp. oversat af Engelsk of Joh. Boye. Kiöbenhavn 1777. (M. Hallæger.)
—— — Prince af Danmark. Sørgespil af W. Shaksp. Oversat af H. C. Wosemose. 12. Köbenh. 1834.
—— — oversat af Oelenschläger. Kiøb. 1846. 2nd Ed. 1847.
—— Julius Cæsar. Sørgespil af W. Shaksp. Oversat af H. C. Wosemose. 12. Köbenh. 1834.
—— Kong Lear. Sørgespil af W. S. Oversat af H. C. Wosemose. Köb. 1854.
—— — Et Sørgespil i fem Optog af W. Shakespeare. Oversat efter N. Tates Omarbeidelse, som spilles paar de Kongelige Skuepladse i London. 12. Kiøb. 1794.

Shakspear's Kong Lear overs. af Foersom. Kiøb. 1850.
— — overs. af S. Beyer. Kiøb 1850.
—— Love's Labours' lost. Lovbud og Lovbrud. Lystspil i 4 Acter. En Bearbeidelse af Shaksp. af S. Beyer. 12. Kiøb. 1853. Schubothe.
—— Macbeth. Tragedie in fem Acter efter Shakspeare og Schiller, bearbeidet til Opførelse paa den danske Skueplads ved. P. Foersom. 12. Kiøb. 1816. 2nd Edition. Foersom & Hoger. 1850.
— — oversat og fortolket af N. Hauge. 8. Christiania 1855.
—— Merchant of Venice. Kjöbmanden af Venedig. Lystspil i fem Acter af W. Shakspeare. Fordansket til Skuepladsens Brug ved Prof. K. L. Rahbek. 12. Kiøb. 1827.
—— Merry Wives of Windsor. De tystige Koner i Hillerød, en Omarbeidelse og Efterlignelse af Shakspears „Merry Wives of Windsor." Skuelspil i fem Acter af Capitain V. H. F. Abrahamsen. 12. Kiøb. 1815.
—— The mundre Konen i Windsor. 1829.
—— Midsummer-Night's Dream. Oversat af Oehlenschlaeger. Kiøb. 1816.
—— Othello af Wulff. 1822.
—— Richard the IIIrd. Shakspeare som Elsker, eller Proven paa Richard III. Lystspil in 1 Act af A. Duval. overs. af Brunn. Kiøb. 1813.
—— Romeo og Julie, af A. E. Boye. 12. 1828.
—— Tempest. Stormen. Et Syngespil i tre Afdelinger af Will. Shaksp. Omarbeidet til Kunzens efterladte Partitur af Levin Christian Sander. 12. Kiøb. 1818.
—— Twelfth-Night. Hellig Tree Kongers Aften eller: Hvad man vil. Lystspil ov. af Boye. 1829. (for det danske Theater bestemte Oversaettelse.)
—— Viola. Romantisk Lystspil i 3 Acter. En Bearbeidelse af Shaksp. ved S. Beyer. 12. Kiøb. 1850.

DANISH SHAKSPEARIANA.

Gervinus. Shakspeare en Karakteristik efter Gervinus von K. Arentzen. Kiøb. 1854.
Hauch. Afhandling om Shakspeare.
Holdt. ditto.
Heiberg, J. L. Anledning af Hr. Zu-Zx's Anmeldelse. Kiøb. 1860.
Sander. Forelaesninger over Shakspeare's og hans Sørgenspil Macbeth. Kiøb. 1804.

SWEDISH TRANSLATIONS.

Shakespeare's Dramatiska Arbeten, öffversatta af C. A. Hagberg. 12 Vols. 8. Lund 1847—51.
—— Antony and Cleopatra, af G. Scheutz. Stockh. 1825.
—— As you like it. Som ni behagar af G. Scheutz. Stockh. 1825.
—— Hamlet. Stockh. 1819.
—— Richard II. Scheutz. Stockh. 1825.
—— Julius Caesar, af Scheutz. Stockh. 1826. 2nd 1831.
—— — Stockh. 1816.
—— — öfversat af P. Westerstrand. Stockh. 1839.
—— Konung Lear. Upsala 1818.
—— Macbeth, ofv. E. G. Geijer. Upsala 1813.
—— — af. H. Sandström. 12. Stockh. 1838.
—— Merry Wives of Windsor, af. Scheutz. Stockh. 1825.
—— Merchant of Venice, af Scheutz. Stockh. 1820. 1829.
—— — af Arfwidsson. Stockh. 1854.
—— Midsommars aftonen? af A. Lindberg. Stockh. 1834.
—— Othello, mohren i Venedig af K. A. Nicander. Stockh. 1826.
—— Romeo och Juliet öfvers. af F. A. Dahlgren. Stockh. 1845.
—— Tempest. Stockh. 1836.
—— Twelfth Night. Trettondags afsom af Scheutz. Stockh. 1825.

Gellersteat. Shakspeare och Skalderna. 4to. Lund 1848.
S's. The Tempest, an ontline Sketch of the Play. 8. Stockh. 1836.
Shakespeare och Hans Vänner eller Det Glada Englands gyllne Alder. 2 Vols. Stockh. 1839.
Högman, Ch. de poësi dramatica G. Shakespearii dissertatio. 4. Upsala 1843.
Hageberg, C. Aug. Shakspeare och Skalderna. (Sh. opinions on poets and poetry.) 4to. Lund 1848.
Romdahl, Axel. Obsolete Words in Shakspeare's Hamlet. 8. Upsala 1869.

DUTCH TRANSLATIONS.

William Shakespear's Tooneelspeelen. Met de Bronwellen en Aantekeningen van verscheide Beroemde Schryveren. Naar het Engelsche en het Hoogduitsche vertaald en met nieuw geinventeerde Kunstplaaten versierd. 5 Vols small 8. Amsterdam 1778 – 1782.
The title of the 4. Volume has in addition: Aantekeningen, enz-van Rowe, Pope, Theobald, Hanmer, Warburton, Johnson en Capell. Naar de uitgaaf van Capell uit het Engelsch vertaald en met aantekeningen van Prof. Eschenburg en van den Vertaaler verrykt. This first Edition contains 15 plays namly:
   Vol. I. Hamlet — de Storm — de vrolyke vrouwen de Windsor.
   Vol. II. Macbeth — Leven en Dood van Koning Johannes — de Kunst om een Tegenspreekster te Temmen.
   Vol. III. Othello — Henrik de Vierde, 1. Deel — De Dwaaling.
   Vol. IV. Marcus Antonius en Cleopatra — Richard de Tweede — de Twee Edellieden van Verona.
   Vol. V. Coriolanus — Koning Hendrik de Vierde, tweede Del — Veel Leven over Niets.

William Shakespear. The Plays of William Shakespeare. Uitgegeven en Verklaard door Mr. C. W. Opzoomer. 1te Stuk Othello. 12. Amst. 1862. 2te Stuk Macbeth. Amst. 1862.
—— Bloemlezing uit de deamatische Werken van William Shakspeare. In nederduitsche Dichtmaat overgebracht door Mr. L. Ph. C. van den Bergh. 8. Amsterdam 1834.
Antonius en Cleopatra. Aegyptica ofte Aegpt. trag. of M. Antonius en Cleopatra, door G. v. Nieuwelandt. 4to. Amst. 1624.
—— door Brunius. 8. Amst. 1781.
—— vertaeld door W. van Loon. 12. Utrecht 1861.
As you like it. Orlando en Rosalinde. Landspel. Vertaald door A. S. Kok. gr. 12. Haarlem 1860.
Hamlet. (Brandt G.) De veinzende Torquatus Amst. Wed. G. de Groot. 8. 1720. (imitation of Hamlet.) 2nd Edit. 1740.
—— de veinzende Torquatus. Treurspil. 12. Amsterd. s. d. (1710?)
—— gevolgt naar het Franch, en naar het Engelsch door M. G. de Cambon. Geb. van der Werken. 12. Gravenhagen 1779.
—— - gevolgd naar het Franch van den Heere Ducis door Ambrosius Justus Zubli. 1 Ed. 1786. Tweede Druk. Amsteldam 1790.
—— vertaald door P. Roorda van Eysinga. Met Inleiding van J. Moulin. 8. Kampen 1836.
—— Historisch Treuspel. Ten gebruike der Gymnasia. Met ophelderingen voorzien door S. Susan. 8. Deventer 1849.
—— overs. door A. S. Kok. Onden toezicht van Dr. J. van Vloten. 12. Haarlem 1860.
—— english, uitgegeven en verklaard door A. C. Loffelt. Utrecht 1867. Beijers.

Julius Caesar. Treuspel van Sh. vertaald door Mr. C. W. Opzoomer. 12. Amst. 1860.
—— door Posthumus.
King Lear. Treurspel in vyf bedryven, gevolgt naar het fransch door mevrowe M. G. de Cambon gebooren van der Werken. 12. Sgravenhage 1786.
—— Koning Lear. Treurspel van W. Shaksp. Uit het Engelsch vertaald door W. van Loon. 12. Utrecht 1861.
Macbeth. Treurspel van W. Shakspeare uit het engelsch door Jurriaan Moulin. 8.
    1te Druk. Kampen bij Tibout 1835.
    2te „ Deventer 1845.
    3te „ on der toezigt van Dr. J. van Vloten. 12. Haarlem 1858.
—— — door Susan. 1. Edit.? 2de Druk Deventer 1842. 3de Druk Dev. 1848.
——. — English Text, Introduction and english Notes by Lindo (A doctors dissertation.) 8. Arnhemiae 1853.
—— Opzoomer, C. W. Aantelkeningen op Shakespeare's Treuspel Macbeth. 8. Amsterdam 1854.
Merchant of Venice. De Koopman van Venetie. Tooneelspel van Will. Shak. door T. N. van der Stok. 1e Druk 1859. 2. Goedkoope uitgave. 12. Rotterd. 1863.
—— van Posthumus. (see Friesic.)
Midsummer Night's Dream. Gramsberger M. Klucht tragoedie of d. Hartoog v. Pierlepon. 4to Amst. 1650. Hetz. Amst. 1657. 4to.
—— Piramus en Thisbe, of the bedrooge Hartog v. Pierlepon. 8. Amst. 1752. (same subject as the M. N. D.)
Much ado about Nothing. Blyendigh. Treurspel van Timbre de Cardone ende Fenicie van Messine. Leeuwarden 1618. (an imitation of the play.)
Othello, de Moor van Venetien door Moulin. 1. Edit. Kampen by Valckenier 1836. 2nd Ed. 1848. 3. Druk van Vlohen. 12. Haarlem 1857.
—— naar Eschenburg. 8. 1781.
—— door J. P. Uilenbrock (naar Ducis). 1790.
—— Muliassus de Turk van Kalbergen. 4to. Amsterdam 1652.
—— door B. Brunius. 8. Amsterdam 1780.
Richard III, Koning Richard III. Treurspel door A. S. Kok. Amst. 1860. 2nd Edit. 1861.
Romeo and Juliet door Jacob Struys. 4to. Amsterdam 1634.
—— door J. van Lennep. Amst. 1853.
—— Tooneelspel, gevolgd naar het hoogduitsche van den Heer Weisse door P. J. Uylenbroek. 2nd Ed. door B. Fremerij. Dordrecht 1786. Derde Druk. Amsterdam 1791.
—— door Moulin. 3de Druk van Vloten. 15. Haarlem 1858.
—— A Tragedy by W. Sh. with explanatory notes and introduction by C. Stoffel. 8. Deventer 1869.
Taming of the Shrew. De Konst om een Tegenspreckster te temmen. Amst. 1780.
Tempest. De Storm door B. Brunius. 8. Amst. 1778.
—— van Moulin 1836. 2e Druk van Vloten. Haarlem 1858.
—— The Tempest, with dutch notes door S. Susan. 8. Kampen 1854.
Titus Andronicus. Aran en Titus off Wraak en weerwraak, Treur-Spel van Jan Vos. l'Amstelredam, gedruckt by Otto Barentsz Smient. 4to. 1st Ed. 1641. 2nd Ed. 1642, 3nd 1644, 4nd 1648, 5nd 1656, 6nd 1660, 7nd 1661, 8th Ed. 1709, 20th Ed. 1726.
—— boertig berymt door Jakobus Rosseau 12. Amst. 1716.
—— Boertige Beschryving van der Amsterdamschen Schouwburg en het vertoonen van Aran en Titus. 12.
Two Gentlemen of Verona. Amst. 1781.

DUTCH SHAKESPERIANA.

Duval, Alex. Shakespeare Minnaar Blijspeel, naar het fransch door C. van der Vijver. 12. Amst. 1810.
Kampen, N. G. van. Redevoering over William Shakespear. Voorgelezen in de Leydsche Afdeeling der Hollandsche Maatschappij van Fraaije Kunsten en Wetenschappen, den 9. December 1814. 8.
—— over Shakspeare. 8. Leyden 1815.
—— Werken der Hollands. Maatschappij (Othello) 1823. VI. pag. 216—17.
Moulin, J. Omtrekken eener Algemeene Literatuur over W. Shaksp. en deszelfs Werken. 8. 1845. Dweede deel. (The first was not published.)
—— Tegen den Heer van der Hoop, als beoordeelaar myner vertaling van Macbeth 1836.
Pennevis, A. Shakspear en de Hedendaagsche Nederlandsche Uitgaven en Vertalingen zijner Tooneelstukke. Kritische Bijdrage tot de Kennis van Dichtkunst. 8. Utrecht 1863.
Sybrandi, K. Verhandeling over Vondel en Shakspeare als Treurspeldichters. Uitgegeven door Teyler's Tweede Genootschap. Haarlem 1841.
Tydschrift, de Navorscher. Several Articles on Shakspeare. Vol. III. Vol. IV. Vol. VI 305. VII.

FRIESIC TRANSLATIONS.

Merchant of Venice De Keapman fen Venetien in Julius Cesar, two Toneestikken fen Willem Shakspeare. Out it Ingels foorfrieske trog. R. Posthumus. 8. Grinz Oonken 1829.
As you like it. trog. Posthumus. 8. Dorkum 1842. (mentioned by Lowndes.)

BOHEMIAN TRANSLATIONS.

Dramatika̋ Díla Williama Shakespeara Nákladem Musea Královstvi Ceského. 25 Vols. 12. Praze 1855—1869, translated by various authors: Doucha, Kolar, Celakovský, Maly, Malého, etc.
—— marná lásky snaženi. Prěložel J. Maly. 8. Praze 1870.
—— Othello, maurenjn Benátský. Truchlohra w pateru gednánj prelozena od. Jak Bud. Malého. gr. 8. Praze 1843. Kronberger. ²/₃ Thlr.

HUNGARIAN TRANSLATIONS.

Shakspeare. Minden Munkái. Forditjäk, Többen. Kiadja a Kisfaludy Tárasag Elsö Kötet. 18 Vols. Pest 1864—1869.
—— transl. by Dobrentei. Kaschau 1824.

WALACHIAN TRANSLATIONS.

Shakspeare. Macbeth Tragoedie in cinci acturi tradure d'in englisesce de P. P. Carp. Jassi 1864.
Romeo and Juliet de Tona Hardam.

MODERN GREEK.

Hamlet. .Ιμλετος, βασιλοπαις τῆς Δανίας, τραγῳδία τοῦ αγγλου Σαιξπερου. Ἐνστιχως μεταφρασθεῖσα ὑπο Ιωαννου Η. Περβανογλου. Athens 1858.*

POLISH TRANSLATIONS.

Shakespeare William Works-Dramata, translated by Józefa Korzeniowskiego. 3 Vols. (Containing 10 plays.) Warsau 1857—1860.
—— by Kefalinski and Dycalp. 3 Vols. 8. Wilna 1840—48.
—— Dziela dramatyczne. 2 Vols. Poznań 1866 & 1869.
— Alls well that ends well; trans. by Dycalp. 12. Wilna 1845.
Hamlet, transl. by Ostrowskiego. 8. Livów 1870.
- Julius Caesar, tr, by Pajgerta. 12. Livów 1859.
—— Merry Wives of Windsor, transl. by John of Dycalp. 12. Wilna 1842.
—— Macbeth, transl. by A. E. Koźmiana. 8. 1857.
Besides these there are other translations published in Polish Literary Journals.

RUSSIAN TRANSLATIONS AND CRITICISM.

Shakspeare's dramatic Works, published by Gerbel. 1866—1869. 4 Vols. 4to.
— Richard the 3rd, translated into Russian by Drushin.
—— King Lear, translated into Russian, with Introduction, by Drushin.
—— Lectures by N. Tickonravof. Moscow 1864, published by Grasunof.
Hamlet and Don Quixote written by Loof. St. Petersburgh 1863. (This elaborate reply to Turgenief's article on Hamlet is published in the first Volume of Sovremennik for 1860.
On the Characters in Shakspeare's Hamlet by Jaroslavtsef. St. Petersburg 1865.
Hamlet. A Criticism, by Bsherka Timovsef. St. Petersburgh 1862.

BENGALEE TRANSLATIONS.**

The Merchant of Venice translated into Bengali, by Hara Chandra Ghose. Calcutta.
Romeo and Juliet. Romiyo-o-Juliyet. Calcutta (1818?)

---

* Lowndes also mentions a translation of the Tempest. (Athens 1855?)
** Both are mentioned by Lowndes; I have not been able to get either in India.

TO SHAKSPEARIAN COLLECTORS.

The Publisher begs to enform Libraries, and Collectors of Shakspeariana, that he has great facilities for supplying any of the books mentioned in the Catalogue English as well as Foreign.

AN SHAKSPEARE-FORSCHER.

Der Verleger erlaubt sich Bibliotheken und Forscher darauf aufmerksam zu machen, dass er mit Leichtigkeit jeden Auftrag auf englische Shakspeariana auszuführen im Stande ist.

ENGLISH SHAKSPEARIANA.

SUPPLEMENT FROM 1864 to 1871.

The *Cambridge* Edition of Shakspeare edited by Clark and Wright was finished in 1866, and is at present the best Edition we possess. — In the last Volume the Editors expressed themselves thus:
Nothing can be more unfounded than the notion so prevalent in Germany, that Shakspeare has till of late years been neglected and undervalued by his countrymen. Even in England this erroneous assertion is frequently repeated, as if it were too obvious to require proof. The Genius of Shakspeare and the stupidity of his commentators is a popular antithesis as trite as it is unjust. In this despised class are found some of the most famous and most accomplished Englishmen of their time. And it is a study of great interest to follow them as they exercise their varied talents on the noblest field which the literature of their country afforded:
Rowe, himself a dramatist of no mean skill; *Pope*, with his deep poetic insight; *Theobald*, with his fine tact and marvellous ingenuity; *Hanmer*, whose guesses, however they may pass the sober limits of criticism, are sometimes brillant, often instructive and never foolish; *Warbourton*, audacious and arrogant, but now and then singularly happy; *Johnson*, with his masculine common sense; *Capell*, the most useful of all, whose conscientious diligence is untiring, whose minute accuracy is scarcely ever at fault; *Steevens*, *Malone*, *Blackstone*, *Farmer*, *Tyrwhitt*, *Rann*, *Boswell*, *Singer* and *Sidney Walker* with all their varied learning, together with their successors of the present generation in England, Germany and America, who have devoted themselves to the illustration of Shakspeare as to a labor of love." —

The wonderful love of Shakspeare shown by the Cambridge Editors, has lately revealed itself in a Copy of Shakspeare of a most unusual kind. Scholars have long collected editions, illustrations and books of their favourite ancient and modern authors, but perhaps no individual has collected more assiduously than
Mr. H. R. Forrest of Manchester
whose Copy of Shakspeare with all its addenda is a marvel, a literary curiosity and a library in itself.
We will endeavour to describe what Mr. Forrest has done.
He took K. Meadow's, Charles Knight's, Staunton's and Cassel's illustrated Editions of Shakspeare and added to these all known

illustrations by Boydell, Fuseli, Howard, Smirk, Chodowicki, Retzsch, Buhl; every other illustration that he could procure, historical, descriptive, and artistic, portraits of all the historical personages of the plays, portraits of the actors, english and foreign, who ever performed in the pieces. Every thing in the way of scenic representation of the plays, and therefore all the customs and costumes of the stage, giving a history of stage costumes and stage performances of the plays — also the historical portraits, collected from Meyrick's Armour, from Boutell's monumental Brasses, and from Copies of old illuminations so that as far as possible the actual times of each piece whether its scenes were laid in England, Italy, Germany, Greece or Denmark is before the examiner of this Copy of Shakspeare.

Next come the erudite and illustrious Annotators and Translators of the text of Shakspeare, whose portraits he added. Then he collected from the carricatures, squibs and periodicals whatever had any reference to Shakspeare; he added Maps of Cities, old Architecture, views of Towns and Castles and Theatres until the Copy of his Shakspeare formed 45 Volumes in quarto, with more than 10,000 illustrations — a marvellous work of never ceasing perseverance. It would be difficult to surpass the diligent research by which this one author has been illustrated, and there can be no question that the
Forrest Copy of Shakspeare
is unique, as a Collection of Illustrations to Shakspeare's plays.

A Copy of *Venus and Adonis* printed for William Leake 1599 has been discovered in an old Library by Mr. Ch. Edmunds, and there is now no doubt that this is the real *4th Edition* and the one of 1600 is a myth.

The Collier *Emendation* Controversy is now fully set at rest. The Corrections have not convinced Shakspearian Scholars[*] that they are of any authority. *Singer* proved that many of the best of the emendations were not new, and that most of the new were uncalled for or absurd. In this estimate of the reading he was supported by *Knight, Halliwell* and *Dyce,* and the result has been that these Collier Emendations have had no lasting effect and are nearly put aside as useless.

Shakespeare's Birth-place and the Museum at Stratford-upon-Avon, are also now in a flourishing condition. The number of Visitors to the Birth-place during the year 1869—70 was about 6,450. The house has been fitted up and two rooms are furnished at the Birth-place as a Shakespearean Museum.

---

[*] Staunton's Preface to Shakspeare.

www.ingramcontent.com/pod-product-compliance
Lightning Source LLC
Chambersburg PA
CBHW020112170426
43199CB00009B/508